ALBERT STRANGE

Yacht Designer and Artist 1855-1917

John Leather

ALBERT STRANGE
Yacht Designer and Artist 1855-1917

The Pentland Press Ltd.
Edinburgh.

© Albert Strange Association
First published in 1990 by
The Pentland Press Ltd.,
Kippielaw, Haddington
East Lothian, Scotland.

Printed and bound by Holmes McDougall Ltd. Edinburgh
Jacket design by Janet Dalgarno

ISBN 0 946270 73 2

CONTENTS

Page

PREFACE   by Maurice Griffiths G.M.   vi

ACKNOWLEDGEMENTS   viii

CHAPTER 1   SMALL YACHTS and BIG CANOES
              A Background Perspective to
              Albert Strange's Yacht Designs   1
CHAPTER 2   ALBERT STRANGE   12
CHAPTER 3   HAPPY DAYS ON THE HUMBER   26
CHAPTER 4   A SINGLE-HANDED CRUISE IN THE
              NORTH SEA   37
CHAPTER 5   AN ALBUM OF ALBERT STRANGE
              DESIGNS . . . 1   47
CHAPTER 6   THE YEARS OF MATURITY   70
CHAPTER 7   MY LAST CRUISE IN CHERUB II   85
CHAPTER 8   ALBERT STRANGE ON THE CRUISING
              YACHT'S STERN   96
CHAPTER 9   A SKETCHING CRUISE ON THE IRISH COAST 105
CHAPTER 10   AN ALBUM OF ALBERT STRANGE
              DESIGNS . . . 2   115
CHAPTER 11   ALBERT STRANGE AS AN ARTIST   144
CHAPTER 12   ALBERT STRANGE — THE MODEL
              YACHTSMAN AND CANOEIST   162

APPENDIX 1   THE ALBERT STRANGE ASSOCIATION   180
APPENDIX 2   A LIST OF STRANGE DESIGNS (Basic Facts) 181
APPENDIX 3   A LIST OF PAINTINGS AND SKETCHES   190
APPENDIX 4   THE STRANGE FAMILY TREE   196
APPENDIX 5   BIBLIOGRAPHY   198
              INDEX   200

PREFACE

Yacht designing, someone once wrote, is a blend of a sense of balance, of a form of sculpture on paper, and a sound knowledge of sea conditions. Born with a love of boats of all kinds, it would not have been surprising if the young Albert Strange had elected to make the sea, or the creation of little ships, his career in life. As it was, his artistic leanings called more strongly, and perhaps wisely he chose art as his career whilst devoting his remaining energies to designing canoes and yachts.

It was an inspiration that, happily, he did not keep to himself, for when he became headmaster of the School of Art at Scarborough in 1882, those of his pupils who showed any interest in boats were treated to special instruction in the theory and practice of yacht design — and how one would like to have sat in on these sessions!

It has been said that anyone can design a good looking bow, but that it takes an artist to produce a really good stern, and it was perhaps mainly in his development of the beautiful canoe stern in his designs that Albert Strange showed the training of the artist, the capacity to observe and appraise the finer points of hull form.

Even his earliest plans for sailing canoes which developed into the celebrated canoe yawls, showed his appreciation of pleasing lines in a hull with well balanced bow and stern. Indeed, he introduced a conception of a cruising yacht's stern which had not appeared before, except in one or two half hearted and regrettable examples. His gracefully curved and beautifully proportioned canoe sterns came as a revelation in an era which accepted long overhangs and flat counters as suitable for a gentleman's yacht. These canoe sterns not only took the eye but they were practical in the sense that above a fine clean run, the stern swelled out on both sides to give the yacht ample buoyancy above the waterline, together with a desirable amount of stowage capacity aft of the cockpit and a useful deck spread for the mizzen and its shrouds.

Recalling that Albert Strange joined the Royal Canoe Club in its early years, later to become an active member also of the Humber Yawl Club, his interest in the design — indeed in improving contemporary designs — of sailing canoes can be well understood. He was also an almost exact contemporary of Harry Fiennes Speed, who was born in 1857 and whose delightful writings on his own cruises in large canoes and small yachts, earned him an enviable reputation as a pioneer small boat cruising man in late Victorian years. It seems more than likely that these two sailing canoeists must have found much in common, and shared notes and experiences.

It is worth considering, too, the possible influence that two other contemporary yacht designers' work probably had on Albert Strange's canoe designs. Linton Hope, celebrated in his day for his many designs of cruising yachts from 3 and 4 tonners to the 52 ton Mollihawk; and G. Umfreville Laws, a versatile designer of cruising yachts in the 3 to 10 ton range, were personally known to Albert Strange. Doubtless the three exchanged views and suggestions over the years.

During the 1880s and 1890s Linton Hope was producing a new conception in lightly constructed racing craft, skimming dishes with metal fin-and-bulb keels and a spade-like rudder without a protective skeg aft. An innovation which rings a modern bell in the RORC, doesn't it? With basket light steambent timbering, shell thin planking and rigged with large standing lug-sails having a number of full length battens, these raters showed an astonishing superiority over contemporary racing boats. They were in a class of their own, and were never entirely equalled in performance until Uffa Fox produced his own version of them, the Flying Fifteens, some sixty years later.

At the same time G. Umfreville Laws was making his name as a successful designer of various types of small light displacement boats, it could be argued that Albert Strange with his ideas on canoe yawls, was perhaps the catalyst who induced Laws to produce one or two canoe sterned yawls of his own. Perhaps the best known design of this type, to present day yachtsmen, is the NEREID II, a pretty 29' 6" canoe sterned yawl of 6 tons TM, built in 1913 and still sailing. She is a design which, in my view, reveals many characteristics of Strange origin.

It is not unreasonable, therefore, to infer that Albert Strange must have adapted some of both Linton Hope's and G.U. Law's ideas in light displacement and lightweight construction for his own canoe yawls, for it is a notable feature of his grasp of the subject that he was essentially a practical designer. His construction drawings and specifications were always thoroughly workable and presented boatbuilders with no problems in following them. In this he was no inexperienced amateur.

Almost all architects, whether concerned with the designs of bridges, buildings, ships or little yachts, gain something from studying the work of other architects. It is not necessarily plagiarism nor the highest compliment which is paid by copying, but rather a crystallisation of ideas through a study of what others are doing. When Albert Strange's beautifully proportioned canoe sterned yacht designs first began to be published, it need not be idle conjecture that they could have had some influence — perhaps only an unconscious effect — on the subsequent work of other designers. And among Albert Strange's late contemporaries there were a number of well known names, such as A.E. Payne, C. Sibbick, William Fife, Alfred Mylne, G.L. Watson, Charles E. Nicholson, Colin Archer, A.R. Luke, A. Westmacott, Frederick Shepherd and T. Harrison Butler.

In his exquisite drawings, Albert Strange showed that the design for a small cruising yacht can be a creation of beauty which pleases the understanding eye from whatever angle she is viewed. He set a high standard in well proportioned hulls and rigs: proportions which hold good to this day, like those of the great architects in history.

In a far more modest way I may be able to claim that in some of my own designs — perhaps the more shapely ones — I have owed a great deal to a study of Albert Strange's plans, even to the extent of designing for my own use in 1948, a 28' Bermuda Yawl called TAMARIS, whose bow and canoe stern and other features, bore a strong resemblance to the Albert Strange model. And perhaps because of this guidance, she proved to be a sweet little boat for cruising, with no notable vices.

It is a privilege, therefore, to be given this opportunity to write the Preface for this book which is a fitting tribute to a fine artist and a great yacht designer.

MAURICE GRIFFITHS G.M.

ACKNOWLEDGEMENTS

Writing a biographical book is rather like designing or building a ship — it is very rarely achieved by the work of one man. In writing of the life and work of Albert Strange, yacht designer and artist, I have been greatly assisted by independent research carried out by members of the Albert Strange Association, in particular by Mark Miller, Richard Blomfield, Don Goodsell and also by Mike Burn. The idea for the book was that of the Association's Honorary Secretary, W. H. (Bill) James, himself a fund of knowledge on the life and work of Strange and a tireless worker in the quest for information on his life, his yacht designs and paintings, and for the preservation and continuing enjoyment of the craft he designed.

Valuable information has also been gained from the pages of early issues of YACHTING MONTHLY, whose editor kindly gave permission for the use of this material, whilst Maurice Griffiths G.M., an earlier editor, consummate cruising yachtsman, designer of yachts and for long an admirer of the designs of Albert Strange, has contributed the preface.

Other material has been obtained from the early Year Books of the Humber Yawl Club which after over a century of activity, remains one of the most practical sailing fraternities. The Mystic Seaport Museum of Mystic, Connecticut has assisted with access to their collection of Albert Strange plans, which were in the possession of the late William P. Stephens, for long a corresponding friend of Albert Strange.

The artistic aspects of Albert Strange's life have been ably researched by Tony Watts and Sheila Willis, who have contributed a chapter on his art and a list of known paintings. Tony is also responsible for the sketch maps and has kindly researched and written Chapter 12.

The publication of this book has been one long-term aim of the Albert Strange Association, under the chairmanship of Ian Taggart and with the enthusiastic support of Martin Strange, grandson of the subject.

The manuscript has been read by Jamie Clay, whose brother Peter has helped in various ways, not least by research at Mystic Seaport Museum. Other members of the Association have kindly allowed publication of photographs of their yachts. I am also grateful to those who have allowed the Association to photograph and list their paintings.

I hope that long into the future, this book will encourage continued use of existing craft and possibly the building of new yachts and boats to the designs of Albert Strange, and to appreciation of his paintings.

JOHN LEATHER,
The Saltings,
Fingringhoe,
Essex.

CHAPTER 1

Small Yachts and Big Canoes

A background perspective to Albert Strange's Yacht Designs

During the past century, small yachts designed by Albert Strange have attracted the attention of sailing men by their reputation of fitness for seagoing. Many of them have a pointed 'canoe' stern and are rigged as gaft yawls. These features have become almost a hallmark of an Albert Strange design, though he also produced many cutters and some sloops and ketches, many having a transom or counter stern. Although he also designed a variety of small centreboard sailing boats, canoe yawls, canoes and a few racing craft, including one 6 metre International Rating Class yacht design, his principal interest was the small seagoing yacht. Strange's personal taste in pleasure afloat contributed to the evolution of his skill as a designer of small pleasure craft, at first as an amateur, then later it bordered on professional status, though his principal occupation was always the teaching of art.

Such was the symmetry of his craft, that for years yachtsmen have claimed to recognise a yacht designed by Albert Strange at sight, in harbour or at sea. That consummate maritime author and cruising man, E. Keble Chatterton, well described the pleasure of finding his Strange designed yawl Charmina in the 1930s.

"I had come in from the Channel one afternoon and was lying in Torquay. In the cool of the evening, whilst lazing round the harbour looking over this craft and that, my eyes suddenly were filled with a perfect picture. I stopped rowing and was infatuated. There, alongside, was the most beautiful little yawl — beautiful in the curves of her hull — beautiful in the way she held her head and sat the water — beautiful in her suggestion of seaworthy strength. I admired the sensible tall mizzen-mast which combined all the advantages of yawl and ketch, without the defects of either. I liked the good sheer and sensible amount of freeboard; she would be delightful in a seaway. But that stern! Only an artist could have produced such perfectly balanced ends. Surely only one man could have produced such sweet lines in a small ship, and that was Albert Strange! It was more than a quarter of a century since I had last talked with this brilliant designer, who was a painter of pictures long before he took to yacht architecture and became the greatest expert in adapting the old Viking stern to the modern yacht.

A head and shoulders appeared at the after-hatch. 'I apologise, Sir, for staring at your yacht' was my excuse, 'but really she's the nicest little ship I've ever seen. Is she an Albert Strange?' 'The last he designed before he died — come aboard.'" (In actual fact, the last was probably VENTURE — J.L.)

Such is the lure yachts by Strange have for devotees.

The story of the evolution of Albert Strange as a yacht designer and of his yachts and boats is a long one, and is mixed with his love of sailing and cruising in small craft. His life was not long lived but encompassed much of the development and active use of the paddling and sailing cruising canoe and its derivative, the canoe yawl. When he died in 1917, aged 61, both types of craft were declining in Britain, though the racing of sailing canoes would flourish to this day and a few enthusiasts continued to cruise in their canoes and others in canoe yawls. Both types of craft have become rare. By 1914, these variants bore little resemblance to their predecessors.

During Strange's lifetime, pleasure sailing, which had been the pastime principally of a limited leisured and wealthy class, moved into the reach and inclinations of the middle classes and some better off working men, besides the many who lived by the water and managed to own and sail a small boat in a frugal manner for their pleasure. Sailing and yacht clubs proliferated in Britain after the mid 19th century and sailing and rowing became a weekend and evening pleasure of an increasing number of people, both here and abroad, particularly in America and Germany. Few of these enthusiasts had much money to spare for their pastimes and their boats had usually to be small and simple. Yet, between about 1890-1914, some of the true classics of small boat sailing had been published and the small cruising yacht, of a size and simplicity still popular today, had been evolved in principle and provided the foundations on which the subsequent development has burgeoned. This led to the thousands of able small cruising yachts which have been the products of evolutionary design over many years and latterly it has witnessed the revolutionary use of glass reinforced plastic (GRP) as a hull, deck and interior construction material, of aluminium-alloy for masts and spars and synthetic fibres for sailcloth and ropes. Many designers, builders and sailing men, professional and amateur, have contributed to this long process and the part taken by Albert Strange cannot be viewed in isolation. His contribution was substantial in the small boat cruising world but can become distorted without historical perspective, for Strange was only one of many talented people who contributed to shaping the future of small sailing boats and yachts.

It is nowadays sometimes stated that small cruising yachts were not designed and built before the last years of the 19th century and that Albert Strange was amongst the first to design them. This is incorrect. Small cruising yachts and many small racers were being designed in detail and built for many years before 1900, by designers who were often also the builders. There were many very talented people in Britain, Germany, Sweden, France, Norway, New Zealand and the United States, with others elsewhere. A comprehensive list would be tedious but confining it to British designers, often also builders of small cruising and other yachts, at the time when Albert Strange was well into his design career, around 1902, one would include Stow and Son of Shoreham, Sussex; Douglas Stone of Erith and later Brightlingsea, Essex; Harold Clayton of Penarth, Wales; J.E. Doyle of Kingstown, Ireland; E.P. and P.T. Harris of Rowhedge, Essex; J. Allen of Poole, Dorset; H.P. Blake of Southampton, Hampshire; Harry Smith of Oxford, later of Burnham-on-Crouch, Essex; C.P. Clayton of Southampton; John Adam of Gourock, Scotland; Forrestt and Co. of Limehouse, later of Wivenhoe, Essex; Linton Hope of Greenhithe, Kent, later of London; Sam Bond of Rock Ferry, Cheshire; John T. Howard of Maldon, Essex; Charles Sibbick of Cowes, Isle of Wight; Aldous and Son of Brightlingsea, Essex; Tom Musslewhite of Poole, Dorset (who had designed the great racing schooner EGERIA in 1865 but continued designing small yachts); Harley Mead of East Cowes and later Falmouth, Cornwall; J. Hilditch of Carrickfergus, Ireland; G.U. Laws of London; R. McAlister of Dumbarton, Scotland; T. Jackett of Falmouth; and others including the notable Arthur E. Payne and his father Alfred Payne of Southampton.

Strange could also be compared with other able contemporary amateur designers of yachts and boats, such as Landseer MacKenzie of Bournemouth, J. Pain Clark of London and H.E. Bayly of Exmouth, Devon, though individually, they did not produce the number of designs which resulted from Albert Strange's transition from amateur to quasi-professional status.

As a comparison, Arthur E. Payne was a good example of the many British professional designers of small yachts, both cruising and racing, who were active during the period when Strange designed yachts and small boats. Born in 1858, three years after Strange, Arthur Payne was one of three sons of Alfred Payne, a yacht designer and builder with a yard at Belvedere, Southampton. Arthur was apprenticed to his father and 'went through the shops' to learn thoroughly the practical side of yachtbuilding in an expanding yard noted for its small racers, cruisers and fishing boats. Arthur quickly showed great promise in the design of yachts and boats, turning out many small craft which were useful cruisers, and others which were prominent in racing. A great many of the best Solent fishing cutters, little craft from 16 to 27 or 30 feet, were designed by Arthur Payne, as others were by his father, and were built alongside the many yachts at their yard. Arthur Payne designed 175 yachts, irrespective of other craft, about the same number as Albert Strange, and would have designed more had he lived beyond 45 years. A fine example of his work in small, practical pleasure craft, was the design of the 20 ft cutter FOAM II, for marine artist Robert Leslie, in 1887. She combined speed, windward ability and grace in an attractive hull typical of Payne's form for small cruising or fishing boats (FIG 1).

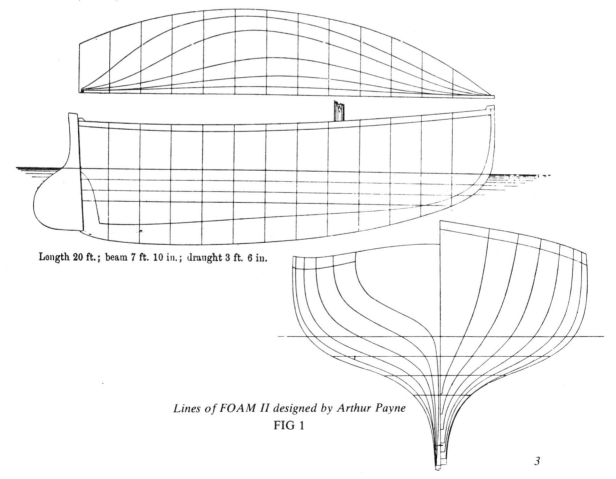

Length 20 ft.; beam 7 ft. 10 in.; draught 3 ft. 6 in.

Lines of FOAM II designed by Arthur Payne
FIG 1

As the Payne family business grew in the 1890s, craft large and small were designed and built in great numbers. It became Summers and Payne Ltd., continuing to build many fine yachts to Arthur's design, from 16 footers to the magnificent 205 ton yawl GLORY, with scores of cruisers and racers in between, all cleverly designed and well built with great attention to detail. Two surviving examples of his small cruisers are the 29ft cutter AYAH, designed and built in 1897 and beautifully formed, and the little 16ft 4in TEAL built in 1902, a year before Arthur Payne's untimely death. Designers such as Arthur Payne and his contemporaries were thoroughly trained professionals, whose work was based on years of close application and was usually backed by study of scientific principles, accurate calculation and excellent draughtsmanship. These men set a high standard against which amateur designers such as Albert Strange were measured, a criterion which enabled Strange's achievements to be evaluated in clear perspective.

A further misconception seems to have arisen regarding Albert Strange's use of the yawl rig in many of his designs. The yawl rig, in small and large yachts, had been in use for many years before the Humber Yawl Club was founded or Strange took up designing. The small cruising yachts of John MacGregor, the ROB ROY, and W.E. Middleton, the KATE, were well publicised examples of the 1860s and 70s. There were many others such as the Marquis of Dufferin's LADY HERMIONE or the venturesome 10 tonner WIDGEON, both well known from their owners' writings. The yawl rig was then also sometimes called the 'Dandy' rig (Dundée is French for a ketch) and was used in many fishing and a few coasting and pilot craft to reduce the length of the main boom and area of the mainsail — for the same reasons it was attractive to yachtsmen. The low centre of area of a two-sailed rig was also obviously desirable in canoes, which have a small range of stability, as was the division of the area into two sails to be more manageable when setting, reefing or stowing by a crew with limited freedom to move when sailing. It is almost certain that the use of the two-masted 'yawl' rig in canoes originated on the Thames and spread to the River Mersey, the Humber, Clyde and elsewhere in the 1870s. Technically, this rig was that of a ketch, as in a canoe, the mizzen mast is inevitably stepped before the sternpost.

Albert Strange was also to be much influenced by the sailing cruising canoe and those using them, particularly by friends from the Humber where a type of pleasure craft known as a canoe yawl flourished for some years after the 1870s, as did the type elsewhere, amongst small boat cruisers of limited means but adventurous spirit. During the 1890s, Albert Strange became gradually closely identified with the canoe-yawl and later the canoe-yacht, a larger derivative for which he became well-known. Both craft originated from the popularity of the paddling and sailing canoe and it is also necessary to understand something of this story to appreciate the background to Strange's career as a small boat sailor and designer.

When Albert Strange was a boy, living by the River Thames, John MacGregor was gathering the experience which would have one of the greatest influences on future small pleasure boats and their use. MacGregor was a graduate of Trinity College, Dublin (then part of Britain) and also of Trinity College, Cambridge, a religious idealist and an untiring advocate of the healthy life. He visited Canada in 1859 and on the Ottawa River saw the birch bark canoes of the Indian tribes. The Indians of North-eastern America, like others on the west coast of the continent, had developed over many years light but adequately strong craft suited to their waters. These were fast, manoeuverable, constructed from indigenous materials and were readily portable when necessary. MacGregor was a keen oarsman who had rowed stroke at Cambridge. He was fascinated by these craft, which were paddled with great skill by the Indians who allowed MacGregor to try several types of canoe. He thought these the most interesting boats he had seen and a type ideal for exploration and modest adventure. He returned to England filled with enthusiasm for canoeing as a sport and with many ideas for a craft which could be built with clinker planking, the widespread method for British small boats at the time, yet which would still be light enough to portage when necessary.

However, MacGregor's entry into practical canoeing was delayed until 1865 when, after recovering from injury sustained in a railway accident, which prevented his participation in another of his sports, competitive shooting, he laid out the basic design for a wooden canoe. He described her as, 'Fifteen feet in length, twenty eight inches broad, nine inches deep and weighed eighty pounds. A paddle seven feet long with a blade at each end and a small lug-sail and jib, were the means of propulsion . . .' The canoe was decked with a small cockpit opening and MacGregor's canoe more closely resembled an Eskimo kayak than the form and arrangements of the Canadian Indian birchbark. She was built with oak planking, unusual in a craft intended to be as light as possible. The deck, more sensibly, was of cedar. This canoe was built by Searl, boatbuilders of Lambeth, an old-established London firm which built large numbers of small boats for the Thames and elsewhere.

John MacGregor lived in an age of adventure and exploration. The world was still full of wonders and parts of North America and much of Australia, Africa and parts of Asia were still unexplored. A few daring travellers were attracted to the Middle East and the Far East, and gold rushes and mass emigration caused by overpopulation, economic depression and famine were rising statistics, swelled by a few with a sense of adventure. Against this international background, John MacGregor sailed and paddled his new canoe through Belgium, Holland, Germany, Switzerland, France and so home. He described his travels in a compelling book, A THOUSAND MILES IN THE ROB ROY CANOE. It was an immediate success when published in 1866.

MacGregor's voyaging and enthusiasm fired the imagination of many, and soon afterwards, a group of enthusiasts met in London to form what would become the Royal Canoe Club. John MacGregor was voted Commodore and Warington Baden-Powell, the barrister brother of Lord Baden-Powell of Boer War and Boy Scout fame, was Vice-Commodore.

MacGregor's canoe cruising had been anticipated about twenty years earlier by Sir Henry de Bathe, who later became a member of the Royal Canoe Club. He had cruised with a paddling canoe on the Thames and there were undoubtedly others of that time, probably more adventurous than de Bathe. But it was the distances covered by MacGregor in foreign countries, his enterprise and ability to publicise his journeys which attracted imitation by many young professional and middle class men who had little other link with going afloat.

John MacGregor followed his European cruise with others in similar canoes, to Scandinavia and to Egypt and Palestine. In 1867, he sailed across the English Channel in a small yawl-rigged yacht, also named ROY ROY, and built to his specification, to attend the Paris exhibition and regatta, again writing a book on his cruising, THE CRUISE ALONE IN THE YAWL ROB ROY.

The Royal Canoe Club was established on the River Thames, and other clubs quickly sprang up in many parts of Britain, notably on the Clyde, Mersey and Humber. A similar enthusiasm for paddling, and paddling and sailing canoes arose in America about 1869 and reached a peak in the 1880s, but it started to decline about

10 years later. Canoe sport also spread to Germany and Scandinavia, particularly to Sweden, and in Holland and Canada and elsewhere, canoeing was soon an established sport. Despite the long cruises by MacGregor, the ROB ROY type of canoe remained best suited to use on rivers. In a seaway these canoes were wet because of the low freeboard and slight sheer, and lacked stability because of narrow beam. When under sail, the canoeist could do little to sit the canoe up, except to lean the upper part of his body to windward of the cockpit and play the sheet. Because a centre-plate was not fitted, sailing to windward was almost impossible.

Whilst MacGregor and others enthusiastically ordered more and larger ROB ROY type canoes, some of their fellows started to develop a type of canoe better fitted for open water sailing but which could still be paddled when necessary. Amongst them were amateurs Walter Stewart and E.B. Tredwen, who were each in later years, to become well known for cruises in small boats and who both designed practical small cruising yachts. An inevitable result of the desire to 'cruise' in a sailing canoe, led to the building of larger canoes which had sufficient internal space to allow sitting up below the deck or under a low cabin top, where two might shelter and sleep in spartan conditions.

The Thames continued to be a centre for pleasure canoe development, well after the 1860s and the little yard of McWhirter at Erith, built some of these larger sailing canoes, which were hybrids between a small cruising yacht and a big canoe. In 1879, McWhirter built the large canoe WATER RAT to the basic specification and outline sketches of the brothers Henry and Lancelot Fiennes Speed. They were typical of many keen amateur sailors of that time — 'Hardy Corinthians' as they were often styled. Their craft was the early form of canoe-yawl, having greater length, beam, depth, displacement and range of stability than the sailing canoes from which they evolved.

Canoe-yawls became popular on the Mersey, on the Humber, to some extent on the Clyde and elsewhere. These were craft suited to the fresher breezes and short seas of exposed estuaries and the coast. But the canoe-yawl lost one of the canoe's principal advantages; it could not be portaged by one or two men, nor could it be so readily carried by the rail or road transport of the time. It was possible for the owner of a canoe-yawl to take a companion with him for a short cruise and still have a lively and responsive boat. Some owners were able to take their wives cruising. Dr John Hayward wrote in 1893, in his comprehensive little book CANOEING that, 'Many ladies become excellent hands, and some are able to steer and even race such craft. I know of men whose wives go quite long cruises with them in canoe-yawls, and one couple sleep aboard under a tent, and declare it delightful and comfortable.'

So, the larger canoe-yawl developed during the 1870s and 80s parallel with the paddling and sailing canoe, though as a type, it became much more diverse in size, hull form, arrangement and rig. It was primarily a cruising craft and was little used for racing, though there was a significant development of fast canoe yawls on the upper Thames. However, the keen small boat racing enthusiast of that time was more likely to put money into ownership of a three tonner, or later a half-rater, if he could afford it, or one of the very few racing dinghy classes if he could not.

There were some attempts made to distinguish between canoe-yawls and canoe yachts. W. Baden-Powell of the Royal Canoe Club held that a canoe-yawl had a '. . . length not exceeding 20ft, beam not less than 5ft, depth from the upper side of deck to underside of keel, measured at any point, not exceeding 3ft . . .' Clubs on the Mersey adopted this definition but Hayward insisted it '. . . will exclude a large number of boats commonly classed as canoe-yawls, some of which are beyond the measurements, some possess counters or transoms, and some (as the VITAL SPARK and some of the Humber yawls) have metal keels.' Hayward was a keen canoeist and canoe yawl sailor, who had cruised widely in small boats under sail and oar and had sailed canoe-yawls for many years. His own distinction between the canoe-yawl and the canoe yacht was rational, though never widely accepted. He held that a canoe-yawl could be brought ashore with reasonable ease whereas the displacement and draught of the canoe yacht forced her to be kept on a mooring. Many canoe-yawls were not more than 18 ft in length, were three-quarter decked and had a centreplate, while the rig was generally removable. But few would try to lift such heavy boats out of the water in the course of use, even if help were available, and most were kept afloat if possible. Size, hull form and rig varied with locality and the owner's desires. Some of the fastest were built at Oxford, many miles from the sea, by two designers and boatbuilders who make another worthy professional comparison with Albert Strange, this time in the design of canoes and canoe-yawls as well as small yachts.

In the 1880s, the fresh water reaches of the River Thames, which run from the heart of England, were entering on their thirty year heyday of boating popularity. The rapid growth of rail travel, often cheaply available to most of the population, led to expansion of the building of skiffs and other boats for hire on the Thames. It also encouraged large numbers of steam launches, houseboats and the building of sailing craft suited to its narrow and shallow waters. Small boatyards were busy along the many miles of river between Lechlade and Teddington, below which the tidal Thames began its course through grimy London, towards the clean water of its estuary. At Oxford, a university city, there were several boatbuilding yards, one, later two, worked by the five Smith brothers, all boatbuilders. Two of them, Theo and Harry, were inventive and progressive. Besides designing and building small boats, Theo also designed and made bicycles, then a new craze in an era when motor cars were just beginning to be thought of. He lived a few doors away from William Morris and for some time they worked independently on cycle manufacture but after a year or two, Theo returned fully to boatbuilding while William Morris went on to found a car manufacturing empire. However, Theo's inventive mind ranged well beyond the repetitive building of clinker planked rowing skiffs and canoes for hire and for private use. He liked to design and build fast boats and many of his clients were young men attending Oxford University, and some were its lecturers. The Oxford University Sailing Club held sailing races on the stretch of the Thames by Port Meadow, where winds were relatively uninterrupted by Oxford's trees and buildings. Several members were keen canoeists and a number of sailing canoes, mostly intended for racing, were designed and built for them by Theo, and others by Harry Smith. Many of these had complete or partial chines, particularly in the after body, to provide sufficient volume of displacement aft, to maintain trim and provide lift when sailing fast. To illustrate their design ability, Theo was producing the detailed designs for a planing, racing canoe in 1888. This light and very fast craft had a hull form with one feature of particular significance. The partial chine aft was designed in a curve depressed to end at the heel of the sternpost. The transverse sections followed this chine profile to produce a lifting force when at speed and so aid the boat to trim level and plane. In this, Theo Smith showed his considerable scientific reasoning, well ahead of the designers of fast steam torpedo boats, torpedo boat destroyers and early motor launches, who were to experiment with similar forms for the same reasons a decade later.

The fame of the sailing canoes produced by the Smith brothers spread and the craft were further developed in hull form and rig. Larger canoes were designed and built by them for cruising, as well as day sailing and racing. They also built many small 'raters' and a few small cruising yachts. Both Theo and Harry also designed and patented collapsable boats for use as yacht tenders, for ease of transport on expeditions, and in larger sizes to be carried as lifeboats on ships. Their larger canoes were so successful, that they became nationally known as the 'Oxford canoe-yawls', a type usually having a well rockered keel profile, reasonable beam and a sloop, sometimes a yawl rig, technically a ketch as with so many canoe-yawls, as the mizzen was stepped forward of the sternpost. The reputation for speed of these Smith canoe-yawls did much to attract notice to the type in other sailing waters, particularly amongst racing and younger owners.

The Oxford canoe-yawls were taken by rail to other places but occasionally sailed the length of the Thames, into the tideway, to sail on the coast. The Solent racing world was shaken by one which was built to sail in the then popular half rater class of small keel or keel/centreplate racers. Her success brought indignant protest from the keel boat majority but raised the sailing world's respect for the speed of the small, fast centreplate craft, of which at that time, the Smiths designed and built the swiftest for their size.

The fame of the designs and the fine construction and finish of the Oxfordshire men is now little known but their advanced ideas, draughted in detail and backed by calculations, were executed well. Both continued as designers and builders of small craft for many years. Harry moved to manage and then own, the Burnham Yacht Building Co. at Burnham-on-Crouch, where he designed many small cruising and racing yachts. Theo moved to Hythe, then to Ashlett Mill, on Southampton Water before settling finally at Yarmouth, Isle of Wight. His detailed proposals for the establishment of an aircraft building factory at Oxford in 1909 and his design of an aeroplane that year might have led him to other things but he died a respected designer and builder of small boats.

The Smith brothers were established designers and builders when Albert Strange designed his first boat, and at the time when his great friend, George Holmes, essayed his first draughting of canoes and dinghies for the Humber. Strange's other contemporaries in the design of canoes and canoe-yawls included professionals, such as Sam Bond of Rock Ferry on the Mersey; Linton Hope of Greenhithe; G.U. Laws of London; C. and A. Burgoine and also Turk of Kingston-on-Thames and others. There were also gifted amateurs, such as W. Baden-Powell, E.B. Tredwen and Walter Stewart. Albert Strange would have been familiar, at first hand or by reading, with the work of them all and with others designing and building small yachts and canoes overseas.

In the course of his life, particularly after the 1880s, Strange made many friends through the publication of his designs and his writings. One was the American, William P. Stephens, a keen canoeist, born in 1854, who was to have influence by correspondence on Strange's thoughts on design. Stephens had studied civil engineering and thus acquired some ability at draughting and calculations. He took early to sailing small boats but did not obtain any professional qualifications. He worked for two years in a shipyard then took up canoe and small boat building for two more. By 1891, he had turned to a combination of small boat and yacht journalism, acting as yachting editor of the influential American journal FOREST AND STREAM until 1903. He also designed and occasionally built sailing and paddling canoes and, after the mid 1890s, small canoe yachts. From 1903 until 1939 he was editor of LLOYD'S REGISTER OF AMERICAN YACHTS and altogether he became recognised as an authority on yachting and small boat sailing and design, rather in the manner of the Englishman, Dixon Kemp. In October 1897, Stephens designed a small canoe yacht of advanced form as a yawl rigged single-hander, 21 ft 9 in overall, 18 ft waterline length, 5 ft 9 in beam and 3 ft draught. Displacement was 2,800 pounds and the ballast keel 0.53 ton (FIG 2). The design of this craft was published in the HUMBER YAWL CLUB YEARBOOK of 1898. She was an attractive and well conceived boat which almost certainly drew inspiration from one of Albert Strange's earliest designs, No 4 in his list. This combined the desirable shallow draught characteristics of the canoe-yawl with a pointed, overhanging 'canoe' stern of what later became known as the 'canoe yacht', though the stern was antedated in principle by the English yawl JULLANAR of 1875 and the Sydney cutter AUSTRALIA of 1858.

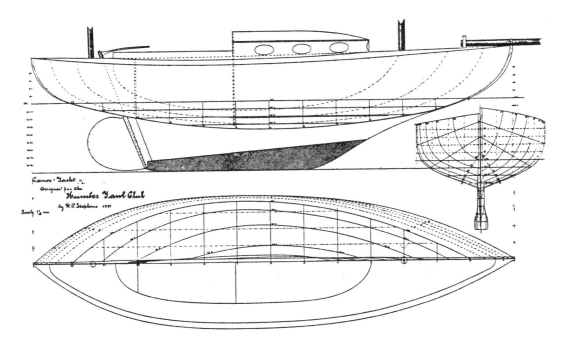

Canoe yacht designed by William P. Stephens

FIG 2

Strange designed this single-handed cruiser in 1891 with principal dimensions of 20 ft 9 in overall, 6 ft 6 in beam and 2 ft draught without the centreplate lowered. The rig was a gaff ketch with a single headsail and the design appeared in THE YACHTSMAN in 1892, the year before the correspondence between Strange and Stephens started. Two boats were built from the design, despite it being in many respects patently amateur. Stephens' canoe yacht design of 1897 came out simultaneously with a very well executed design for a canoe yacht named CATRIONA by Louis N. Sanderson of Scarborough, who was an art pupil of Strange, who had encouraged him in yacht design. The CATRIONA had some of the characteristics of Stephens' yawl but Sanderson declared he was unaware of the American's work. The design of the CATRIONA won second prize in THE

YACHTSMAN Design Competition No 2 in 1898 and quite independently, another entry had a very similar stern in plans submitted by Charles V. Johnson of Brighton, Sussex who preferred a sloop rig. A year later, George Holmes entered a shallow draught canoe yacht design in another of the magazine's competitions — a 30 ft yawl with a canoe stern very similar to Albert Strange's style of overhang and cleverly worked in on a draught of 2 ft with the centreplate raised.

So how does the work of these many talented designers, professional and amateur, stand in the history of yachting and small boat sailing, and in comparison with that of Albert Strange? Some of the small cruising yachts, a few racers and even fewer canoe-yawls designed and built by able men, such as Payne and the Smiths survive, as do some of their larger yachts, but their designer's names are now barely recalled and their creations are certainly not as well known as the design work of Albert Strange or his friend, Dr T. Harrison Butler. There are two main reasons for this. Strange's major design output took place from the mid 1890s to his death in 1917. This was a period, particularly before 1914, when the growth of British yachting magazines was rapid and spread news and opinions on the work of yacht designers widely, to a yachting public which was broadening from the earlier wealthy and leisured classes to the less well off, mainly professional men who usually had less time for their pastimes. They, accordingly, wanted smaller yachts or small boats and many were out of sympathy with the world of established yachting, its customs, traditions and expense. Many took readily to the publicising of amateur cruising expounded by a few of their fellows, such as Albert Strange and Harrison Butler, who also designed small yachts based on their sailing experience and probably did not charge realistic design fees, because of their other income.

In his design career, Strange was also greatly helped by his friendship with Herbert Reiach, a competent professional naval architect, designer of yachts and one time manager of the Southampton yacht yard of J. and G. Fay. Because of ill-health, Reiach became the founding editor of YACHTING MONTHLY the magazine which would become the principal outlet for Albert Strange's published designs.

There was also, I suspect, benefit from that peculiarly British trait of admiration for the gifted amateur who appeared to keep up with the professionals. An ability also usually admired by the professionals, who knew well the skills needed to succeed, but also the burdens, perhaps unknown to the amateur, of earning a living from their work and in many cases the further burden of managing the vagaries of a yacht building and repairing business.

Albert Strange started designing small yachts as a pastime in the late 1880s, at a time when the methods of design calculation, of fine wooden construction, refinement of rigs and rigging and the development of many yacht fittings, all of which Strange was to use in his yacht designs, had been evolved and were in widespread use. The great majority of designers of even quite small yachts and pleasure craft were using calculations and draughting to ensure satisfying characteristics in their output. He would not, therefore, be an innovator but rather a contributor to and a refiner of a certain style of small cruising yacht to which, like the practice of cruising in small yachts, Strange devoted much thought. His first commissioned design was for a centreplate sailing cruising boat whose hull form was developed from a lines plan appearing in Dixon Kemp's MANUAL OF YACHT AND BOAT SAILING. This WREN, ". . . is now incorporated amongst the designs given in Mr Dixon Kemp's latest edition of YACHT ARCHITECTURE." (Extract from a paper read by Strange to members of the Royal Yorkshire Yacht Club published in THE YACHTSMAN Jan 14th 1892.)

From that modest beginning, influenced by other reading and his own sailing experiences as a young man, Strange began thirty years of yacht and boat design. He gradually became acknowledged as a master of conceiving able and attractive small cruising yachts, resulting in a following of admirers which persists to this day and is the cause of the writing of this book.

This is intended to be an overview of the life of Albert Strange and of his yacht and boat designs and cruises. It is not meant as a comprehensive biography, much of which would be tedious to the average reader interested in sailing and small craft, but offers a review of his life and work which may encourage others to research in more detail.

CHAPTER 2

Albert Strange

Albert Strange at the tiller of the yawl CHERUB III

Appreciation of the work of a designer of small craft is helped by knowing something of his personal background and experience, particularly if, as with Albert Strange, his vocation was different from the hobby which he developed to almost equal his employment, in the time he devoted to it, and for which he is best remembered.

Albert Strange was born on 29 July 1855, into an England fighting alongside France against Russia in the Black Sea and the Baltic, a struggle which became known as the Crimean War. To give a wider historical perspective, that year explorer David Livingstone discovered the Victoria Falls, named for the great Queen who had been 18 years on the throne, ladies of fashion wore the crinoline and although Trafalgar had been fought fifty years earlier, many warships remained fully rigged despite the advance of steam and iron.

His birthplace, the small town of Gravesend, was then a busy community on the south bank of the Thames tideway, east of London. It looked to the river for most of its living. Shipping, large and small, of a still growing empire passed it each tide and the foreshore had several boatbuilding and small shipbuilding yards.

Albert Strange was born at 30 Queen Street, one of a row of small houses many of which were demolished in 1970 when flats were built in the area, though number 30 was still standing in 1983. His father, George L'Strange, was a shopkeeper of uncertain lineage, whose forebears may have been immigrants from Europe. He had two children by his first marriage — Charles, who became a Thames River Pilot at Gravesend, and a daughter Elizabeth, a spinster who trained as a nurse in Winchester and subsequently became a sister at Queen Charlotte's Hospital, London. George's first wife died and his second wife was Sarah Elizabeth Jarman. It was about this time that he changed his name from L'Strange to Strange. Albert was one of four children of George and Sarah. The others were Frederick, (who trained for the Ministry at St Augustine's Missionary College at Canterbury and later became the British Chaplain at Port Said, Egypt), Emily and Florence Sarah. Their mother died young and George Strange married again, this time to Anne Blundell who was a nurse at St Thomas's Hospital where she nursed and met George. The one child of this marriage was Ethel, born in 1877.

George maintained that all his children should have a good education. He paid for his first daughter, Elizabeth, to be trained as a nurse and her brother Charles had to have his apprentice's premium paid for him. Albert's brother, Frederick, was supported during his training at the Missionary College and George was also prepared to pay for Albert to study for a legal career, but as he wished to study art instead, his father helped him to study at the Slade School of Art in South Kensington. The last child, Ethel, went to a private school. Albert's father was not only a good parent but must have been successful in business. He owned a shop and dealt in china and general hardware.

It is probable that young Albert attended a local school, of a type then common, where a small weekly fee paid for a basic education. Whatever it was, he showed early talent for music. His parents encouraged him to develop his ability at the piano and this remained throughout his life. However, the sullen, grey river was calling to Albert, as rivers do to many boys in many ages. He began to spend much of his spare time by it, watching ships and boats and the work in the yards of the town, asking questions and probably being a nuisance to the workmen, though perhaps he was able to run an errand or two.

Boys usually thoroughly absorb things which really interest them and the sights, sounds, smells and noises of the Gravesend yards and the way of life of the men working there became etched on his memory. Although content in his studies and developing a love of music, Albert Strange was possibly happiest about the boatyards of the shore.

His musical leanings led to his joining the church choir, which held an annual outing in summer. In 1869, when Albert was 14 years old, the choir outing was to be on the river, sailing aboard the craft of a local fisherman (referred to in Chapter 7). Probably she was a transom sterned, clinker planked and bawley rigged Gravesend shrimper, about 28 ft long, perhaps a little larger. On the day, Albert took with him a model sailing yacht to tow astern on a line. It seems he had made the model and the skipper of the shrimper noted with interest that its details were unusually correct for a boy's model. Because of this, he took an immediate liking to Albert and perhaps discussed sailing and the shape of craft and their rigs with him. He also allowed Albert to go fishing with him in the bawley at times.

This fisherman was one of a few on the lower Thames who were engaged to act as local pilots by the skippers of the large class racing yachts, when these raced in the various annual Thames matches which, until 1914 and particularly before 1900, started off from Gravesend or nearby, at the start of the yacht racing season of the big yachts each May. They raced seawards down the Lower Hope and Sea Reach, usually to round the Mouse light vessel and return. New fliers showed off their form, or not, depending on their design, construction, handling, and the competition, which was invariably very keen in those days of professional crews which might number between thirty and forty men in the bigger yachts. The professional skippers were in full charge of these great vessels, their handling and tactics. They needed expert local advice on depths and tidal sets, exact locations of banks and shoals and local weather patterns which could only be learned in a lifetime afloat in a locale. Local fishermen were the choice for this work and usually one of them sailed on board each of the big racers so his advice was available to her skipper who with his hands on the tiller lines, eyes on his sails, his rivals and his crew, besides the winds and thinking his tactics out ahead, needed all the assistance possible to squeeze the most out of his command. These local pilots took no part in handling the yachts. The yachts were large but not as big as they would become in the 1890s and 1900s when draughts of 18 to 20 feet were common and sail plans reached over 150 feet from bowsprit end to boom end and spread over 10,000 square feet of working sail, without the great spinnakers of almost equal area.

Albert's friend, the Gravesend fisherman, was one of these yachting pilots and rather unusually was able to invite Albert to join him on one of his engagements as his "boy". The boy enjoyed it immensely and evidently did not get in the way — the greatest sin on board a racing yacht. Perhaps he also made himself useful, taking round the beer and sandwiches to the crew with the steward. As a result, Albert was invited to sail with the fisherman on other yachts when he acted as pilot, and so he sailed on several of the big cutters and perhaps also a few schooners and yawls of the mixed fleets of the big class of the 1860s and 1870s. The large schooner EGERIA was his favourite. He also sailed in the schooner SEA BELLE.

Three years later Albert Strange owned his first craft, an old Thames peter boat named DAUNTLESS. According to an article Strange wrote in THE MODEL YACHTSMAN AND CANOEIST of April 1893, he acquired her via his fisherman friend (again referred to in Chapter 7) after the peter boat sank whilst racing off Gravesend in a local knockabout class. Excessive sail area and an inexperienced crew caused the accident. The fisherman, helped by Albert, rescued the four occupants who left the sunken boat to the bawleyman in gratitude. He passed the refloated boat on to Albert for a modest sum, and with the spritsail reduced in size and the foresail set she became Albert's 'Yot'. She was 18 ft in length and 6 ft beam, clinker planked and with a pointed stern. Originally an open boat with a wet well amidships as a relic of her fishing days, Strange fitted her with a cabin and altered the rig. Not having a centreboard or false keel she would reach and run quite well but be slow turning to windward, even with a fair tide. However, she could also be rowed. Albert's plan of the DAUNTLESS appears here (FIG 3). The boat had a lifelong effect on Albert Strange's designs for small sailing yachts.

In her he set off with that wonderful self-confidence of youth to explore the

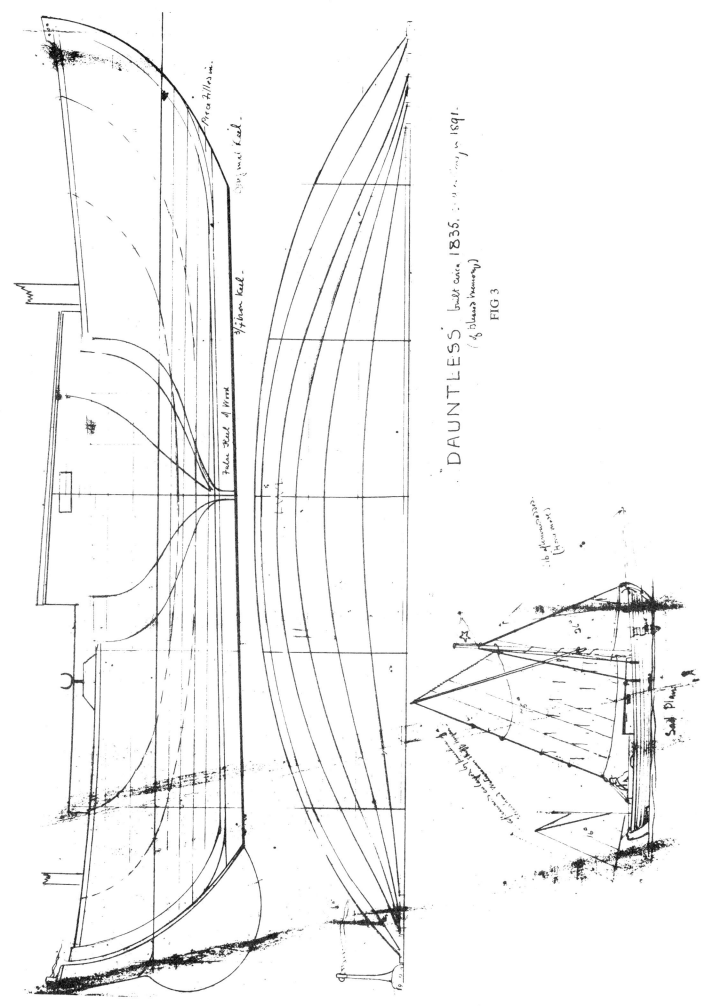

DAUNTLESS – a Peter boat – Albert Strange's first boat

rivers and creeks of the Lower Thames area and its tributary river the Medway. Narrow waters with swift tides breed good fore and aft seamen and Albert Strange started a long apprenticeship in learning the ways of small boats.

George Strange, his father, hoped Albert would study for a career in law and tried to arrange his later education to suit. Albert must have disappointed him greatly when, aged about 18, he declared that he wished to become an artist and enrolled at a local art class. Despite family opposition, he persevered and embarked on a way of life which was regarded as particularly precarious. However, Albert became disenchanted with the tuition available locally, so his father paid for him to attend the Slade School of Art in South Kensington, London. It is also known that he was a student, and presumably later an Honorary Associate, of Leicester College of Arts and Crafts.

About 1875, his father's fears appeared to be justified when Albert, then 20 years old, became restless and set off to study in France, sailing over in his boat, on board which he proposed to live whilst there, though he, with other students, was soon painting and sketching in Lombardy and Picardy and the boat must have been laid up. It was a happy time for him. He progressed well in art studies and developed an individual style, stimulated by his surroundings, a typical experience of many young art students in France.

In 1880, aged 25, Albert Strange returned to England to live at Little Buckland near Maidstone in Kent and about 15 miles from Gravesend. He sought work in the art world and was lucky enough to be appointed Second Master at the Liverpool College of Art, part of the Upper School of Liverpool Collegiate.

Strange had gone into partnership with a friend over a 26ft cutter called QUEST. She was reputedly an ex-Government vessel, though she seems very small for such service, as a cutter. In her they cruised the lower Thames, the Medway and the Kentish and probably also the Essex coasts. In 1881, they sailed her to northern France. The first of Albert Strange's cruising accounts, written many years later as, "A Winter's Tale", was a retrospect of the return of the QUEST early in 1882. That was a notable year for Albert Strange since for the first time, he had a painting exhibited at the Royal Academy, where he would exhibit annually during many of the following ten years. Then, in August, he married Julia Louisa Woolard, a member of the Society of Friends, or Quakers. This was made possible by a further step in his career. He had applied for the position of Headmaster of a government school of art which was being established at Scarborough on the Yorkshire coast. The small seaside and fishing town with its harbour was becoming a mildly fashionable resort and was much frequented by artists.

Albert Strange's application was successful and at 27 and with only two year's teaching experience, he took up the position in September 1882. It is possible he may have known of the opportunity through W.S. Caine, a Member of Parliament and a sailing acquaintance of Albert's. It may be that Caine also had some influence in the appointment as he was to open the school formally in August 1884, two years after its foundation.

Albert and Julia Strange took a house in Scarborough and immediately became enthusiastically involved in the operation of the Art School. Their future appeared secure, no mean achievement at an early age in the Victorian era. The School was to grow and flourish, eventually receiving 250 pupils in a year. The curriculum gave particular attention to the design of textiles, wallpapers, pottery and book illustration, no doubt strongly influenced by the ideas of the prevailing arts and crafts movement. These early years were ones of development and Albert's energy and foresight were a strong part of the Scarborough Art School's quickly growing reputation. He became a well known and respected local figure.

In 1884, Julia gave birth to a daughter, Dorothy, and two years later, to their first son, George Frederick. But, despite the cares and duties of a young family, Albert Strange's interest in sailing, in boats and the sea remained strong and with an apparently secure job, he joined the Royal Yorkshire Yacht Club which was based at Bridlington Harbour. The harbour at Scarborough fascinated Strange. It was visited by many types of small vessels, including sailing and steam drifters, trawling cutters and ketches and a few of the then new steam trawlers, besides regular calls by brigs and brigantines and barquentines, usually bringing house coal or stone for the roads. A few yachts also visited the harbour which had its own fleet of fishing cobles. In summer, in fine weather, these also took parties of visitors for a sail from the harbour. But in winter, with the wind onshore, this coast is a desolate and dangerous place where wrecks were fairly commonplace. Altogether, Scarborough offered much to an artist with seagoing inclinations.

Albert Strange was a visitor on many yachts and other craft in the harbour and retained his early liking for single-handed sailing but with a young family to support, he could not afford to own a large craft. He had visited the Humber, winding inland and dividing East Yorkshire from Lincolnshire. It was a wide and windy estuary with tide ridden lower reaches. There at Hessle he had met with some members of the Humber Yawl Club, whose canoe-yawls were of robust dimensions, hull form and rig to suit local sailing conditions. Members also owned a variety of other small craft.

Albert was familiar with craft having a small mizzen of yawl proportions from his Thames experiences. He produced a design for a small cruising gaff cutter to be built for himself and in 1888, placed an order for her with James Frank, a Scarborough boatbuilder. The CHERUB, as she was named (Plate 1) proved successful and

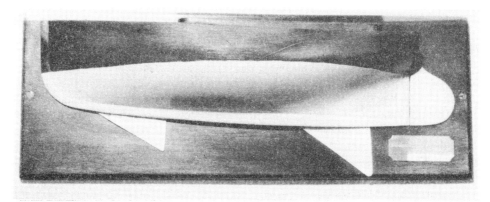

CHERUB I – the first small cruiser designed by Albert Strange for himself and built by James Frank at Scarborough

PLATE 1

suited Strange as a single handed boat. He kept her at Scarborough harbour and sailed along that exposed north-east coast, often wracked by strong winds and cold, boisterous weather.

In 1891, Strange joined the Humber Yawl Club and almost immediately became a close friend of George F. Holmes, an engineer of Hull, then a substantial fishing port on the north shore of the Humber, with a large deep sea trawling fleet of sailing and steam vessels. George Holmes was from the 1880s to the 1930s a prolific designer of small sailing and rowing craft in his spare time, all of them sound, practical boats. He also had considerable artistic talent and was a founder-member of the Club. Their friendship lasted until Strange's death and in the 1890s, the two men often sailed together, usually in Holmes' little canoe-yawl EEL (FIG 4). These were sociable little cruises during which both men sketched and painted wonderfully atmospheric records of small boat sailing.

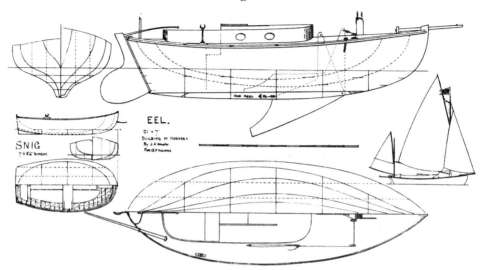

Canoe yawl EEL designed by George Holmes

FIG 4

Albert read the American periodical FOREST AND STREAM of which the notable American canoe designer and yachting journalist, William P. Stephens was yachting and canoeing editor between 1883 and 1903. In 1893, Strange wrote to him regarding some opinions expressed in an article and a corresponding friendship developed and continued until Strange's death. It was also to lead to an unexpected preservation of many of Albert's original design drawings, as we shall see.

In 1893-94, Albert Strange replaced the CHERUB (which was not actually sold until 1896) with a slightly smaller craft, the CHERUB II of 22 ft 2 in length overall (FIGS 5, 6 & 7). Next summer in 1895, full of resolve to visit old friends, he sailed her down the east coast to the Thames, via the Humber and Trent and described this six week cruise in the first of the several illustrated articles he wrote for YACHTING AND BOATING MONTHLY (later YACHTING MONTHLY) some years later.

Scarborough harbour was a meeting place for many artists and amongst them were several with sailing experience and inclinations. There was enough interest to form a local sailing club and Albert Strange acted as Chairman at the inaugural meeting of the Scarborough Sailing Club in May 1895. That year he was elected Captain of the Humber Yawl Club which continued to grow. By publication of an attractive little Yearbook, the Club became well known in British sailing circles for the practical approach to the sport by its members and for their artistic and design talents. By then Albert Strange was well established at Scarborough.

In 1896, he arranged for the CHERUB II to be transported by the ship LADY MARTIN from London Docks to Portsmouth to attend a meet of the British Canoe Association at Wootton, Isle of Wight. This Association, of which Albert was a member, comprised an active and enterprising group of canoeists of the sail and paddle, holding "meets" in different places each summer at which the members, and sometimes their wives, lived in tents ashore. They held paddling and sailing races, talked canoes and equipment and exchanged ideas in an apparently delightful fraternity which has been so well recorded by Dr John D. Hayward in his books.

After the meet, Strange sailed the CHERUB II along the south coast, around Dungeness and along the east coast of Kent into the Thames and Gravesend, a trip of some 200 miles which forms the subject of Chapter 7.

Soon afterwards, the CHERUB II was sold and in 1897, Albert Strange and George Holmes set off by steamer from Hull taking Holmes' canoe yawl EEL as deck cargo to Germany for a cruise from the river Elbe and into the ever alluring Baltic. Strange had begun designing in the 1880s and this hobby developed gradually from boats designed for himself, to craft for friends and fellow club members and to commissions from others. By 1898, when he became Captain of the Scarborough Sailing Club, he had designed about forty small craft, the then most recent for a Canadian owner. That year the Strange's last child, Albert Richard Hugh Strange was born.

Aged 43, Albert Strange had a happy family and his work at the school of art was successful. He had become well known in the locality and had been Captain of both the Humber Yawl Club and the Scarborough Sailing Club, an unusual distinction. Strange's artistic work was rewarding intellectually and financially. His watercolours

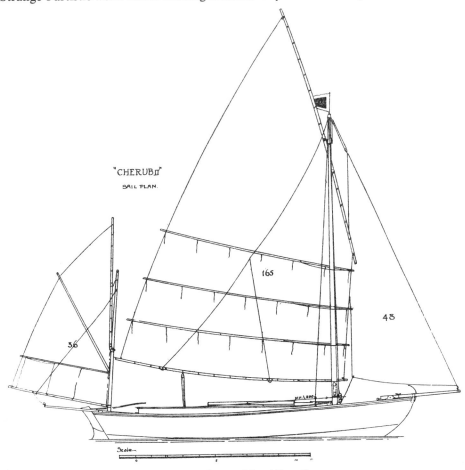

CHERUB II designed by Albert Strange

FIG 5

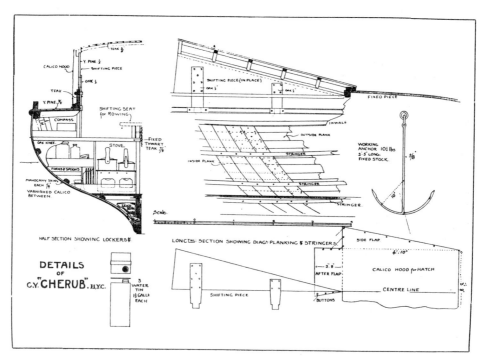

FIG 6

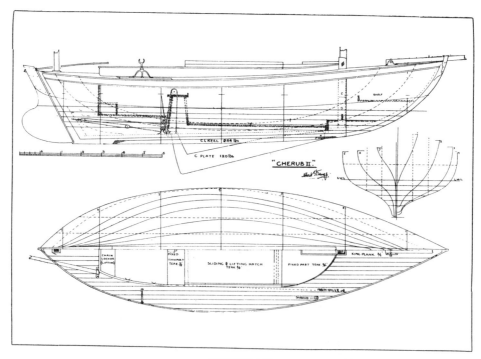

CHERUB II
FIG 7

were clear and carefully executed. These sold well, particularly scenes of country or coast which were known and liked by local people. His work kept him in contact with youth and brought the pleasurable task of helping them to improve their talents and advance themselves generally. He found enjoyment in this and spent many summers painting in the countryside, afloat or alongshore.

Like many men of that age and settled and successful background, Strange developed a quick wit and an inclination to speak at dinners. He spoke frequently at dinners of his two sailing clubs. Sometimes he also contributed a musical piece and in all ways, enjoyed the company of fellow members.

So far, Albert Strange had achieved most of his aspirations and good standing in the community. Besides being increasingly recognised as a designer of small craft — he was also developing as author of pleasing illustrated articles on small boat sailing. At middle age, he could not foresee the continuing increase of interest in his small craft designs, which was to dominate the last third of his life and bring lasting recognition. There were also further developments in art. In 1900, Strange was asked to become visiting art master to Bootham, the noted Quaker school at York, then temporarily quartered at Scarborough. Possibly his older son, then 14 years of age, was a pupil there, as the younger would be from 1912 to 1914. It might possibly have been from one of his wife's connections, but however obtained, Albert Strange enjoyed his weekly one day visits to Bootham, although the journey of forty miles or so to York and the return, would take considerable time by train and this additional appointment probably restricted his sailing club and Humber Yawl Club activities.

In May 1901, Albert Strange was elected the first Honorary Life Member of the Humber Yawl Club and was presented with a copy of Folkard's book, "The Sailing Boat" in commemoration. It was an honour to be treasured. During the following years, he continued to design small boats and yachts at an average rate of one per month. The probable development of his ideas for small cruising yachts and boats are discussed in Chapter 6. By 1903-04, when he designed the yawl SHEILA for use on the west coast of Scotland, Strange had become well known in British sailing circles amongst cruising men and his creative ability was of interest to other designers of small yachts.

His family progressed. In May 1909, Strange's elder son was admitted to the Roll of Solicitors, giving great satisfaction to his parents and contrasting with Albert's problems in settling his own future career.

In 1910, Albert Strange designed another small yacht for his own use. The CHERUB III was built at Dickie's yard at Tarbert, Loch Fyne, Scotland and embodied Strange's best ideas for a 6 ton cruising yacht. He took lodgings in the village to oversee her completion but his delight in this had to be curtailed as Julia became ill. After her recovery, the Strange's next summer holiday was taken on board the new boat, with their family. They cruised in the Western Isles and greatly enjoyed that summer. Perhaps they were all never to be so happy again. In November, Albert suffered a mild heart attack. It was the first of a series of unpleasant events.

Albert's doctor, knowing his patient's activities, forbade sailing in the future and recommended the immediate sale of Strange's beloved new yacht. However, Albert decided to keep the CHERUB III for a while in hope of an improvement in his condition. A few days later, news came that his brother, Frederick, Canon Strange, had died suddenly as British Chaplain at Port Said. Albert felt this loss deeply. Worse was to come. In May 1912 the Strange's daughter, Dorothy, died, aged only 28, from tuberculosis. She had married but evidently lived apart from her husband, not far from Scarborough. Two months later, Albert's old friend W.I. Beaumont, for whom he had designed the yawl HAWKMOTH, was drowned.

Despite all these misfortunes, Albert Strange tried to keep cheerful and to ease the sadness, he plunged into his creative work. Soon he was painting more than ever and ten or so yacht and small boat designs came from his drawing board each year. A notable commission was from Claud Worth, an eye specialist and amateur cruising yachtsman. For him, Strange designed the cutter TERN III, perhaps the peak of his yacht design attainments, although in contemporary yacht registers she is credited as designed by Worth. However, it seems that like many amateur 'designers', Worth's part went no further than laying out the design parameters which Albert Strange developed into a detailed design (FIGS 8 & 9).

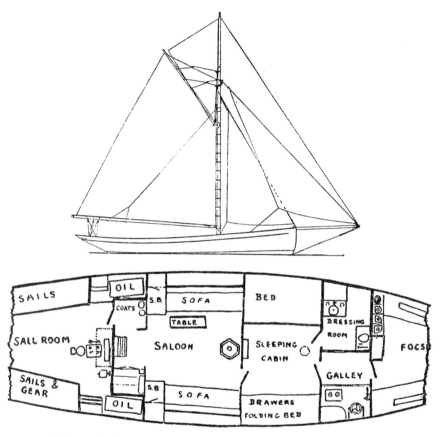

Lines, sail plan and accommodation plan of 53 ft cutter TERN III

FIG 8

But all was not well with Albert Strange. Worth wrote that year to W.P. Stephens, their mutual American friend, ending his letter, "I suppose you have heard about our good friend Strange. He had a severe attack of influenza and it has left his heart weak, so that he will never again be able to do any sailing single-handed. Poor fellow, I am really grieved about it, for a better man and a keener sailor there surely never was." Gradually Albert faced the reality of his condition and he sold the CHERUB III to W. Murdoch, a schoolmaster of Campbeltown, Scotland.

1913 brought a visit to England by Willam P. Stephens, who had long corresponded with Albert and with George Holmes. Stephens sailed from New York

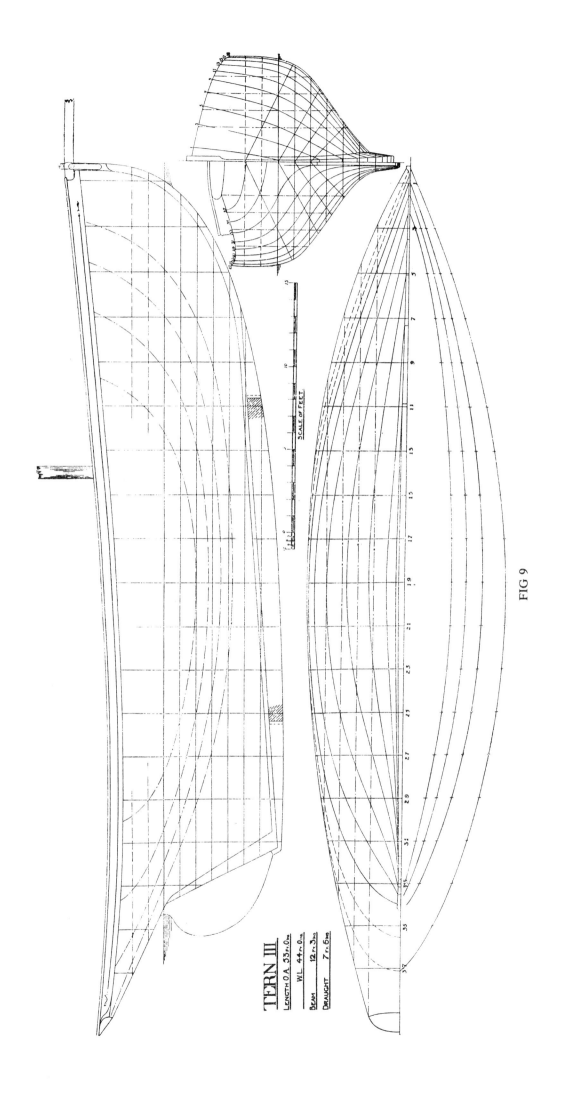

TERN III

LENGTH O.A. 53ₙ.0ₘ
WL 44ₙ.0ₘ
BEAM 12ₙ.3ₘ
DRAUGHT 7ₙ.6ₘ

SCALE OF FEET

FIG 9

on board the British cargo steamer PASCAL in August, enjoying a fifteen day passage to Manchester. From there, he took the train to London and did some business at Lloyd's Register of Shipping office. A few days later, he travelled by train to the village of Hessle, on the north bank of the Humber, near where the Humber Yawl Club had its headquarters. He was met by George Holmes and stayed at his quaint stone house in the village, which overlooked the river and was shadowed by a large windmill. They spent a weekend cruising on board Holmes' new canoe yawl SNIPPET, sailing about the Humber and into the river Trent, before returning to Hessle for Stephens to go to London by rail for more business. After it, Stephens joined Ernest Hicks Oliver, then editor of the British LLOYD'S REGISTER OF YACHTS, for a two week cruise in Oliver's recently purchased canoe yawl EEL, obtained from George Holmes earlier that year via indirect correspondence with William Stephens, who had introduced them by letter. The EEL was now kept at Burnham-on-Crouch, the largest sailing centre on the east coast of Britain. They sailed about the rivers Crouch and Roach and afterwards, ventured across the Thames estuary to the river Medway, before returning to Canvey Island where Stephens left to return to London en route for America. Sometime during the visit, the only one he seems to have made to England, Stephens visited Albert Strange as he recorded, "I only had a few days to visit him personally." During that visit, it is possible that Strange handed over to Stephens a number of his designs, probably with a view to their publication in a projected book which was never completed. Perhaps Strange expected their eventual return, but because of Stephens' interest and care, they have happily ended up in the archives of Mystic Seaport, deposited there by Stephen's daughter, Eleanor, after his death. There are also later plans by Strange in the Stephen's Collection, including one incomplete at his death.

Despite his condition, Albert maintained hope and enthusiasm for small boats and their sailing. He wrote to William Stephens in April 1914, "I went to see my doctor the other day and he found my wretched heart was rather better; I promptly put it to him: 'Was it enough better for another boat?' But he demurred. However I got out the lines of a little chap 21' × 7' 6" × 2' 9" and am going to ask Dickie at Tarbert for a price; then, when you come over next year (1915) you can come for a cruise about Loch Fyne." Alas, Strange never got his boat or the cruise as the Great War broke out four months later, on August 4th 1914. Yachtbuilding and yachting ceased almost entirely in Britain for four years. Albert continued to design small boats and cruising yachts, some of them commissioned work. Others were prepared for his own satisfaction. He also continued to write to and for yachting journals and in particular for the YACHTING MONTHLY.

The war though, brought more worry to Albert, as it did to all. He was deeply moved by it, not least because of his naturally patriotic interest in that greatest and most destructive of wars. His younger son enlisted as an army cadet. In 1915, a German battle-cruiser squadron attacked seaside towns on the east coast of England in a demonstration of defiance of the British Grand Fleet. Lowestoft, Yarmouth and Scarborough were shelled in a raid which had no military significance but considerable effect on British morale. One shell, believed to be of 150 mm calibre, fell on Strange's house, but luckily he and Julia were unhurt. One assumes they were not at home, though not far away.

In 1916, Albert Strange retired from his position with Scarborough Education Authority and this seemed to improve his health. He was again elected Captain of the Scarborough Sailing Club, which was operating on a 'caretaker' basis during hostilities, as were all yacht and sailing clubs in the absence of most of their members on war service. He devoted much of his now considerable spare time to designing yachts and boats.

In the North of England, the early summer of 1917 was hot — perhaps this contributed to his deterioration as on July 9th Albert Strange suddenly collapsed and was put to bed. He died two days later, July 11th, and was buried next to his daughter in the village churchyard of Hutton Buscel, a few miles from Scarborough.

Strange's life was recalled with sadness by many friends. W.P. Stephens wrote:—

"I came to know him intimately and to esteem him not only for many sterling qualities as a man, but as a devoted yachtsman and a disinterested worker for the good of the sport. His work as a designer appealed to me as based on actual experience at sea and a broad and comprehensive view of the whole subject of design; while recognising the value of racing as an essential part of yachting, and giving much time to the study of measurement (for rating) he had no use for the racing machine, the freak or the rule cheater."

Julia Strange passed her husband's considerable library to the Scarborough Sailing Club, where it was unfortunately destroyed by flooding during the 1939-45 war. His drawing instruments were given to various friends who also designed craft. Dr T. Harrison Butler received his planimeter and cumbersome wooden dividers. What happened to his design drawings is not clear. Fortunately, a number of these had been given to W.P. Stephens, probably during his visit to England. Stephens in turn left them as part of his collection deposited at the Mystic Seaport, the noted maritime museum at Mystic, Connecticut in the United States of America. This has ensured their preservation.

Albert Strange's estate was valued at £6,500, at that time a substantial sum for anyone other than a businessman or those in upper social levels. More important for posterity, he left a considerable influence in art, as amongst his students were J.H. Inskip, Harry Watson, Fred Appleyard and those two notable marine artists, Frank H. Mason and the incomparably accurate Charles Pears, keen sailing men both, whose love of the sport was doubtless enhanced and encouraged by Albert Strange.

His yacht and small boat designs have delighted hundreds of yachtsmen and over the succeeding years have continued to attract attention. Harrison Butler put it, "His influence on the design of the small cruiser was far reaching and will be permanent." Although this statement has lost some of its force with the years, and many contemporary sailing people have never heard of Albert Strange, his designs contributed to the steady evolution of the small cruising yacht at a crucial time in its development and many of the craft built from them are still sailing.

Julia Strange survived Albert by about 15 years and his elder son, George Frederick, lived to 83, dying in 1969. Strange's old friend, George Holmes, was also blessed with a long life of sailing and small boat design. He died in May 1940, the father figure of the Humber Yawl Club, which he and Strange had done so much to encourage and sustain as a true centre of practical small boat sailing. This ideal shared by these two friends still shines out from their now dated but still attractive designs and in their writings.

CHAPTER 3

Happy Days on the Humber

When Albert Strange settled in the Yorkshire coast town of Scarborough, he must have sought a congenial venue for continuing his sailing of small boats. The North Sea is uninviting along the Yorkshire coastline, which has few natural anchorages, rivers or creeks to explore. It was therefore natural that Strange should also seek the occasional companionship and modest facilities of the group of small boat sailors, established on the muddy waters and swift tides of the Humber, which forms a boundary between the East Riding of Yorkshire and Lincolnshire.

The Humber Yawl Club was the principal sailing club on the estuary, founded in 1883 by enthusiasts from the town of Hull and its locality. Hull was then one of Britain's largest fishing ports, besides being a centre for manufacturing and cargo trades and some shipbuilding. The club members were principally local shopkeepers and other owners of small businesses, managers and clerical workers of the area, with a few 'artisans' who were keen sailing men and had saved sufficient for ownership of a small boat. It was a democratic membership and like many sailing clubs and particularly those whose members own small craft, it quickly developed a warmth of fellowship. This seems to have been particularly marked during the three decades before the 1914-18 war. The Humber Yawl Club burgee has flown from the mastheads of some notable personalities then and since, and it remains a vigorous organisation. When Albert joined the Humber Yawl Club in 1891, the Club Captain was H. Munro and the Mates were George F. Holmes and A. Mills. All were to become firm friends of Strange. George Holmes is the best remembered. Born in 1861, he sailed as a schoolboy with the fishermen of Hornsea beach, on the sweep of coast between Spurn Head and Flamborough Head and about 15 miles from Hull. Later he owned a 20 ft coble, rigged for pleasure sailing with two spritsails. During the subsequent fifteen years, he owned many small boats until in 1894 he designed the EEL as a cruising canoe-yawl. Holmes was a founder member of the Humber Yawl Club and had earlier been a member of the eastern branch of the Royal Canoe Club, formed on the Humber in 1872, though the interests of the parent club remained firmly on the River Thames. The eastern branch canoe club members owned a variety of small craft, including several 'Rob Roy' type clinker planked paddling and sailing canoes of the type developed by John MacGregor in the 1860s. There were also some of the more powerful NAUTILUS type canoes evolved by Warington Baden Powell. Humber canoeists also designed their own paddling and sailing canoes, but all these craft were really only suitable for sheltered waters and the Humber can be rough at times for even sizeable craft, and the tides run strongly.

Perhaps it was this desire for a more powerful type of sailing craft which prompted the formation of the Humber Yawl Club in 1883. Members desired longer, beamier, deeper and more able small sailing craft, but wanted to retain the pointed stern hull form. They were probably also influenced by developments elsewhere, on the upper Thames by the 'Oxford Canoe Yawls', developed by the brothers Theo and Harry Smith, and by similar craft evolving on the River Mersey. Some members draughted their own ideas and a few had new style canoes built. The resulting craft were well represented by the 14 ft × 3 ft 4 in CASSY, designed by George Holmes in 1883 (FIG 10). She had all the features of what was to become a recognised type of fairly seaworthy sailing canoe, but the paddle had been discarded in favour of a pair of oars to better combat the tides.

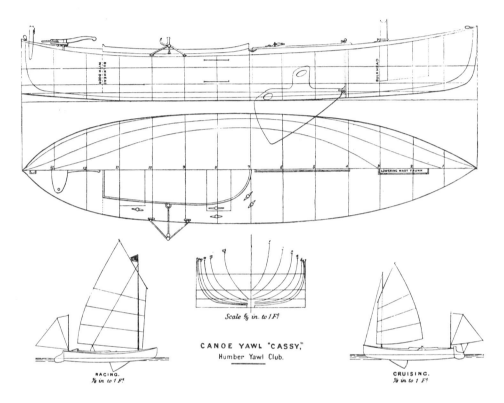

Canoe yawl CASSY designed by George Holmes

FIG 10

By the time Albert Strange joined the Humber Yawl Club, George Holmes and other members had developed their canoe yawls to a larger size, such as the DAISY of 1890 which had lost the paddling facility of the earlier craft, to emerge as a sailing boat *per se*. At that time, Albert Strange owned the small cutter yacht CHERUB, built in 1888 to his design. This first CHERUB was an unusual hybrid. Her plumb-stemmed, shallow draught hull had a straight keel, a transom stern and a fairly full body of conventional form, but two centreplates were fitted, one forward and another deeper one aft. Her plans cannot be found and only a well made half model remains, salvaged by Mrs Bill James from a discarded oven! The model was restored by Bill James and is now in the Scarborough Yacht Club. It is therefore not possible to appreciate fully the design, though the principal dimensions of 21 ft length × 7 ft 3 in beam are healthy.

Forward and aft centreplates were sometimes used in larger sailing canoes and Strange may have got the idea from that source. What is more likely is that he was following the experiments of another contemporary artist-yacht designer, Landseer Mackenzie of Bournemouth, who used the same arrangement in the 25 ft lug-rigged 2½ rater HEATHEN CHINEE, built in 1879, and in one or two of his other designs. Two centreplates allow variable increase in the immersed lateral plane and in the position of its geometric centre. This is useful when sailing on a reach and at times when going to windward. However, when turning, the forward plate has usually to be raised as otherwise the craft will not come about. Strange probably chose the two plates to allow a single-hander to trim the boards and sheets so the boat would keep a straight course for periods without needing a helmsman. It is unfortunate we know no more of this first CHERUB as she appears to be one of Strange's most interesting designs.

The Humber Yawl Club took pride in publishing a well illustrated annual year-book and that of 1892 contained Strange's account of CHERUB's cruise in 1891, illustrated with black and white drawings in a style which would soon become familiar to his fellow members. He kept the CHERUB at Scarborough, at least for a time, as the cruise of 1891 started there and continued by way of Filey Brigg, then south to Boston in Lincolnshire, to Blakeney on the north Norfolk coast, on south to Harwich in Essex, before doubling back into the Deben to lay up at Woodbridge.

This CHERUB, first of three yachts of the same name, was the last cutter Strange was to own as he was quickly converted to the local advantages of the Humber type of centreplate canoe yawl — it appears by the considerable influence of George Holmes. Strange essayed the design for a shallow draught canoe yawl for his own use and the 1893 year-book contained the plans of the CHERUB II (FIGS 5, 6 & 7). She was built at Scarborough by James Frank and was 20 ft 2 in LOA × 17 ft 7 in LWL × 5 ft 10 in beam, 1 ft 9½ in fixed draught, 3 ft 2 in with C/P. The lines were those of a sailing craft with easy sections, a slackly rounded bow profile and fine ends; a hull likely to be wet in a seaway. The rig was originally designed with a gaff mainsail and mizzen, with a single headsail, but was changed to a standing lug mainsail and a 'batswing' gunter mizzen, again with a single headsail set to a short bowsprit. The change may have been made from considerations of the hull's limitations of power to carry sail, as a gaff rig would be heavier than the lug and these small centreplate canoe yawls were tender in strong winds.

While the CHERUB II was being built, Albert Strange continued to sail the cutter CHERUB along the Yorkshire coast and into the Humber and River Trent. Later that season, Strange and George Holmes cruised in Holmes' canoe yawl DAISY on the Zuider Zee, in company with the other Humber Yawl Club craft OPOSSUM and GODIVA, each boat having a crew of two. The three boats were shipped from Hull and across the North Sea to Antwerp. They sailed down the River Schelde to Hansweert, through a canal to Wimeldenge, into the Waters of Zeeland to Dordrecht. Canals took them on to Utrecht, to Weesp, Muiden, Edam and Hoorn, on to the Zuider Zee, before making for Amsterdam, where the boats were shipped back to Hull. This ambitious cruise demonstrated the principal advantages of such small, transportable craft for limited cruising abroad.

One of the delights of this cruise was the chance Strange had to make many drawings and paintings of Dutch scenes and craft. He also recorded the club boats and one painting entitled DAISY IN FULL FLIGHT, showed the canoe yawl reefed and going well in a Zuider Zee chop with her companions turning to windward in the background (Plate 2).

George Holmes, too, found much to draw and paint. His great love of small boats and his ability as an artist, coupled with an amiable disposition, cemented a lifelong friendship with Albert Strange. Holmes published many charming illustrated accounts of his cruises over many years, in the form of black and white scripted logs. These were profusely illustrated with vignettes and incidents of these trips and with sketch plans of the boats involved and sometimes of craft encountered.

DAISY in full flight
PLATE 2

In 1895, Albert Strange made a single-handed voyage in the new CHERUB II, south to the Humber, then via the River Trent to Boston and on into the Wash, that treacherous waste of shallows and strong tides between the coast of Lincolnshire and north-Norfolk. He continued coastwise to Brancaster, to Yarmouth, and along the Suffolk coast to the difficult haven of Southwold and to Harwich, in brisk conditions, ending that part of his cruise at Brightlingsea, in north east Essex. As a holiday cruise, it provided him with an ideal opportunity to develop his skills even further at single-handed sailing, in which for many years he had been particularly interested.

These experiences in sailing canoe yawls encouraged Strange to continue designing the type. In 1894, he built the centreplate canoe yawl ETHEL to the lines of Design No 4 built in 1891 (WREN) and also in 1895 made a cruise from Scarborough to the Thames in the CHERUB II, single-handed except for part of the trip up the River Trent, a tributary of the Humber, then via the Foss Dyke waterway and the River Witham to the Lincolnshire port of Boston. The CHERUB II faced strong winds on the seagoing part of this venture and Strange caught the atmosphere of an east coast squall in his painting LUFF BOY! (Plate 3) showing the yawl off Walberswick, Suffolk. He averaged twenty miles each day on this trip.

Strange's ability as a small boat sailor and his strong support for the Humber Yawl Club led to his being elected its Captain in 1895. He had then completed another design, for the 19 ft 3 in × 5 ft 9 in canoe yawl WAWA for Henry Hughes. She was also built at Scarborough by James Frank. As Club Captain, Strange had to take the lead in social events such as a magic lantern show, then a popular form of entertainment, with slides projected on a screen; evenings enlivened with recitations, solos on the mandolin, songs and much good humour. The winter programmes of such clubs played a vital part in their continuance and popularity, sustaining the members' interest and providing welcome amusement in an era when entertainment had to be almost totally self-generated.

In 1896, he and a friend, probably George Holmes, took the CHERUB II to the British Canoe Association meet in the Isle of Wight and afterwards sailed her to the Thames (Chapter 7). In 1896-97, George Holmes took delivery of the canoe yawl EEL which he had designed for himself. The 21 ft × 7 ft centreplate EEL had a gaff yawl rig (FIG 4) and her snug cabin was an improvement on earlier Humber yawls which had only temporary sleeping accommodation. She was to prove a successful and long lived little craft and is still sailing.

Luff Boy!
PLATE 3

Albert remained active on the draughting board, preparing plans for the 3 ton centreplate yawl TAVIE II and the following year, he designed the centreplate sloop MONA as a small day sailer and overnight cruiser, an unusual design for him, having a very shallow hull with a spoon bow and flat-sectioned counter. These features, coupled with a gunter sloop sailplan of considerable area and a long bowsprit, radiused cockpit coamings and a low shelter roof, gave the craft an American appearance. Her design may well have been influenced by transatlantic tastes, as Strange was then in correspondence with American designer, W.P. Stephens. She was designed for the man who looked over the quay at Lincoln (in A SINGLE-HANDED CRUISE IN THE NORTH SEA) and who asked Albert to design him a boat. A rough draft was done on a piece of paper and the plans were drawn later, probably with the influence of American practice in mind.

Albert seems to have again cruised to north Norfolk in 1897 and that season George Holmes' EEL was shipped to Hamburg, from where he and Albert Strange cruised down the River Elbe, through the Kiel Canal into the Baltic. Strange recorded this in two delightful illustrated articles published in YACHTING MONTHLY. Such voyages are the essence of small boat cruising. One has to have cruised under sail in that way to appreciate fully the snug enjoyment which would be that of Holmes and Strange, each seated on his bunk after a day's passage, the evening meal consumed, washing up done and pipes alight for a yarn before turning in. They would be tired with sun, spray and salt air and with an ache or a bruise here and there from the little craft's liveliness in a breeze. But what satisfaction — and what expectation of the morrow! There is nothing to compare with this and they knew it.

At that time Albert was also producing the illustrated covers for the Humber Yawl Club yearbooks, in the arts and crafts movement style, and later showing the influence of *art nouveau*. His various sailing and club activities led to his elevation to life membership in 1901, coupled with the presentation to him of a copy of that fascinating book by Henry Folkard, THE SAILING BOAT. That season he and George Holmes sailed the EEL to the Wash by way of the Humber, along the coast, to return by the waterways from the Wash to the River Trent, and so back to the Humber. This was a favoured cruise of the Humber-based small boat cruisers as the coast of Yorkshire north of Spurn Head was relatively inhospitable and often dangerous for small craft.

The 1901 yearbook included some notes by Strange TO SINGLE HANDERS, which remain valid.

"Almost more important than even the possession of a first rate craft is the knowledge of how to utilise the forces of nature to your own advantage. In coast cruising, the utilisation of the tides is of the greatest importance, and the cruiser should obtain all possible information about them. Start at night with a fair tide rather than wait 'til daylight to work over a foul one. On long cruises do not try to turn to windward over an adverse tide. Bring up and rest, for by turning the whole tide you will make but few miles on your way, and you will be too tired to make the best of the fair tide when it does come. Keep yourself in first-rate condition by getting a proper amount of rest and food. The tides give you this chance. Do not drive your boat too hard; press her to gain a point, but don't press her all the time. Canvas and sail her with a seamanlike judgement and you will get as far as the man who drowns his craft and wears himself out, while you will be fresh and dry, and he will be well salted and very damp. Always 'keep a bit in hand' — a bit on the weather side — a bit of room to swing clear in harbour — a bit of spare when cutting things fine across shoal patches — a bit of cable to slack out if necessary. In fact, always have a bit to spare of everything you know you will want the most — CHERUB."

Even in an age of universal use of auxiliary engines and yachts of excellent windward performance, this wisdom remains sound for those who would cruise comfortably.

The club yearbook of 1900 contained Strange's NOTES ON CRUISING IN THE WASH, a detailed account with pilotage directions. The following year he gave NOTES ON THE NORTH SEA COAST, describing ports and roadsteads alongshore.

In 1901, the Humber Yawl Club was enjoying three principal activities. Besides the cruising in small boats for which it was principally formed, there were races for small boats on the Humber and for a club one-design class on landlocked Hornsea Mere, about 15 miles north-east of Hull and close by the shore beloved of George Holmes' boyhood. A small secondary clubhouse was erected there and even an occasional ice-yacht was tried on the Mere in hard winters.

The club dinner closing the 1902 season typified the vigorous spirit of the time. It was held at the Imperial Hotel. The room was decorated with signal flags and half models of members' canoe yawls. Club Captain J. Hamilton Jnr was in the chair. Guests included J.F. Ingleby, Vice Commodore of the Royal Yorkshire Yacht Club and owner of large cruising yachts, the Captain of the Scarborough Sailing Club and the Commodore of the Humber Sailing Club. One speaker remarked that he had sailed for many years in the Solent and on the south coast generally but found that Humber Yawl Club members were more practical amateur sailors than he found there. A toast to, 'The spirit of sailing', coupled with, 'Our visitors' was proposed by Albert Strange and there was music and song in the manner of the time, when sailing men were not backward in giving voice to a tenor or baritone solo or in bringing a musical instrument to enliven the evening.

Albert continued to develop his interest in yacht design. Amongst others, he produced plans for the 5 ton cutter KOTIK (later PINCHER) in 1902 and the keel canoe yawl SHEILA for Scottish artist, Robert E. Groves in 1903-04, as his design No 70. She continued the development of his style of stern and hull form in his cruising yacht design, as described in Chapter 6. The Humber Yawl Club organised several design competitions for its members over a long period and the resulting craft were often of a high standard. In 1905, Albert Strange acted as judge and chose the design of GULL by G. McLean Gibson as the best submitted. She was very similar to Strange's designs but then, Strange's canoe yawls were similar to the designs of George Holmes, who had been *his* mentor in the type, and Albert's entry GRAYLING came second to that of George's TROTTER in the following competition.

As well as east coast cruising and a few trips in European waters, Albert found he particularly enjoyed cruising on the west coast of Scotland, with its deep, clear waters. He described such a cruise in the FULMAR (which he owned for one season) at a 1907 lecture to the club. This enjoyment of Scottish waters grew, encouraged by his friendship with Robert Groves, their mutual artistic interests, and the peace of almost deserted anchorages.

Strange had a change of craft by 1908 when he owned TOPSY a 17 ft × 6 ft sloop of his design. The Humber Yawl Club design competition that year was for a small barge yacht and perhaps to show his strict impartiality, Strange, who was acting as judge, set aside George Holmes' entry as being not a barge yacht at all but a 'nice specimen of a flat floored vessel of Humber Yawl Club type.' The prize went to another member but the two old shipmates remained firm friends.

1908 marked the beginning of a period of seven years of intensive activity by Strange in the design of small yachts. The range of his work extended and varied examples included the 6 metre International Rating Class yacht DESIRE; HAWKMOTH, a 5 ton auxiliary yawl; the 30 ft keel canoe yacht SHEELAH II as design No 98 and THORN, a 4 ton yawl; which was entered for the club's 1910 'Keel canoe' design competition, but was placed second to George Holmes' TRENT. It is interesting to recall the comment of judge Harold Clayton on THORN, 'A fine little

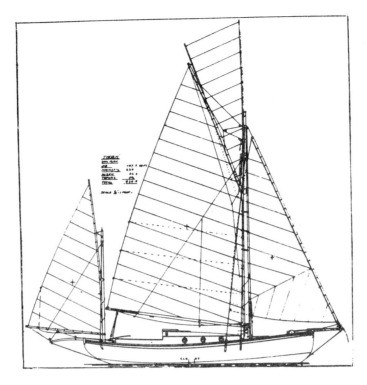

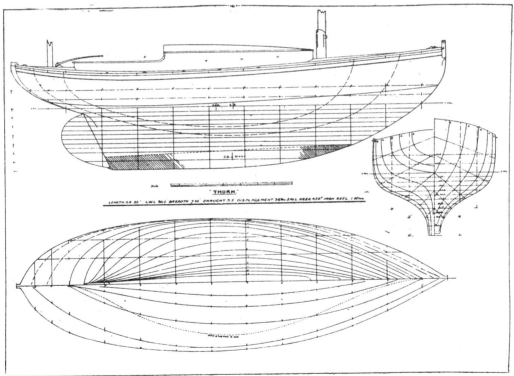

The yawl THORN was Albert Strange's design for the 1910 Humber Yawl Club Competition

FIG 11

cruiser, well thought out and drawn, but spoilt by the ugly and hard midship section, a flat side and rather hard quarter; the draught is a little deep under her mast which would make her rather hard and wild, running before any sea, not necessary for windward work; good headroom, comfortable cabin with plenty of locker space, main sheet block on horse would be liable to jamb, the topsail as shown would not stand and the yards would always be in the way on deck; she would be better with a smaller mizzen and would balance better. The C.G. of the keel would be better if a little further forward.'

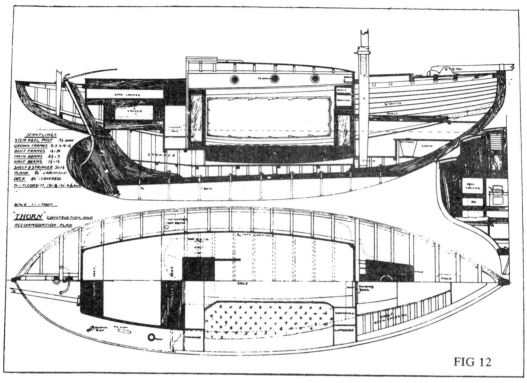

FIG 12

Harold Clayton was experienced in yacht design and owned the 51 ton yawl ZINITA. The design repays study in relation to his comments (FIGS 11 & 12).

By 1911 the little TOPSY was replaced by Albert's new yawl CHERUB III, Design No 112, a 29 ft keel canoe yawl, regarded as a very fine addition to the club list. His great hopes for cruising her extensively in the Western Isles were short lived due to the onset of his illness, which may have been accelerated by his increased activity in yacht design. Two years previously, he had designed the cutter BETTY, later renamed TALLY HO, a powerful craft which was to win the Fastnet race in 1927, then owned by Lord Stalbridge. The fifteen starters included a variety of yacht types, including the schooner LA GOLETA, designed by American John G. Alden, and the race, in wild weather, became a final struggle between these two, a refined type of English cutter and a then 'state of the art' American offshore schooner. The schooner was first round the Fastnet Rock but the TALLY HO was close astern in a wind which had attained near hurricane force at times during their outward passage but was then easing. There was anxiety for their safety as all other competitors had retired with damage or defects. LA GOLETA crossed the line first (at Plymouth), with TALLY HO 52 minutes astern, but the winner on handicap of the Fastnet Cup. In this race, JOLIE BRISE was also a starter but was forced to retire. It is a pity that

Albert Strange was not alive to know of this achievement of one of his designs, with a good crew, in the days before the designing of specialised offshore racing yachts in Britain.

Strange's illness forced the sale of his CHERUB III in 1912 but he continued to design yachts and boats until his death in 1917. Despite restrictions on physical exertion, he maintained membership and close links with the Humber Yawl Club, which continued to grow and extend its influence amongst small craft cruising men and to receive wide publicity in yachting periodicals.

The 1914 club yearbook had a note that, '. . . our dear CHERUB has prevailed upon his doctor to let him go in for a boat — a very little one it has to be — and we have wheedled out of him the lines to which he proposes to build, as we thought they would interest fellow members.' The plans of the 3 ton gaff sloop BEE were dated April 1914 and were featured in Humber Yawl Club's Yearbook 1914. She was transom sterned, a 21 ft 6 in centreplate cruiser, having a small ballast keel and had similarities to the work of George Holmes. Unfortunately, Strange was never to have her built. Soon after, in August 1914, the outbreak of the war stopped all active

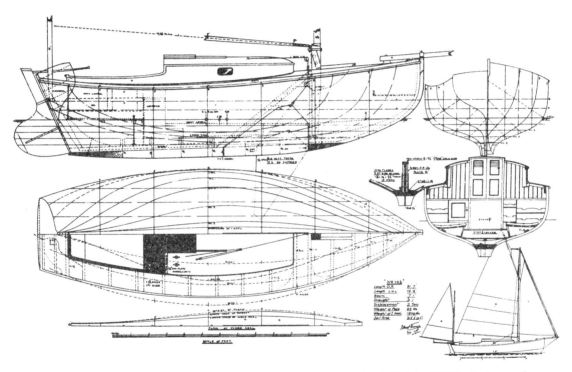

Design No 146 was prepared for a member of the Humber Yawl Club in 1915 in the hope of being built after the war. The main features sought were accommodation for two and light draught on a displacement of two tons, but having potential for reasonable speed and handiness. The transom stern provided maximum volume in the length of 21ft 7in but the beam of 7ft 1in could with advantage have been increased to, say, 7ft 6in to increase the range of stability in strong winds. The draught of 2ft 1in is realistic for the size of hull but the 1800lbs iron keel is perhaps a little ambitious if draught was to be maintained with two people and all cruising gear and stores on board. The centreplate is small in area and would have been better arranged as "L" shaped and lowering from aft with the upstanding part under the thwart at the cabin entrance. The sail plan of 315.5 sq ft was too generous and about 250 would be ample for the size and form of hull. She would be best rigged as a cutter leaving the bowsprit length as shown.

FIG 13

yachting around the British coast and the Humber Yawl Club members went to war, many never to return from that most horrific of conflicts.

Albert Strange and George Holmes, both elderly men, 'carried on' in the spirit of the home front. Both continued to design small craft — Holmes, when time permitted, and Albert much as usual. His friend, Herbert Reiach, founding editor of YACHTING MONTHLY, encouraged him to prepare a series of articles on the design and construction of small cruising yachts, which appeared in its pages during the war. Albert judged a club cruising competition in 1915 and the following year published the lines of Design No 146, with a description of the craft, a pretty transom sterned yawl, but having the then fashionable snubbed stem profile (FIG 13). His last contribution to the Humber Yawl Club was the cover of the 1917 yearbook.

George Holmes and Albert Strange exerted considerable influence on the progress of the Humber Yawl Club during its early years. It provided a focus for their interests afloat and an outlet for their designs, particularly valuable to Strange during his formative years as a designer of small yachts. It also brought contacts and the friendship of many like-minded sailing men. Holmes and Strange both benefitted from sailing together and discussing their common interest in the design of small, practical sailing boats and cruisers of modest cost. These designs were moulded by their sailing grounds, often subject to demanding conditions for small craft. Many of their designs are still sailing, cared for and continuing to give pleasure. Both men did much towards improving the small cruising yacht at a time when these were more individual craft than now. They did not live to see how efficient a seaboat the type has become and in such numbers, yet now rarely designed with the attractive appearance and character of the many craft from their drawing boards.

CHAPTER 4

A Single-Handed Cruise in The North Sea

Albert Strange was an observer of detail, both in his painting and in his appreciation of small craft. This enhanced his ability as a designer of small yachts and boats, and supplemented his practical experience of handling small craft and of their behaviour at sea. Strange wrote several accounts of his cruises, and the charm of these pieces, besides his pleasant style of writing, was in his recording of the many events and small incidents which might have gone unnoticed by others. His cruise accounts were lively stories of minor adventure, written by someone who savoured his changing surroundings and who found pleasure in the experience. Strange was a philosopher afloat.

He could at times be sentimental about yachts, places and people. He accepted what fate sent and could endure his own company for periods but was at ease with new acquaintances or old friends.

Reading these accounts of cruises almost eighty years after they were written, reminds us that the way of life ashore has changed out of all recognition but that in many other ways, little has changed in the sailing environment. The winds blow with the same vagaries and the sea responds in its old capricious ways. Yachtsmen can still experience all that Strange described.

An aspect of pleasure sailing which has deteriorated since his day, is the self reliance which was expected and accepted in those times, and indeed until about twenty years ago. The safety of a yacht and her crew was entirely the responsibility of those on board. In Strange's day one navigated by the winds, the tides, and the best seamanship which could be achieved by the crew — auxiliary motors were only just beginning to be installed in existing yachts. The commonplace use of engines, the calling of coastguards and lifeboats by radio transmitters, and the expectation that somebody else, lifeboat, helicopter or other vessel, will in extreme need provide salvation, has all too frequently replaced the judgement, seamanship, skill and endeavour of earlier times.

Many of Albert Strange's accounts of his cruising were written several years after the events described had taken place and this emphasises the strong impression these experiences must have made on him at the time. Although the original sketches for the illustrations were contemporary, as he always carried drawing and painting equipment with him on a cruise, those actually published were sometimes worked up at a later date.

Space only permits a very few of Strange's narrative writings to be reproduced but it is hoped these will re-create the pleasure these accounts brought to the early readers of the YACHTING AND BOATING MONTHLY and YACHTING MONTHLY, from whose pages they are reproduced with the Editor's permission.

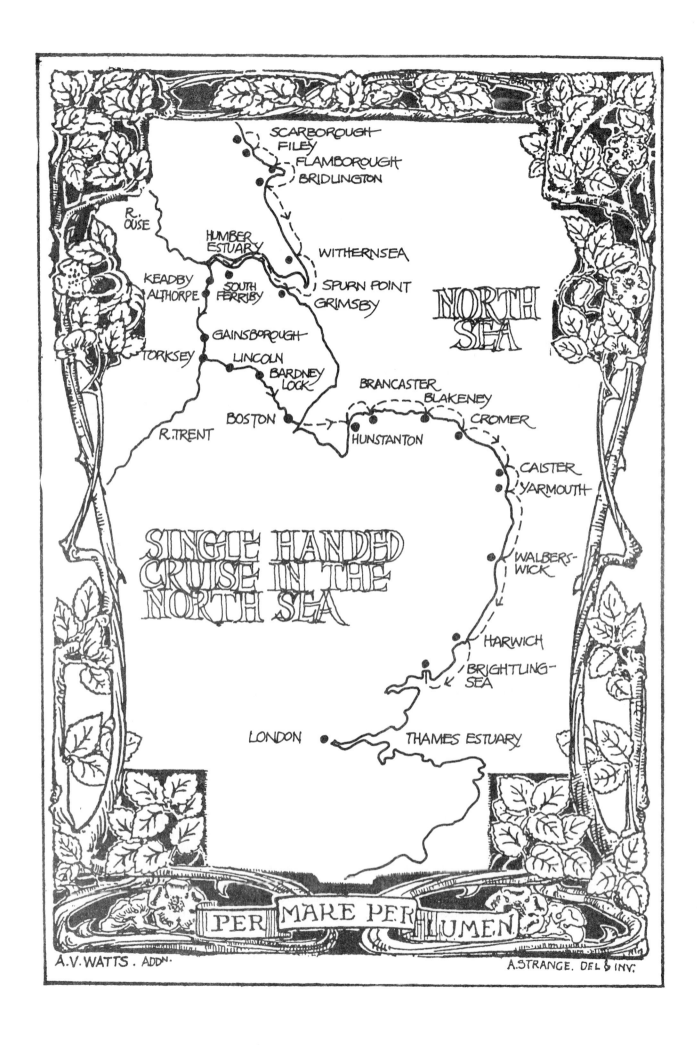

SINGLE HANDED
CRUISE IN THE
NORTH SEA

NORTH
SEA

SCARBOROUGH
FILEY
FLAMBOROUGH
BRIDLINGTON

R. OUSE

HUMBER
ESTUARY

WITHERNSEA

SPURN POINT
GRIMSBY

KEADBY
ALTHORPE
SOUTH
FERRIBY

GAINSBOROUGH

TORKSEY
LINCOLN
BARDNEY
LOCK

BOSTON
BRANCASTER
BLAKENEY
CROMER

R. TRENT
HUNSTANTON

CAISTER
YARMOUTH

WALBERS-
WICK

HARWICH
BRIGHTLING-
SEA

LONDON
THAMES ESTUARY

PER MARE PER LUMEN

A.V. WATTS. ADDN.

A. STRANGE. DEL & INV.

The first, which is the subject of this chapter, appeared in the issue of February 1908 and describes a cruise in the CHERUB II, from Scarborough to the River Thames. It was a single-handed cruise, except for the trip up the River Trent and via the Foss Dyke and the River Witham to the Lincolnshire port of Boston. In the coastal part of the cruise, hard winds necessitated two and sometimes three reefs and the average distance sailed each day was twenty nautical miles. However, the cruiser's maxim should always be, "Enjoyment is not proportional to distance covered".

"A few weeks ago there was much talk, and almost as much writing, on what Mr Chas Pears in his delightfully written and illustrated article called "the most fascinating form of madness". Today a certain decline seems to have come on this mania, but, though we hear less about it, I am not sure that there is less done. We all occasionally in our cruises meet the solitary voyager, and I must plead guilty to having supplied certain solitaries with designs of floating asylums suited to their particular form of the disease.

But at the time of which I write the craze caught me as badly as it did most others. My own private mania was to discover and build as small a boat as was possible to do mad things in. All, or nearly all, the others seemed to want something as big as possible. Mr McMullen's boats (especially the biggest ones) appealed to them. "Rob Roy Macgregor's" yawl appealed more to me, but yet seemed almost too large for real comfort in working, and too permanently heavy to be as properly amphibious as a single-handed cruiser really ought to be.

So after laborious comparisons with known boats there was at last growing towards completion in a boat-builder's shed the outcome of a winter's planning and thought, and the dear old thing still exists somewhere in the vicinity of Mersea Island to prove how kindly the fates are to single-handers — both men and boats.

This does not seem exactly the place to give a full table of sizes, weights or areas. Perhaps I may be allowed later on to give these things in detail; but for the present it will suffice to say that she was 20 ft overall, 17 ft 9 in waterline, 5 ft 8 in beam and 1 ft 10 in fixed draught, with a small narrow centreplate. Her total weight, fully equipped, was 22 cwt and her sail area 250 sq ft. A hard trial assured me that she was uncapsizeable, but any simpleton could lay her down and fill her if he wanted to. The hull and fixed ballast weighed a little over 8 cwt of which 3½ cwt was keel and centreplate. The rest of the ballast was of lead cast to fit on the keel inside. Her mast, spars, sails and gear were light, as was also the structure of her hull — this being as necessary in a small cruiser as in a racer, so long as there is reserve strength enough to meet all possible emergencies.

And so one fine but breezy morning in July the CHERUB and I left Scarborough bound for London. As is so often the case in our climate, it was cool enough to have been November instead of July; and the wind was fresh from the north-east, which makes much commotion on the sea in these parts. Nothing but ourselves was bound out, and a big Norwegian schooner lay rolling and pitching in the bay, most anxiously waiting for water into the harbour. The long seas broke here and there and licked long white tongues of spray up the cliffs. Filey Brigg was one smother of spume as we raced past on the last of the flood with quite as much sail as was wanted under double reefs. And then when the ebb began to make, what a variety of motion the boat put on as the long sea broke up in Flamborough race! The thought involuntarily arose that if she would go through this she would go through anything short of Corrievrechan, and it was with great relief of mind when at last, after standing a good way off the land to avoid the worst of the race, we were able to head west into Bridlington Bay and spin swiftly on a broad reach into the harbour. CHERUB was a new craft to the Bridlington boatmen, and they gathered round to look at her as we moored. The general opinion was well expressed by one who ejaculated, "Come fra' Scarbro' te-deaa! Bar goom, she's a good 'un!"

We had had a good deal of sailing under varying conditions in our various trial trips, but never such a hard, long run before so big a sea, and I naturally felt very pleased as I turned in that evening to find how well the boat had answered my expectations. I wished, above all things, to have a boat that would be fast, easy, and dry when running and reaching in disturbed water, and nothing could have been better than the boat's behaviour that day — though the motion had been very violent and every muscle of my body ached. It was the first day of a holiday after a long season of indoor work, and I was far from the perfect fitness and hard 'fettle' gained after a week or two of life afloat.

The next day it blew less hard from the same quarter, with fog added. We remained in harbour and experimented with the stove, a methylated-spirit affair — also a 'little thing of my own', very nice to look at, but much like the little girl in the poem who, 'When she was good she was very, very good, But when she was bad she was horrid!' It used to go splendidly for days together, and then give up in a general conflagration. I felt that it was a stove of much originality of character, and one which required sympathy and intimate knowledge. It is very regrettable to have to add that, to the end of our acquaintance, this knowledge was never really thoroughly attained, and the stove's behaviour added a speculative aspect to the always difficult science of cookery which was not always desirable.

On awakening at 4 am the next morning I found that the fog had gone, and this determined me to get away as soon as possible; so we got out our stove and commenced to make breakfast. Here perhaps I may be allowed to say, once for all, what was my method of feeding, and so do my best to preserve from this plain account the reproach sometimes, with justice, levelled at cruising records — that an intolerable deal of space is usually devoted to the matter of meals. But it is important and helpful to know how this great question is dealt with by others, because the single-hander, like an army, 'moves on his stomach'. Well, with me breakfast was the big meal; one never knew when the next would arrive. This first meal, as a rule, consisted of eggs, bacon, or cold boiled beef, cocoa (one pint), bread, butter, and fruit of some sort or another. Then a good lunch of bread, butter and cheese — usually Dutch cheese or Gruyère — was wrapped in a napkin, which in turn was wrapped in American cloth and placed where I could reach it when sailing, together with a bottle of beer or a good-sized flask of claret with some water added. This would be urgently needed about 12 o'clock. When I had made my port and was anchored, the dinner consisted of soup (generally oxtail), more cold beef or a steak, bread, butter and jam, and fruit. To make sure of having fruit, I took a great store of the best French plums, which always came in handy. For supper, biscuits and cheese with cocoa, and if cold or wet, as it was usually on this particular cruise, a tot of whisky of very moderate amount on turning in. I do not set much value on tinned things, except of the simplest sort, and whenever I could catch or buy fish (which is surprisingly seldom on a cruise) I always had it either for breakfast or dinner. Cheese, for those who like it, is an astonishingly sustaining food, as is also plain chocolate in bars. If ever I felt that a complete change of diet was desirable I got it at an hotel; but the cruiser ought to be content with plain food if he gets plenty of it.

Well, having put away breakfast and got outside the harbour, I found that there was so little wind that the boat did no good turning over the ebb, so we anchored again and waited. It was not until nearly low water that there was a chance to get to the southward, and then we began to turn to windward over the slack, making long boards off the land in the rather vain endeavour to cover the 30 miles between Bridlington and Spurn before high water. I hoped that the wind would veer to the westward but it did not, and when we had drawn abreast of Withernsea, after a steady 6 hours beat, it was perilously near high water, and it began to look as if we should not get around Spurn Point before the ebb made. Then at last the wind came from the NW and we reached along quite fast for about 20 minutes, and then to my great disgust, it fell calm. I rowed hard, but without much success, as the swell was still large from the eastward, and at last I saw coming out of the Humber a smack or two, which showed plainly that the chance was over and there was to be no snug harbour for me that night, for the ebb had bent and the tides were nearing springs. Still, I went on rowing and got a little beyond Kilnsea before it was evident that no further progress was being made. So it was 'down anchor' and prepare for a night at sea, or at least to wait until midnight and go into the Humber by the ordinary channel. I sounded and found about 4 fathoms — which would leave me ample water at low tide — let go anchor, and started the stove. It was now about 6.30 pm, a fine evening, but the glass slowly falling and the surf beating heavily on the shore some 300 yds inside me. After dinner I sat in the cockpit and smoked my pipe. Whilst so occupied I saw two or three people on the beach waving. Of course I could not reply, which seemed to distress them, for they waved still more vigorously. Then they tried to launch a small boat, which was promptly capsized in the surf. It seemed very kind of them to take all this trouble, and I thanked them, though I doubt if they heard me. Presently they went away, and I lit my riding light, made a bed on the floor with wedges of kit-bag and sail-bag to keep me from rolling about, and then turned in, very much 'rocked in the cradle of the deep', and slept until midnight. It was still calm then and nearly low water, and the rolling of the boat was much less violent, the swell being broken by the now partly uncovered Binks, a shoal of rather large dimensions lying just outside Spurn Point. Another snooze until the first faint light of dawn spread in the sky, and then breakfast and up anchor. The flood tide soon whisked me through the narrow channel into the broad Humber, and on a close haul I stood across to Grimsby and made fast in the outer harbour, which I soon found was a wretchedly uncomfortable place wherein there was no peace. So I ran outside again and brought up on the edge of the flats, where I could sketch the big tower and the incoming craft in peace on my own anchor, and debate inwardly on the grave question as to whether I should go on outside, round to Wainfleet, or try a round up Humber and Trent to the Wash via Lincoln and Boston.

A fall of three-tenths in the barometer since the previous night almost decided me, and as the morning wore on the wind hardened and kept backing, while the sun grew dull and watery. Long before the low water the wind had risen to the force of a gale and the squalls were very heavy. In one of the worst a sloop, which was turning down over the last of the ebb, refused to stay and became completely unmanageable. She finished her career by getting athwart hawse of a barque, and the frenzied struggle to get her clear was a most interesting sight. The general outlook being so unpromising, I decided to go round to the Wash by way of the Humber and the Trent, and soon after the tide had begun to make, set off up river with two reefs and whole mizen, almost as much as she wanted, but by keeping a weather shore aboard, got fairly smooth water, and we smoked along at something like ten knots over the ground. On the way up we overtook and passed a cutter yacht some sizes bigger than CHERUB, but not without a struggle, though I was abreast of Hull some half mile ahead and to windward. There was a nasty lop of sea in Hull roads and all beyond, but long before high water we were safe inside Ferriby Sluice in fresh still water, and alongside a grassy bank — a great contrast to my two previous days' experiences. The weather continuing very bad, I stayed two or three days at Ferriby, and was the unworthy hero of two adventures. The first was the rescue of a small boy who had, no doubt inadvertently and in pure lightness of heart, jumped off a high wall into 10 ft of water, where he appeared likely to stay, as he seemed unable to swim. My boathook came in very handy, and after emptying several quarts of water out of him, I took him home to his mother, followed by a large and sympathetic crowd. Oddly enough, his mother seemed grateful, and invited him to go to bed and me to have tea with her, which I did, she meanwhile freely watering hers with her tears. When I left she blessed me, which was very embarrassing, for the crowd still lingered outside her cottage. That very night, somewhere about eleven o'clock, when all good persons should have been in bed, and I certainly had been for at least two hours, I was awakened by a call of 'Doctor! Doctor!'. On looking out I saw the moonlit figure of a young woman standing on the bank who implored me to come and heal her brother, who was very ill. It was in vain that I assured the damsel that I was no doctor and that my powers in the direction of medicine might be dangerous to anyone really ill. She still implored and even wept. As there seemed to be no real doctor nearer than Whitton, which was miles away, I reluctantly dressed, and taking my small sea stock of drugs, consisting of chlorodyne, some pills (whose maker's name wild steam-tugs shall not drag from me), and a little brandy, I followed the maid to her mother's cottage, where I found the little household in wild commotion and a stalwart young man lying on a couch groaning loudly. He certainly looked very ill, and I began to feel nervous, but put on the best professional air that I could manage. A little enquiry enabled me to diagnose the case — the young man had been eating very freely of gooseberries — and then the way seemed clear. It is not necessary to go into details of the remedies used, though mustard and hot water played a large part. In an hour the young man confessed to feeling better and wanted to sleep. When I left that cottage I was again loudly blessed by the whole family, and the mother delicately enquired what my fee would be. *She* also wept copiously. As I walked back to my little ship I took a dislike to that village — it seemed to have more than its proper percentage of weeping and grateful mothers — and I shuddered at the thought that I might be again 'called in' if I stayed much longer, and the next case might be more serious for both doctor and patient. So, early next morning, after a call to inquire after my patient, who was up and about, we left about half flood bound to Gainsborough. But a calm, accompanied by furious rain, only allowed us to get just below that most horrible bridge which spans the Trent above Keadby, and we had to spend the next nine hours at anchor, for the ebb runs that length of time in the Trent. The afternoon being finer, I walked to Althorpe, a picturesque village a little higher up, and made some sketches.

I ought to say that I had a passenger for this part of the trip — a young lad, with a passion for boats and sailing, whose parents rashly trusted me with him for the voyage to Boston. He managed to enjoy himself and was a very interesting study, so fearfully keen was he to learn everything about boats and all that pertains to them, and I much enjoyed his company.

The next tide took us to Gainsborough, turning to windward all the way; and the next, after a night's stay at that interesting town, took us to Torksey where fortunately I found a man with a horse going on to Lincoln. We bargained, and I got the tow for three shillings, which, considering that there was a very light wind dead ahead, was a blessing without any disguise. We got to Lincoln about dusk and anchored in the middle of Brayford Water, surrounded by nothing more dangerous than pleasure-boats and swans. Here we were visited by a good many people, who were interested to see a 'sea-going' sort of boat so far from her proper element. CHERUB had to be explained, and I made several converts — one very notable one, who is now one of the hardest sailors on Trent and the district. But the next morning awful news awaited us. We were actually told that we could not go on, as Bardney Lock, below Lincoln, was under repair, and nothing — not even water — could get through! The gross impropriety of such an event was too horrible for words of more than one syllable to express. After having come all this way round inside, to have to go back again and round outside in such weather as

Below Lincoln

we have been having was not to be accepted without a struggle, and I was determined to go on to Bardney and to get through somehow, even if I had to use dynamite. And so we went on, determined that nothing would send us back, saying the very hardest things we could think of about railway companies — for a railway company owns the bridge at Keadby, which drowns on an average a man every year, and doubtless the same horrid company owned the lock at Bardney.

It is well to have a lowering mast if you wish to leave Lincoln via the Witham, for this canalised stream burrows under the High Street and winds in a semi-subterranean manner through the suburbs for some distance before it reaches the open country. There are locks, too, to negotiate, and we found these, at any rate, in good order, and passed slowly along in a steamy, grey, misty, rainy atmosphere. Above us rose the hill on which stands the cathedral, looking this morning like a dream palace, pale and unsubstantial. On the banks were many anglers, doubtless enjoying the weather as being the most propitious for their gentle art, and far off awaited us the ruined lock at Bardney and the unsolved problem as to how to get through it. The very faintest of airs gave us bare steerage-way, and it was noon before we finally reached the problem which it was necessary to solve or else retrace our way to Grimsby.

Yes, alas, it was there, bolted and barred by big balks of timber! The lock-keeper came out and looked at us, shook his head, and said he thought we should have to go back. I had forgotten to purchase dynamite, and it really looked as if all progress was impossible. We made fast, however, and Fred, my youthful companion, began to fish for perch, whilst I suggested lunch. After this meal had been completed we sat and looked at the forbidden lock again, more in sorrow than in anger, and whilst we were thus engaged a large Lincolnshire man strolled up. He heard our tale of woe, bit a large piece of tobacco off one of my plugs, and then said, "Might pull her over if we'd some help." Grand — nay, superbly magnificent idea! But where to get the help? For no houses were visible. Oh, he'd just look up some friends of his who would come along (it being Saturday) and give a hand if there was anything forthcoming for their trouble! Good heavens! I would give untold gold rather than go back, and speeded him on his way with large promises and a three-finger nip of whisky as an earnest of good things to come. So off he went, and we began to strip the boat and carry the things beyond the lock. Presently he returned with four other men like unto himself in stature. The five of them solemnly undertook to haul the CHERUB over the bank, along the lock side, and launch her again for the sum of two shillings each and a quart of beer apiece, and to exercise all due care in the operation. We had only the oars to roll her on and our own cables to haul with, but, after much pulling, splashing, and sweating, we succeeded in getting that 8 cwt of bare boat out of the river, dragged her some hundred yards through nettles, weeds, and rushes, and launched her into her native element below the lock. Never was boat fitted out in so short a time. In half an hour or so we were being towed down the river to a little 'pub' that must have depended upon the beasts of the field and the birds of the air for its customers, for it stood quite alone, hiding behind the river-bank, and in its modest parlour I settled up with my helpers, the sum of 11s 8d satisfying all their claims, and, to judge by their remarks, leaving them my debtors. A little breeze springing up, we went on our way, the five stalwarts lined up on the bank watching us disappear into the rain and mist, and the crew of the CHERUB certainly very light-hearted.

We got to Boston next day in a howling gale, a wintry blast from the north lashing the river into wavelets. I saw Fred off at the station, and returned on board after a tramp through the town, feeling that the gods were making sport of all sailors in sending such weather.

I shifted the boat a little lower down to a better berth, and found a smart little steam-yacht to lie alongside of. Presently the owner invited me on board, and I learnt that he was bound out as soon as he could get away; but his skipper had no fancy to tempt Providence by an outsize passage in such weather. I spent a pleasant evening on board, and left with the promise of a tow down the Cut when they could continue their voyage.

It was two days before that happened, and when we left the locks the skud was still flying across the sky from the north, and the day promised to be anything but fine. At a speed of about 9 miles an hour CHERUB towed beautifully, and we were soon at the lower end of Boston Deeps. My mast had been lowered before starting, and whilst towing there was no chance to raise it. When they said, "Good luck!" and cast me off, I had a lot of trouble to get the stick on end in the jump of sea that was fast making, and there was more wind than I had bargained for to make the passage to Blakeney in. However it was a fair wind, and, with two reefs in, we were soon scudding through the Bennington Swatch and into Lynn Deeps. Going across towards Hunstanton the wind hardened and veered a point eastward. If it was going to do this I should find myself on a dead lee shore at low water off Blakeney, and the prospect was not a pleasing one. But it had to be faced as there was no getting back with the ebb tide drying the swatches and making a bigger sea every hour. When off Hunstanton I came up to a smack or two dredging; they had two reefs down, and were pitching into it pretty well.

I hailed one of them to ask for the position of the Sunk Sand Buoy, which I could not pick up owing to the lowness of CHERUB's side and the height of the sea, which had grown very much during the last hour. A man popped his head above the smack's bulwarks, and, instead of replying to my inquiry, asked me what the 'Hades' I was doing off there in a little thing like that; and when I told him I was bound for Blakeney he grew almost angry, and tried to persuade me to run for Lynn, whither he was bound after he had made his haul. " 'Tis no place for any man to go for in weather like this, isn't Blakeney. You come along arter me!" But I wanted to be in Blakeney, not at Lynn, and after he had told me that the Sunk Buoy had broken adrift, but that I was alright for the 'Bays,' I waved him farewell and left him in a sort of angry sorrow at my pigheadedness.

Along through the 'Bays,' which is a channel inside the Woolpack Sand, we had much less sea, though the wind kept freshening in squalls. The boat reached along beautifully — easy and

"What the 'Hades' are you doin' off here?"

dry — and I took the chance to get some food, especially as I felt rather downhearted after the fisherman's warning, and I always find that things look 'rosier' on a full stomach than on an empty one. We were now dead to leeward, and when off Brancaster I pulled down the third reef, because I knew what awaited us when we should have cleared the Woolpack and be at the mercy of the full fetch of the sea across the Well. I had lost my proper account of the tides, and had no desire to get to Blakeney too soon. But there was no holding the boat; the full ebb seemed to be still with me, and the miles sped away astern very quickly, and early in the afternoon I was off Blakeney, much too far inside the Bar Buoy, and with a young flood tearing up towards the channel bearing me fast to leeward. It was now blowing very hard, and the surf to leeward making the air misty, everything looked as if at least an hour's wait outside was imperative if we were to get inside safely. But, with the staggering sea and the strong lee-going tide steadily sucking me ashore, the boat made nothing at all to windward, and would certainly bear no more sail in the broken sea that was there.

I tried her on both tacks, but lost ground each time, and things looked very black. So, with my heart in my mouth, I pulled up the centreplate and pointed for the place where, amidst all the breakers, there seemed to be most water. On she ran, past the first outer buoy, then the second, and then, as she sank in the hollow of a sea — bang! she touched, and a walloping sea burst over her stern. But in bursting some of it lifted her along, and, as well as I could, I crawled forward and managed to keep her from broaching to with a long, strong boathook, when she touched aft again. The same business was repeated, but I felt that only a few more doses would fill her, and our last cruise would have been finished. Still, the strong flood tide kept her square to the sea, as she only hung on her keel, and after one or two more hard knocks she went over the Bar into smoother and deeper water, and, intensely thankful to the kindly powers that had preserved us, I ran her into the Pit, let go the anchor, and looked below. The water was just up to the floorboards, but the bed, stowed under the foredeck, was untouched, and the stove in its locker was dry and ready for action.

Going over Blakeney Bar

I have always felt that I owed my escape to the fact that the boat's greatest draught of water was right aft, and also to the strong (six knot) tide that had held her straight. With a level keel or more draught amidships she would certainly have broached to and been rolled over by the tide and sea, and, as Blakeney Bar is miles away from all living beings, there was but faint hope of rescue, though the lifebuoy I had ready *might* have floated me to the sands, from which I could hardly hope to escape unless someone had seen us coming in, which I afterwards heard was not the case.

So, after returning the water to its proper place outside, I rested, refreshed myself with hot drinks, and waited for the tide to rise sufficiently to enable me to get to the quay, which would not be before dusk.

When I came on deck to get under way for a really safe spot the sky had lifted from the horizon, and an angry glare spread in a bar above the sea to the westward. And, creeping round the point, there came a little mournful procession — a lifeboat under reefed sails escorting some half-dozen of the Sheringham fishing-boats, which, unable to beach, had either to be abandoned and the crews taken out by the lifeboat, or run the gauntlet of the Bar — as I had done — to get shelter at Blakeney.

It was not until after four days had passed that I ventured down towards the Bar again. The harbour-master, an old friend of mine, came down with me. Though the gale had subsided, there was still a heavy breaking sea on the coast and Bar, and, on his advice, I anchored again in the Pit for the night. On leaving me he said, "If there's a chance I'll hoist my flag." This was to be done because I could not see the state of the Bar from where I was anchored, and when I awoke early next morning I saw with my glass the welcome sign. We were over the Bar by 7.30, after a smart tussle against the tide that had so well befriended me on entering; and an uneventful run of ten hours took me to Yarmouth, where I made fast near the harbour mouth for the night. It seemed quite strange to set whole sail again, which I did off Cromer, and still more strange to find a calm at Caistor. Calms, however, were things that existed only in the intervals between gales, for I left Yarmouth next morning with two reefs again turned in with a sky full of portents and fearful signs, and the presentiment that I should not get very far that day, which presentiment was fulfilled off Walberswick, where a thunderstorm reduced me to bare mizen for a full half-hour, after which I could just carry a three-reefed sail into the old-world little harbour. Fortunately, the wind was S.W. in the said squall and thunderstorm. If it had been on-shore I do not know what would have happened.

Next morning broke a lovely day, with a west wind of whole-sail strength. It was a jolly six hours' sail to Harwich, where I spent the afternoon and evening. The wind having backed to the S.S.W. determined me to go no farther that day, though I might perhaps have managed to get to Brightlingsea twenty-fours earlier than I did.

It was twenty-three days since I had left Scarborough, and yet I had arrived at the 'oyster port' before a coal-laden sea-barge that was expected from Seaham, and which did not arrive until ten days later. The old salts shook their heads and said that this was the worst summer they had ever known — but they always say that, so soon do we forget the bad weather of the past in the bad weather of the present. After my experiences in the Wash, bad weather that was merely made up of thunderstorms seemed almost too good to me, and it is certainly remarkable that for the remainder of my cruise, which lasted three weeks longer, I was able to carry whole mainsail almost every day."

CHAPTER 5

An Album of Albert Strange Designs . . . 1

Most of these plans (and those in CHAPTER 10) have been taken from Humber Yawl Yearbooks or early editions of YACHTING MONTHLY. In many cases they are signed by Albert Strange and the reader will appreciate the high standard of his draughtsmanship which is to be expected from an artist of his calibre.

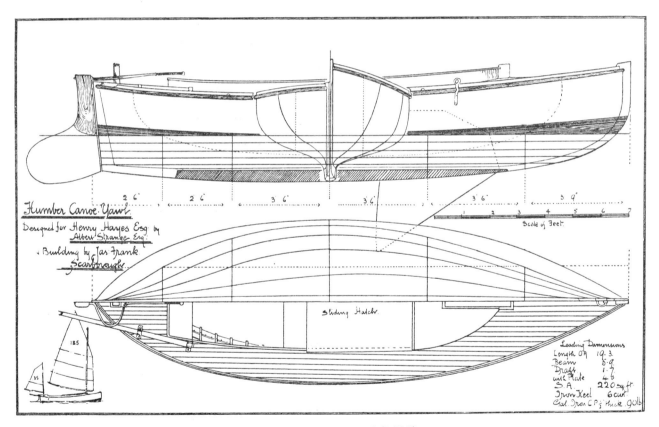

Humber Canoe Yawl (1895)

This is a typical canoe yawl by Strange, designed and built in 1895. Hull sections are fairly fine and she had a small ballast keel of 672 pounds weight. She probably needed additional ballast in the bilge to carry the 220 sq ft rig of battened balance lug and gunter or batswing mizzen. A fast and able seaboat in the right hands.

FIG 14

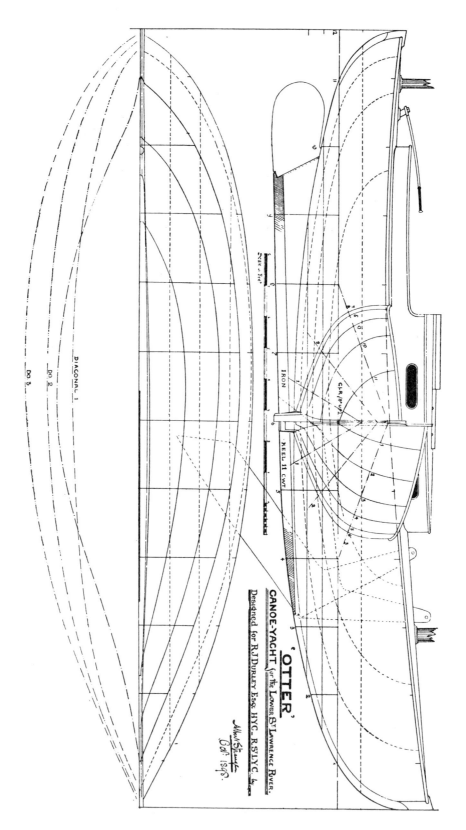

Otter (No 40/1898)

This canoe yacht has been described in chapter 6. She has a considerable rise of floor, easy bilge sections and a fine fore body. She would probably be fast but lack power to carry sail in strong winds and be wet in a head sea. The salient keel and deadwood would enable her to sail fairly well in shoal water with the centreplate only partially lowered. Its case is carried to the deck and is raised by a tackle from the mast to the top of the plate arm.

FIG 15

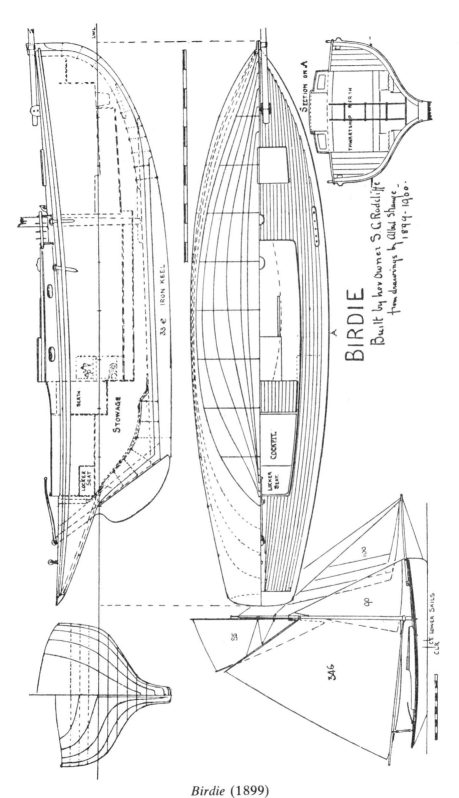

Birdie (1899)

The BIRDIE has the lines and sail plan of a typical small cruising cutter of the 1890s. She would probably sail well but the freeboard aft is rather low for a cruising yacht and the counter has the usual potential for slamming before a sea or when at anchor.

FIG 16

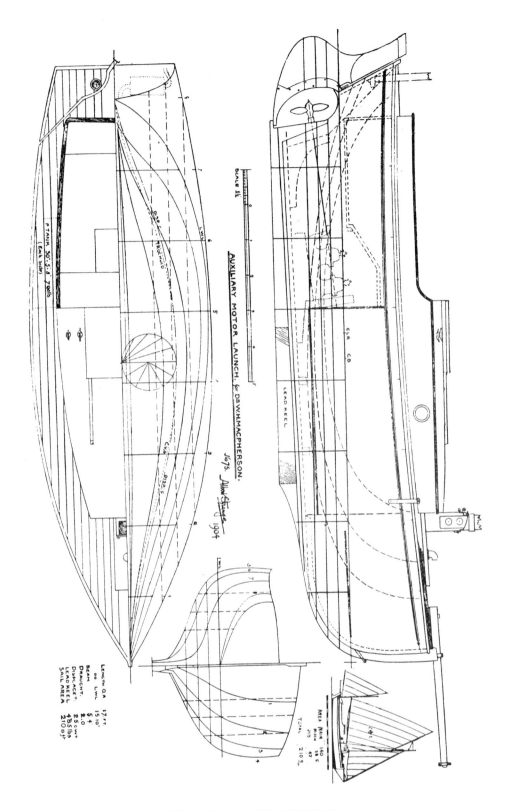

Motor Launch (No 75/1904)

This 17ft auxiliary yawl has a slender hull form, probably dictated by the motor's low power. The hull draught of only 2ft would make her a poor performer to windward, where the motor would be necessary. Nevertheless, a lead keel of 2438 pounds was fitted and a large sail area of 210 sq ft — an unusual combination. The offset mizzen still required the tiller to be cranked to obtain hard over.

FIG 17

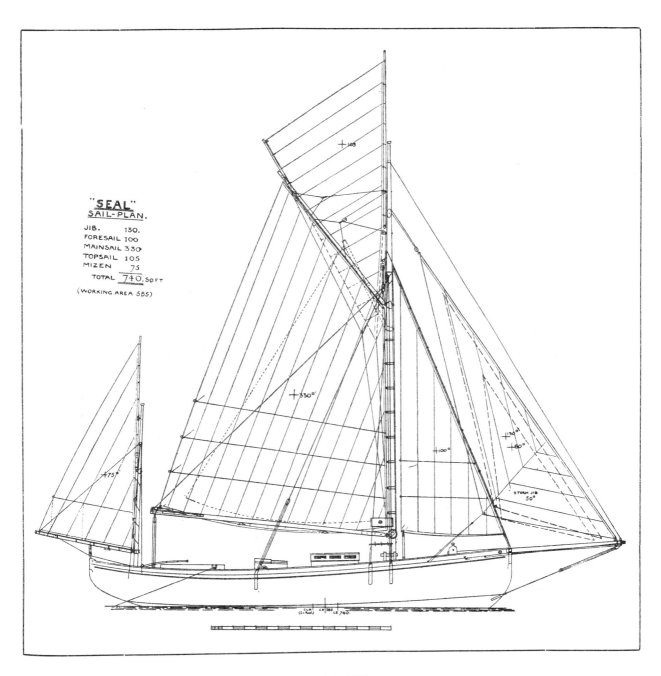

Seal (1907)

The SEAL is a good example of a Strange design for all round cruising, without a restriction on draught. The design won second prize in a design competition of 1907. She had the usual features of Strange's canoe sterned yawls but with proportionately less beam and more draught than many. A flush deck was achieved with the draught of 6ft. Reefing arrangements and a variety of jibs suggest this yacht could be kept going under almost all conditions. The 9ft dinghy, the yacht's tender, included in the drawings, is a delightful study in itself, and should encourage someone to build her.

FIG 18

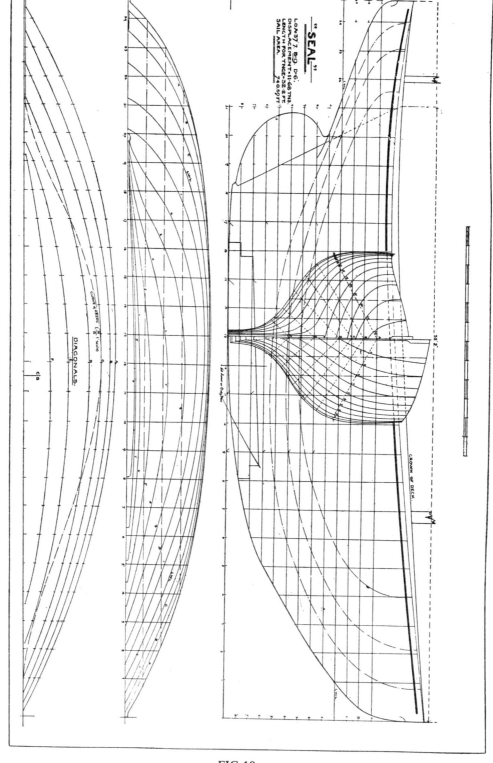

"SEAL."

L.O.A.37.7. B.9. D.6.
DISPLACEMENT-11.68 TNS.
LENGTH FOR TNGE-32.2 FT.
SAIL AREA. 740.5 □ FT.

CURVE OF AREAS (□ ' FEET)

DIAGONALS.

CROWN OF DECK.

SEAL.
Designed :by Albert Strange.

FIG 19

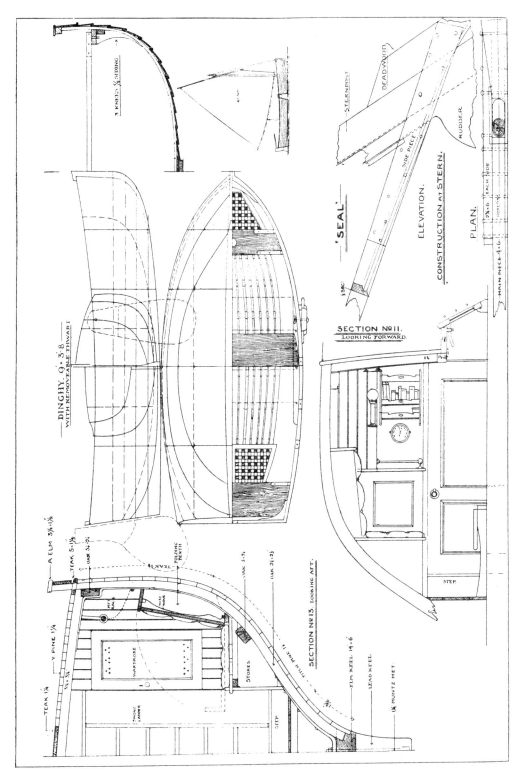

FIG 20

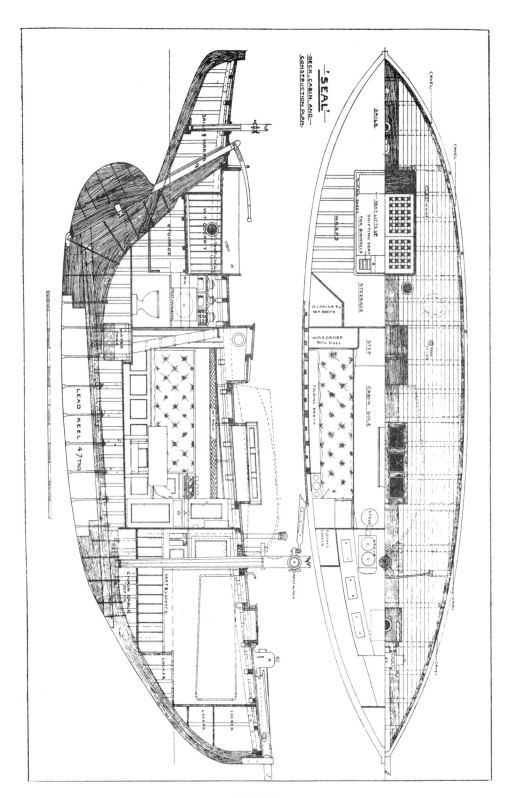

FIG 21

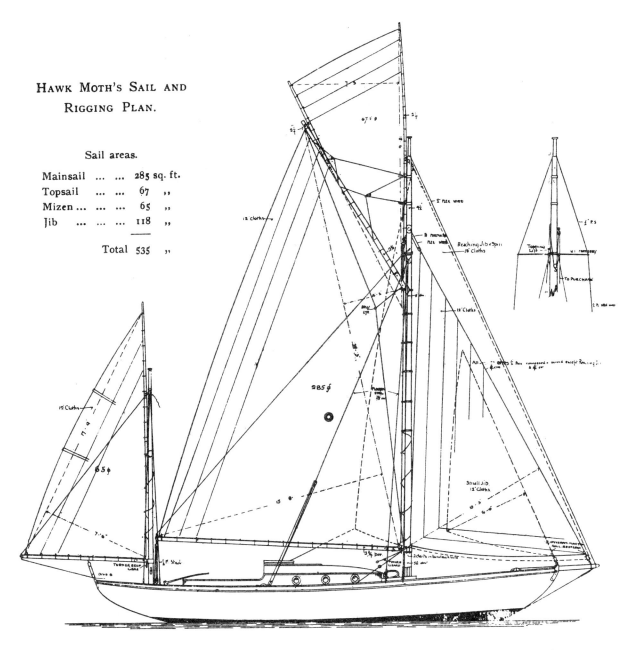

HAWK MOTH'S SAIL AND
RIGGING PLAN.

Sail areas.

Mainsail	285	sq. ft.
Topsail	67	,,
Mizen	65	,,
Jib	118	,,
Total	535	,,

Hawkmoth (No 85/1908)

This canoe yacht was a fairly fast and seaworthy small cruiser, for use on the Scottish West Coast by an experienced cruiser. She sailed well under headsail and mizzen which not all yawls will do and was also handy when reefed. With ample headroom she was a comfortable cruiser for two, though three could be accommodated. Her appearance would have been improved had the bowsprit been eliminated and the headsail set to the stemhead, with the mizzen being a bermudian sail.

FIG 22

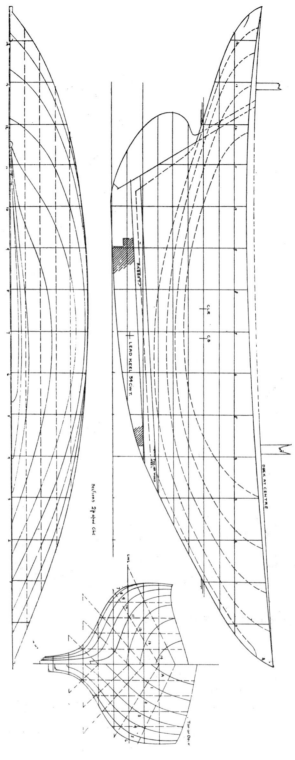

6-TON CANOE-YAWL HAWK MOTH, DESIGNED BY ALBERT STRANGE FOR MR. W. I. BEAUMONT.

L.O.A., 31·75ft.; L.W.L., 22·25ft.; beam, 7·6ft.; draught, 4·58ft.; displacement, 4·7 tons; lead keel, 34cwt.

FIG 23

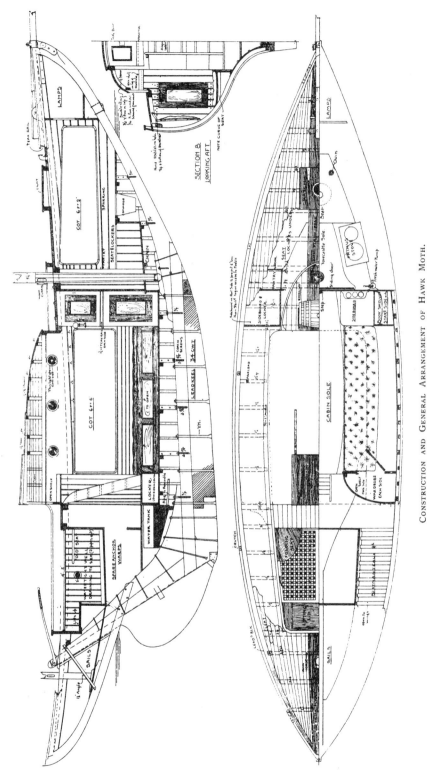

CONSTRUCTION AND GENERAL ARRANGEMENT OF HAWK MOTH.

FIG 24

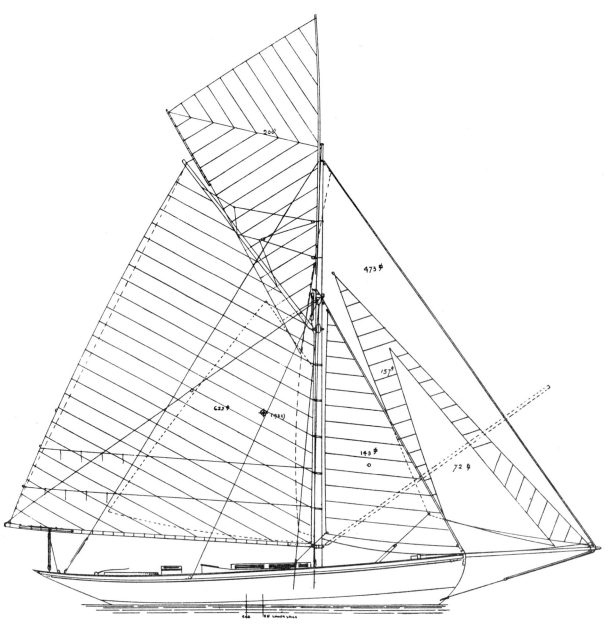

INNISFALLEN'S SAIL AND RIGGING PLAN.

Innisfallen (No 95/1909)

This cutter was designed for cruising and handicap racing about Table Bay, South Africa. She was built by Dickie of Tarbert, Loch Fyne and was shipped out to the Cape. The accommodation was for an owner's party of five, with a couple of natives as crew. The skylights and hatches were larger than in contemporary English yachts, to provide adequate ventilation and light in the high temperatures of the South African yachting season. Special attention was also given to the deck construction. The deep hull had a small iron keel of 2 tons with additional internal ballast. Local winds were either strong or very light and the rig had plenty of hoist, a large yard topsail and sizeable spinnaker and could also set a trysail of modest area for the heavy blows, when her sensible beam and draught would be needed. A powerful and interesting fast cruising yacht needing smart handling.

FIG 25

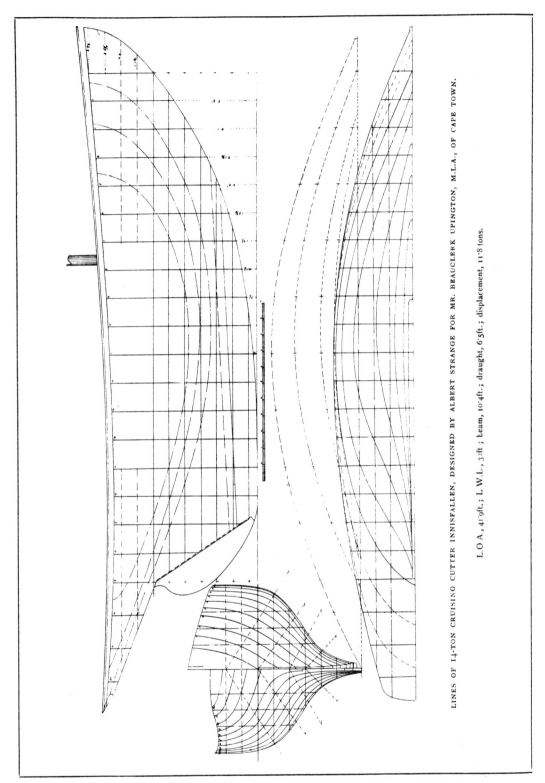

LINES OF 1¼-TON CRUISING CUTTER INNISFALLEN, DESIGNED BY ALBERT STRANGE FOR MR. BEAUCLERK UPINGTON, M.L.A., OF CAPE TOWN.

L.O.A, 41·9ft.; L.W.L., 32ft.; beam, 10·4ft.; draught, 6·5ft.; displacement, 11·8 tons.

FIG 26

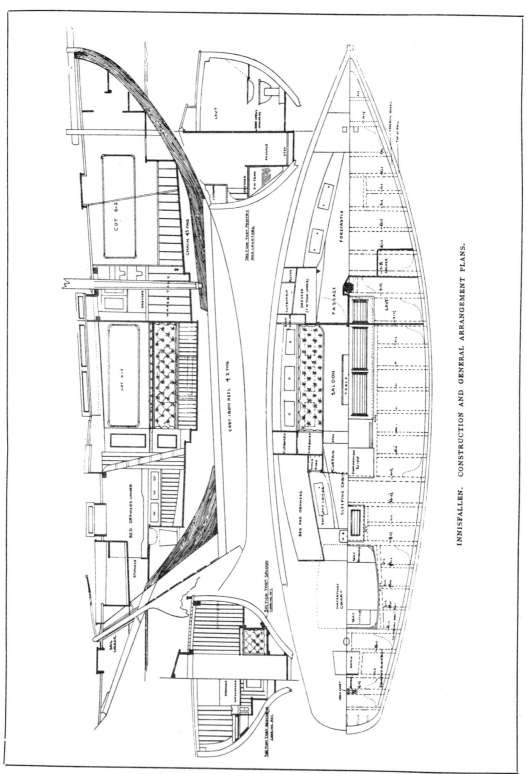

INNISFALLEN. CONSTRUCTION AND GENERAL ARRANGEMENT PLANS.

FIG 27

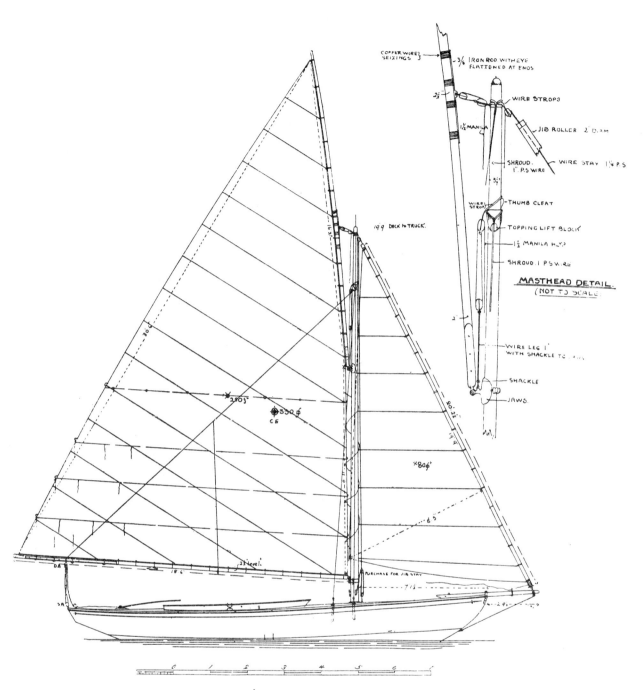

DRYAD'S SAIL AND RIGGING PLAN.

Dryad (No 101/1909)

This dayboat was designed for summer use on Lake Simcoe, Canada, which has shallows and thus forced a shallow draught hull with a centreplate. She was intended to race in handicap events, mainly against similar sized craft. She could also carry from two to four people for day sailing. A small ballast keel was fitted to aid stability, and displacement was 1.2 tons. The owner requested that the underwater body be as much like Strange's own CHERRUB II as possible. She was built in Toronto and the sails were sent out from England. Nowadays she would be a fine little dayboat if rigged as a bermudian sloop, without a bowsprit.

FIG 28

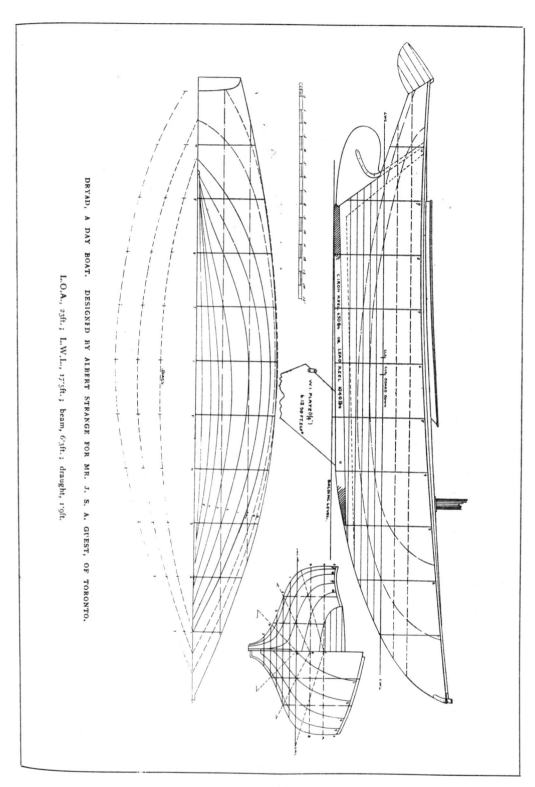

DRYAD, A DAY BOAT. DESIGNED BY ALBERT STRANGE FOR MR. J. S. A. GUEST, OF TORONTO.

L.O.A., 23ft.; L.W.L., 17·5ft.; beam, 6·3ft.; draught, 1·9ft.

FIG 29

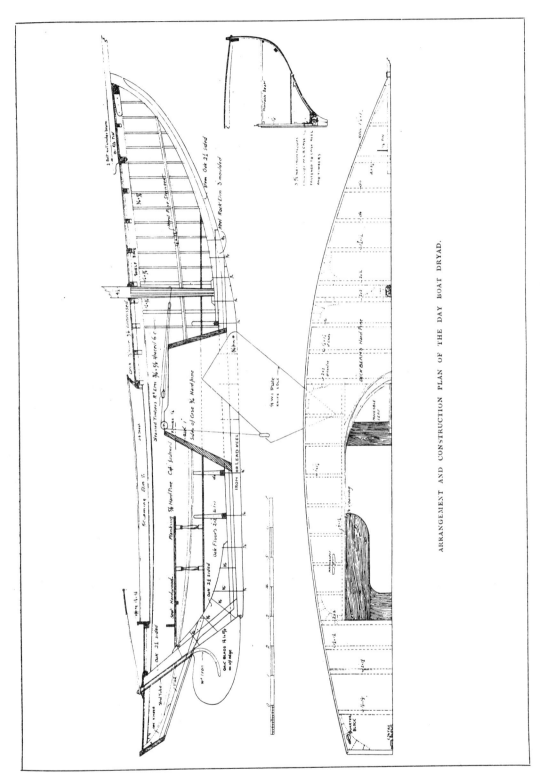

ARRANGEMENT AND CONSTRUCTION PLAN OF THE DAY BOAT DRYAD.

FIG 30

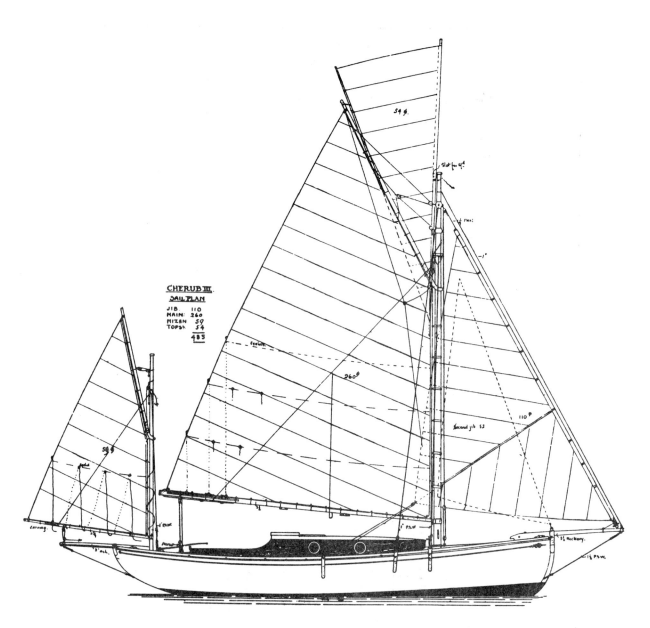

CHERUB III
SAIL PLAN
JIB   110
MAIN: 260
MIZEN   59
TOPST   54
         ̄4̄8̄3̄

Cherub III (No 112/1910)

This yawl was designed by Strange for his own use and was his last yacht. She was handy, very stiff and had sufficient speed for cruising. She would lay-to well, could turn to windward in a channel only 25 yards wide and would handle under jib and mizzen alone. The CHERUB III was originally designed with a transom stern but the design was altered before building. Her lines are, I think, the best of Strange's canoe-sterned yawl hulls, spoiled only by the then fashionable snubbed bow profile above water. The divided arrangement of the accommodation was devised to suit the use of his family.

FIG 31

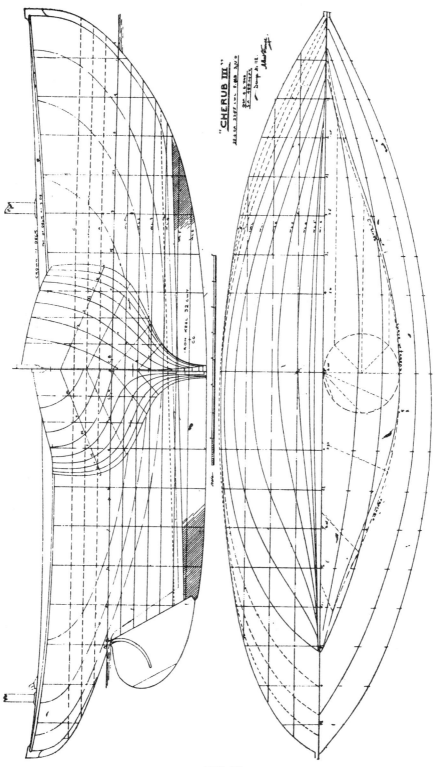

FIG 32

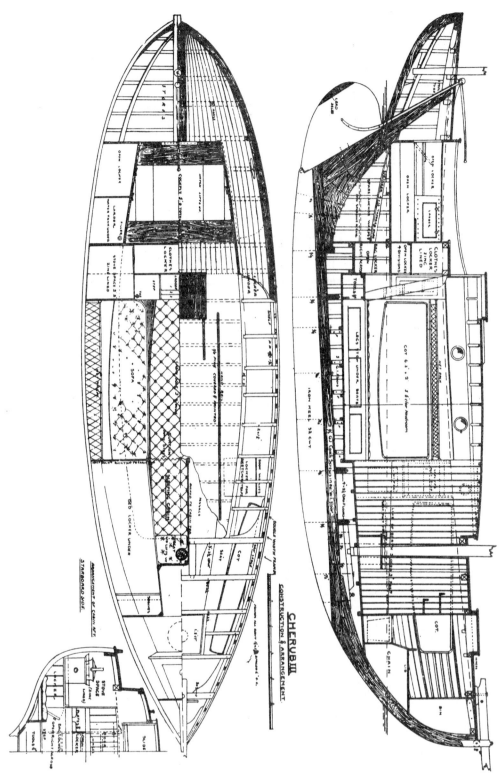

FIG 33

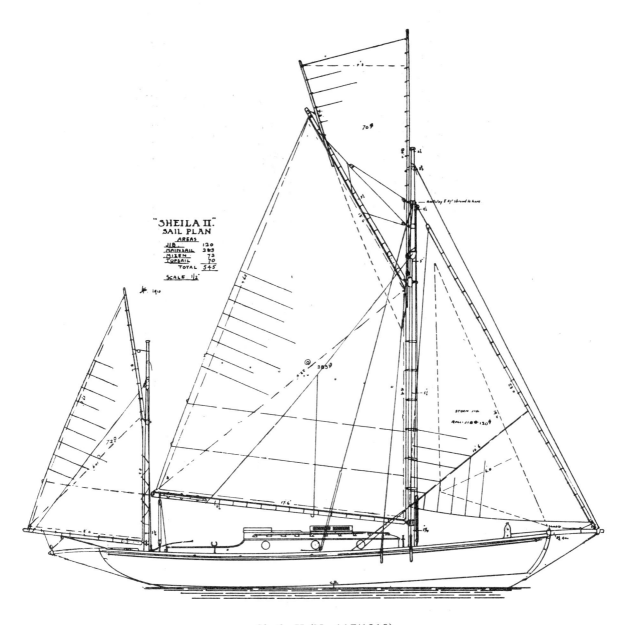

"SHEILA II."
SAIL PLAN
AREAS
JIB   120
MAINSAIL   283
MIZEN   72
TOPSAIL   70
    TOTAL   545
SCALE 1½"

Sheila II (No 117/1910)

The SHEILA II was designed for Strange's friend, artist Robert E. Groves, to be a similar but larger yacht than Strange's own CHERUB III. Grove's boat was a more stable and perhaps slightly faster craft. An alternative setting of a small jib to the stem head for strong winds is shown, though how well it would stand without being hanked to a stay is uncertain. The gunter mizzen would have been better as a bermudian sail, which came into fashion a few years later.

The SHEILA II has sailed long distances and proved to be a good sea boat.

FIG 34

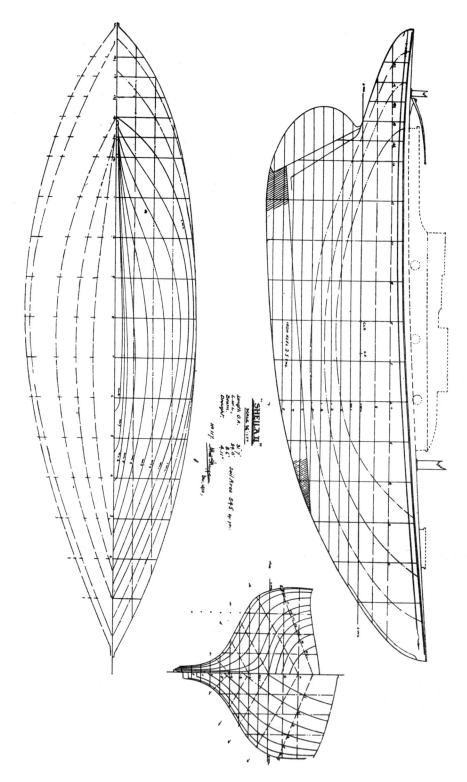

"SHEILA II"

SCALE ¾ = 1"

Length O.A.   31'7"
L.W.L.   25'0"
Beam   8'0"
Draught   5'11"

Sail Area 545 sq.ft.

FIG 35

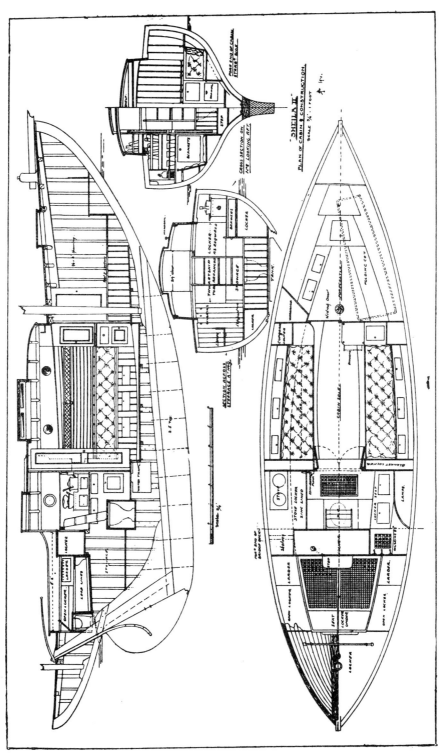

FIG 36

CHAPTER 6

The Years of Maturity —
Designs from 1898-1917

To many, the name of Albert Strange is synonymous with gaff rigged yawls having a canoe stern, probably because these were of a size which appealed to many observers. From study of his designs, it will be seen that Strange produced several types of yachts and boats. For example, his plans in the W.P. Stephens collection at Mystic Seaport Museum in Connecticut, include designs ranging from a 9 ft sailing dinghy to a 98 ft counter-sterned hull and also a small motor yacht. Albert Strange produced many attractive craft across this range of size, and most have a feeling of fitness for purpose.

Stern shape is always interesting in yacht design and generally, Strange's designs with a transom stern have a firmer bilge shape than those with a canoe or counter stern. These were usually slacker in the bilge and of generally easier hull form because of their greater draught and less reliance on hull form for the range of stability than most of the transom sterned boats, which were usually smaller and of less draught.

For the past eighty years, yachtsmen have been recognising yachts designed by Strange in anchorages or at sea, and have exclaimed on their attractive appearance and have been inspired by their apparent fitness for cruising under sail. However, Strange did not always design canoe-sterned yawls or other cruising yachts of fixed draught. Most of his early designs were of small, light displacement centreboard craft. The change to larger, but still small, cruising yachts with ballast keels, occurred about 1898-99. Thereafter, this trend was gradual but was still influenced by his earlier designs, his sailing experience and his general philosophy towards the sport.

From childhood, Albert Strange was interested in the design, construction and sailing of model yachts. He designed several and sailed them in competition at various times, besides writing letters and articles on the subject. Designers of model sailing yachts have considerable success in predicting the performance of their creations and it is probable that Strange's interest in models contributed to his ability when designing full scale craft.

It may surprise some that Albert Strange was keenly interested in the development, application and effects of various rules for rating yachts for racing. It suggests a more mathematically inclined mind than is usually found in an artist. He wrote many letters to journals giving criticism and views on rating rules and also designed some small racing craft, including canoes and a six metre, in response to competitions. It is unfortunate that he did not live in the era of the early development of the offshore racer, as the general style of healthy, fast cruising yachts designed and built in the period from 1930 until about 1960, would have delighted him and it would have been fascinating to see what he would have produced for that purpose.

Until the mid 1890s, his interest was in the type of small craft sailed from the Humber Estuary, particularly the developed style of sailing canoe known as a Humber Yawl. The Humber Yawl Club, of which he was a member and for a time the Captain, encouraged its members to design and often to build their own boats. It organised designing competitions to further this activity. The winning entries were published in the club Yearbook which, although a club journal, was also available for purchase by non-members. For his own use and for some of his friends, Albert Strange designed several Humber Yawls, as described in Chapter 3. The design of these small boats followed his earlier efforts which stemmed from his experience with the DAUNTLESS and the adapted design of the WREN from Dixon Kemp's MANUAL OF YACHT AND BOAT SAILING. (Not to be confused with WREN/ETHEL.) Through them and the study of Kemp's text, Strange began to develop individual procedure in small craft design and perhaps an individual style of appearance in his creations.

Contemporary with those of his friend George Holmes, the writings of Albert Strange in the Humber Yawl Yearbooks and in the yachting journals of Britain and America, resulted, in 1898, in an order from a Canadian sailing enthusiast for a larger craft than Strange had hitherto designed, which was to be used on the Lower St Lawrence River. This 25 footer, named OTTER, was to have a modest but yacht-like accommodation. Strange was unfamiliar with the St Lawrence, which is a considerably greater river than the Humber, and he took care to design a more powerful craft than he had hitherto done for his home waters. The OTTER hull form had fuller sections than was then usual in his designs, with increased fullness forward, greater displacement and a modest amount of salient keel and deadwood, as well as the centreplate, to achieve weatherliness. She was given the form of pointed stern which was to become his most widely known hull design feature.

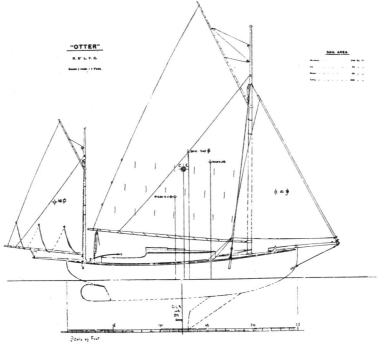

OTTER designed by Albert Strange in 1898

FIG 37

Reputedly, Strange intended to design the stern as the then usual canoe or canoe-yawl style, with a straight sternpost on which the rudder was hung, operated by a tiller which, to clear the mizzen mast, had to be made with a considerable crank in it to enable the helm to put over to an effective angle on one side. This was then usual practice in many canoe yawls, but was cumbersome and unsightly. L.N. Sanderson, one of Albert's young art pupils, is said to have suggested the problem might be solved by, 'drawing a bow at the stern and setting the mizzen aft the rudder post'. Strange is supposed to have been attracted by the idea and to have followed the suggestion, to produce the stern shown on the lines of the OTTER (FIGS 15 & 37). However, this does not accord with the design of an 18 ft centre-plate, canoe-sterned single-hander, Strange's Design No 4, which he produced in 1891. This boat is described in Chapter 8 and FIG 42 and appears to have been the earliest use of this form of canoe stern by Strange. This, and the stern of the OTTER, were similar to that of a small cruising yacht named CATRIONA, designed by Louis Sanderson as an entry in a design competition by THE YACHTSMAN magazine for a single-handed cruiser. It won second prize. The plans of the 24 ft 6 in yawl were published in March 1898 and show a canoe-sterned hull and a single headsail rig, the whole comparable with several later designs by Albert Strange (FIGS 38 & 39). Sanderson was then only 17 years old, an architectural student who was studying drawing under Strange. Her other principal particulars were LWL 20 ft, beam 7 ft, draught 3 ft 8 in, displacement 3½ tons, total sail area 310 sq ft. The accommodation was comfortably arranged for two and the coachroof was unusually swept down at the forward end. This yacht could be compared with Strange's later Design No 70, SHEILA, of October 1903 (FIG 40) and there was obvious interaction between the design philosophy of Strange and Sanderson.

Interest in 'canoe-yachts' was stirring in several quarters in the late 1890s and Sanderson's design had some similarities to a yacht designed in America by Strange's

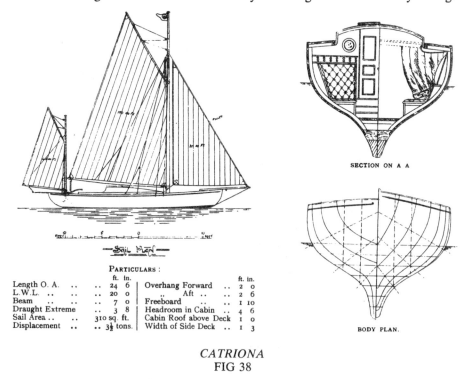

SECTION ON A A

BODY PLAN.

PARTICULARS :

	ft. in.		ft. in.
Length O.A.	24 6	Overhang Forward ..	2 0
L.W.L.	20 0	„ Aft	2 6
Beam	7 0	Freeboard	1 10
Draught Extreme ..	3 8	Headroom in Cabin ..	4 6
Sail Area	310 sq. ft.	Cabin Roof above Deck	1 0
Displacement ..	.. 3½ tons.	Width of Side Deck ..	1 3

CATRIONA
FIG 38

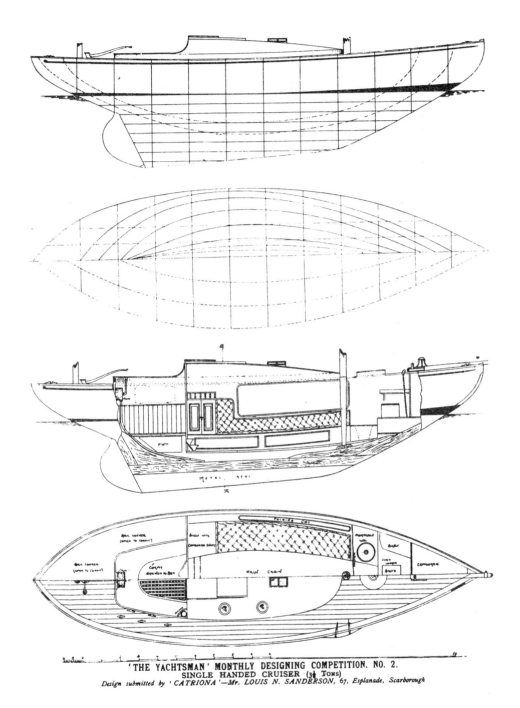

'THE YACHTSMAN' MONTHLY DESIGNING COMPETITION. NO. 2.
SINGLE HANDED CRUISER (3½ Tons)
Design submitted by 'CATRIONA'—Mr. LOUIS N. SANDERSON, 67, Esplanade, Scarborough

*Lines plan, sail plan, sections and general arrangement of CATRIONA designed by L. N.
Sanderson 1898*
FIG 39

friend William P. Stephens, who, as we have seen in Chapter 1, was a noted canoe designer, builder and writer, having great knowledge of yacht design, construction and sailing. Like Albert Strange, Stephens was also a member of the Humber Yawl Club, albeit at long range, and in the Club Yearbook for 1898, he published an article on his design for a small canoe yawl to be built by and for himself. This boat had been designed in 1897, the year before Strange used the same type of stern in the OTTER.

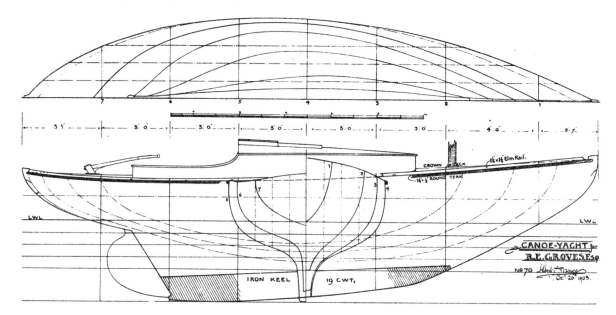

Canoe yacht SHEILA design No 70

FIG 40

It is therefore correct to assume that both Strange and Stephens evolved this form of stern for their own purpose independently of each other. Stephens, writing in the HUMBER YAWL CLUB YEARBOOK for 1898 said of the SNICKERSNEE, as she was named, "In working out the design last fall, it seemed that a double advantage could be gained by the short after overhang (which though unusual, is not inconsistent with the canoe type) both in a better ending of the fore and aft lines, and in a secure step for the mizzenmast well clear of the rudder head and tiller. It was believed at the time that this idea was original, and it is only lately that I have heard from CHERUB of a similar plan first devised by him some years ago but never put into practice." Stephens had designed a slippery looking small cruising yacht of pleasing appearance and with the fin keel then in vogue in smaller racing boats. She had well formed hull sections and a neat canoe stern of the type with which Strange was to become associated. She makes an interesting comparison with Strange's work.

William Stephens wrote of his design, "An attempt has been made to utilise the modern lines of form in producing a faster and far abler boat on about the same dimensions as the old VITAL SPARK; and for the same purpose of single handed cruising. On a waterline 18ft, which may be taken as the favourite size for this type of craft, by virtue of the moderate overhangs and the very full level lines, it has been possible to obtain a hull which will compare favourably in size with the yawl-yacht ROB ROY and the canoe-yacht VIPER on much smaller nominal dimensions. At the same time the form is such as to give promise of an all-around advantage over the older boats in speed, handiness, and ease and power in a seaway. If these results are not obtained, it must be laid to the individual defects of this particular design, and not to the type which it represents. This design is intended to be well within the ability of any single hander, and at the same time to give reasonably good accommodation for two persons in a permanent cabin that shall at all times be dry and cosy. The draught of three feet, quite enough for power and lateral plane, is not too much for convenient use in many localities, and has certain advantages of its own as compared with the two feet of the centreboard type. For one very important point, the middle of the cabin is left entirely clear, greatly increasing the room.

"The dimensions are:—

Length over all	. . . .	21' 9"
Length LWL	. . . .	18' 0"
Overhang bow	. . . .	2' 0"
Overhang stern	. . . .	1' 9"
Beam, extreme	. . . .	5' 9"
Beam LWL	. . . .	5' 3"
Draught, extreme	. . . .	3' 0"
Freeboard, least	. . . .	1' 7"
Displacement, 2800 lbs	. . . .	1.25 tons
Ballast, iron keel, 1184 lbs	. . . .	0.53 tons

"The construction is essentially that of a canoe, with flat bent keel, the fin being added after the hull is completed. The iron keel is of course bolted up through the deadwood of the fin and the main keel and floors. The headroom is 3 ft 8 in under the roof of house, which is shown as 6 ft long, leaving a cockpit 4 ft 5 in long.

"About Long Island Sound and New York Bay, in summer, a total area of 300 sq ft would be none too much with adequate arrangements for shortening sail quickly, and the tabernacle might well be dispensed with. The masts are shown placed for such a rig. In English waters this might be reduced to less than 250 sq ft."

Her rig was a gaff yawl with single headsail, copied from that of the EEL. Stephens was well pleased with the SNICKERSNEE and after a few ballast alterations, kept her for the rest of his long life. The author owns a sloop of very similar shape and size, except that she has a short counter stern, and he can vouch for the seaworthiness of the type.

Neither Stephens nor Strange were the first to design such an ending for a yacht. A notable earlier example was the 100 ft yawl JULLANAR, designed and built in 1874 by John Harvey, a Wivenhoe ship and yacht designer and builder, for Edward H. Bentall, the owner of an agricultural engineering works at Heybridge, Essex. The cut-away profile of the JULLANAR was based on Bentall's ideas for reducing the wetted surface of a sailing yacht and perhaps also reduce her wavemaking. The owner's concepts were further developed and mathematically proved by Harvey, who was a scientific designer of great experience with ships and yachts. His partner, Mr Pryor, also a naval architect, had great faith in the design which in its final form, as built, was less extreme than Harvey had intended, but was modified to suit Bentall's desires. The lines are shown in FIG 41. She proved successful as a cruising yacht and for one season in handicap racing. Although not identical to the stern shape of the OTTER, the profile of the JULLANAR's stern is similar, in that it placed the rudder and stock under the hull, and allowed the tiller to work forward of the encumbrance of the mizzen mast which had an improved step. As the JULLANAR was a celebrated yacht in her day and for some time after, it may be that Sanderson's idea sprang from his reading of her. However, it is equally probable that Strange would have been familiar with the JULLANAR's design from reading about her and possibly by having seen her in the mid 1870s, when she was successfully raced for one season.

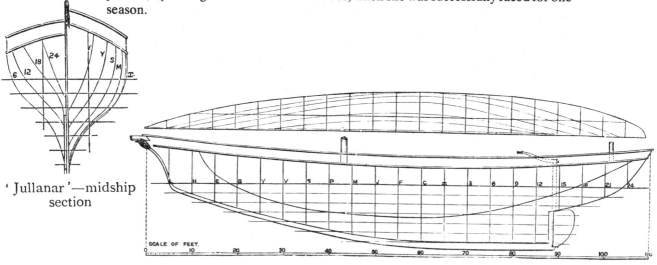

' Jullanar '—midship section

JULLANAR designed and built at Wivenhoe by John Harvey

FIG 41

The canoe stern was also developed earlier and independently, in Australia, when in 1858 the cutter yacht AUSTRALIA, LOA approx 60ft, was built at Sydney with an advanced hull form to reduce wetted surface, and which also ended in a canoe stern.

The pointed form of stern, with the rudder, stock and tiller arrangement, as drawn for the little OTTER, intrigued Albert Strange and in various forms in many yachts, was to become a well regarded feature of his designs. However, the stern of the OTTER was the Strange canoe stern concept in its early form. He was to develop the principle in following years, probably helped by his knowledge of civil architectural proportions and use of the hyperbola or parabola in the curves of its design.

A well-shaped canoe stern of this style is a subtle creation and although many yacht designers have used it in various yachts, it is not easy to achieve satisfying grace and balance in the form when built. Generally, Strange seems to have achieved this successfully, as did his contemporary, J. Pain Clark, who also developed canoe yachts, many of which were notably fast, including the little LORA. A detailed discussion on Strange's views on stern shape follows in Chapter 8.

There was neither an immediate or universal acceptance of this style of canoe stern. Strange reverted to the older style of pointed stern in his design for the IMOGEN (later BOREAS) of 1899 which also had reverse turn in her bottom sections, in contrast to the exposed deadwood arrangement in the OTTER, which was a much less expensive construction; but the fixed hull draught (without centreplate lowered) was intended to be increased to 3 ft 2 in on an overall length of 22 ft.

With these two designs, Albert Strange ventured beyond the small centreboarders of the Humber Yawl Club type of craft, into the design of small cruising yachts. He probably did not foresee this would happen and one supposes his hobby of designing was intended to remain only a pastime. However, correspondence on the design of small yachts and boats in various journals was gradually followed by offers of commissions to design for people and waters of which he had no experience and little knowledge. This advancement must have forced an appraisal of where these new developments might lead. With apparently secure artistic employment and an established way of life, it may be that he found the further role of yacht designer a pleasing confirmation of talent and another means of expression of his creativity, to parallel his sailing activities. Also, in the age in which he lived, to have an activity which could be carried on in spare time and which would also bring some financial return, was certainly worthwhile. It was evidently the case that after the design of the OTTER, Strange seems to have applied himself vigorously to spare time yacht design.

Wisely for his peace of mind, he apparently decided to continue to design *small* cruising yachts for owners of modest means. Many professional yacht designers had designed, and yacht yards had built, large numbers of cruising and racing yachts of all sizes, mainly for wealthy men who, though in many instances were keen and able seamen, were in the majority enthusiasts who liked the idea of owning a yacht and of belonging to one, if not several, prestigious yacht clubs and of being seen to be taking part in a manly sport, but who had little practical experience. They relied on the seamanship and skill of an experienced skipper and crew who navigated and handled the yacht and made life on board, for the owner, his family and friends, as pleasant and comfortable as possible. The owner might take the helm at times and enjoy a turn to windward or a race where, if the yacht was not too large, he could be seen to be handling her under the watchful and experienced eye of the skipper, ever ready with a, 'A little too near, Sir' or, 'Ready about now, Sir or he'll have our weather.' Such owners enjoyed their yachting in their own way in large numbers but others, almost invariably men with much less means, sailed smaller boats themselves or with the aid of friends. They were usually keenly aware of new developments, in the sorts of yacht or small boat they could afford, through articles and illustrations which appeared in yachting journals or on boatyard notice-boards. From the 1890s, the number of those journals increased, THE YACHTSMAN, YACHTING WORLD, MOTOR BOAT and YACHTING and BOATING MONTHLY (later YACHTING MONTHLY) came on the market in Britain, RUDDER and YACHTING, in America, with others elsewhere. These magazines opened a new exchange of information and ideas on pleasure sailing and eventually also on motor craft. They were widely read, as the earlier HUNT'S YACHTING MAGAZINE and its American contemporaries had not been.

Albert Strange's involvement with small yachts, after 1898, started at a time when big class yacht racing in Britain was temporarily at a very low ebb. As a result, smaller yachts and the 'Corinthian yachtsman', as the amateur was then called in magazines, were starting to receive much more attention than before in the British yachting periodicals. The publication of some of Strange's designs, together with those of many other small yachts became more frequent and encouraged greater interest in sailing than had existed previously. This had a snowball effect and gained a momentum which has never stopped since.

Designs for small yachts had been published since pleasure sailing had its own press but these were usually by professional designers who in some instances were also yacht builders. Able small sailing/cruising yacht designs were developed to a fine standard by professionals such as Arthur Payne.

A few cruising yachts were designed by their owners, as canoeists had done since the 1860s. In taking up the design of small cruising yachts for a fee (although we have no proof of this), Albert Strange was straying from a truly amateur status before he drew his designs for the OTTER, into a semi-professional standing thereafter. Cruising in small yachts with an all amateur crew was obviously developing fast and as a participant, he realised that there would be continued expansion of this aspect of sailing. He had progressed from the small centre-board canoe yawl type to the ballasted yacht and set about developing his ideas for craft with a spoon bow, cut away forefoot, moderate draught and often a canoe stern; small yachts which could be afforded by numbers of keen sailing men of moderate means. The canoe yawl SHEILA was typical of his new output. She was designed by Strange in 1903-04, for artist and ornithologist, Robert E. Groves and is one of Strange's best remembered craft, if only from her owner's enthusiastic accounts of his cruises in her. The SHEILA's dimensions were 25 ft overall, 19 ft 6 in waterline length × 6 ft 9 in beam × 3 ft 5 in draught (FIG 40). She was to be sufficiently seaworthy to cruise about the often difficult and dangerous west coast of Scotland, which is subject to considerable variation in weather.

Like most owners of these small cruisers, Groves sought a cheap building price and obtained one from Robert Caine, a builder of fishing boats at Port St Mary, Isle of Man. However, she seems to have been well put together as ten years after her launch in 1904, the SHEILA was wrecked off Dublin and although written off as a total loss, was salvaged and rebuilt after the insurers had refused to do so. Many years' later, she was badly damaged by fire but after repair still survives in use as a yacht. The SHEILA typifies the small cruising yacht of Edwardian times and remains complete with that most impractical of containers, a water barricoe, usually carried in chocks on deck forward of the mast.

After the launch of SHEILA, Robert Caine offered to build another to the same design and quickly, — 'A good plain job for £100 complete.' An attractive offer for contemporary yachtsmen but a sad commentary on the shockingly low wages paid at the time to skilled shipwrights for very long working hours — something of which the gentlemen owners had little knowledge. It is interesting to note in connection with Caine's offer, that Mystic Design 1,752 shows, in addition to the name of R.E. Groves, that of W. Booth, with a later date of 1905.

For these small yachts, Albert Strange had to develop a greater knowledge of wooden yacht construction. As he had not served an apprenticeship in a ship or yacht building yard and had only drifted into a quasi-professional standing as a designer, he must have acquired this by observation at various times when craft were being built and, more probably, from reading. Also, it is very likely that the builders of his yachts made constructional alterations as work progressed, despite what was shown on the plans. Strange probably learned from this process too and in discussion with some of the builders. However, in his lecture to the Royal Yorkshire Yacht Club in 1892, Strange seemed to show detailed knowledge of scantlings etc. which he discussed at some length.

As an example of Albert Strange's design work at that time, the plans of MIST (FIG 41) show a small yacht which was developed from the SHEILA but was just over one foot longer. She was intended for cruising on the Clyde and the west coast of Scotland, was built in 1907, and is still sailing.

The Humber Yawl Club was not alone in organising design competitions. THE YACHTSMAN magazine, YACHTING MONTHLY, YACHTING WORLD and others overseas, such as THE RUDDER and DIE YACHT also gave prizes for competitive designs of various specified pleasure craft until the 1950s when, because of plagiarism, this popular feature of the yachting press was abandoned. This is a loss to both yachtsmen and designers, particularly younger ones. The average sailing man obtains much pleasure from studying the plans of his favourite types of craft and can gain in technical appreciation as a result. This improves his knowledge of craft and his ability to discuss improvements and ideas, which in turn improves an owner's perceived and specified desires when deciding on a new boat or instructing a designer.

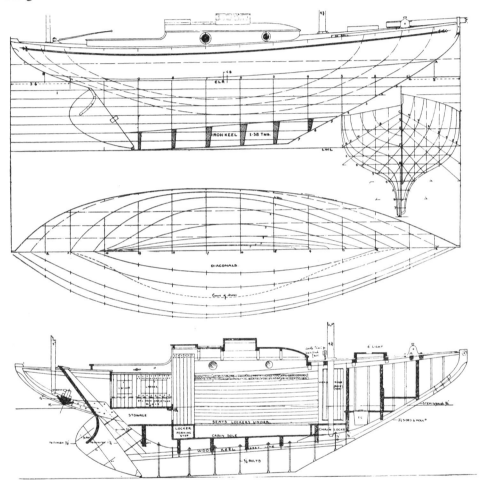

Lines plan and profile arrangement of canoe yacht MIST designed by Albert Strange in 1906

FIG 41

Many yachtsmen before about 1960, were able to discuss details of design and construction in a way superior to those who have come after, many of whom cannot even obtain a copy of the lines of the boat they own, as these are increasingly regarded as commercially confidential.

Yacht designing competitions also provided a chance for younger designers to show what they could do and they might sometimes find their efforts compared with entries of more experienced men. Most beneficial of all was the criticism of established experts on the merits or otherwise of their designs. Such competitions gave opportunity for those little known to bring their names forward, without having to wait for the commission of a patron willing to risk his money to build the first craft from their design, the young yacht designer's most difficult achievement. So these competitions were both a testing ground and a means of advertising.

Albert Strange's success in various design competitions in middle age contributed considerably to advancing his name as a designer of yachts. For an amateur, he was a prolific designer, completing up to ten detailed designs in a year, a reflection on the amount of spare time his employment must have allowed. As he was not making his living from designing, he could devote more time to each than a professional could afford for such small craft and consequently, his attention to detail and the standard of draughtsmanship, equalled that of many professionals, sometimes though, there was the amateur's usual lack of dimensions. Entry of the design competitions extended the circle of admirers of his work and also his experience of tackling the design of various types of small pleasure sailing craft specified in them.

Strange also designed many small boats with a transom stern. These had a robust quality about them, little yachts meant for knock-about sailing at week-ends snatched from 'weather windows' or, rare to Edwardian sailing men, for a week's holiday. Smallest of these was the TOPSY (FIG 51), only 17 ft long. The BEE at 21 ft 6 in length overall was typical (FIGS 70, 71 & 72). But there were much larger designs with a transom, e.g. BETTY.

An interesting example of one of his competition designs is CLOUD (FIGS 52, 53 & 54) which won the first prize of ten pounds in the YACHTING MONTHLY competition of September 1908.

Contestants were invited to design a 30 ft waterline single-hander, wholesome in type with good accommodation and simple rig. Drawings had to be submitted by early October. Twenty-two entries were received.

CLOUD'S dimensions were LOA 38.75 ft, LWL 30 ft, Beam 9.58 ft, Draught 5 ft, Displacement 10.13 tons and Sail Area 777 sq ft in a gaff ketch rig.

It is believed that this design was based on a somewhat larger canoe sterned ketch, QUEST II, designed during the winter of 1906 for his friend and fellow artist, C.W. Adderton (see Chapters 8 & 9) built by Dickie at Tarbert in 1907.

These two successful designs are the first of what might be called his 'blue water yachts'. They show how competently Strange had developed his ideas from centreboard canoe yawls through small canoe yachts to vessels capable of long offshore passages, though these were rare during his lifetime, when ocean voyages in small yachts were regarded as extremely hazardous.

Albert Strange amended the design of CLOUD in 1912. He increased the displacement and drew a yawl rig of greater area. Later that year she was built by W.E. Thomas of Falmouth to the order of Lt A.W. Gush RN and G.D. Stanford.

A second example, BLUE JAY, this time with the original ketch rig, was built by the same builder in 1926 for Norman Dinwiddy. She was cruised widely, circumnavigating Great Britain in 1927 and Ireland in 1929. For each of these cruises her owner was awarded the Claymore Challenge Cup of the Royal Cruising Club. Later owners took her even further afield and she was recently based in Malta.

He also produced designs with longer bow overhangs and counter sterns. These too developed his search for, and understanding of, harmony of hull form and the potential speed which such craft can achieve. These were in the broad tradition of the deeper, narrow cutter yacht type which had pretensions to speed. Amongst these were Design No 119, Mystic 1.744 (1911) and VENTURE (built 1920).

Subsequently, CHARM I, CHARM II, and SEA HARMONY were built basically to VENTURE's lines but in different sizes, drawn by the Sufflings after Strange's death. FIREFLY was based on Design 119 but evidence suggests she was radically altered by Harrison Butler — again after Strange's death. The Suffling Brothers were east coast timber importers and enthusiastic, talented sailors and amateur designers.

Although the above were yawls, many of his counter-sterned designs were sloops or cutters, e.g. INNISFALLEN, DESIRE, DRYAD, AFREET, FLAPPER, NURSEMAID and MONA.

Strange had early come to appreciate the usefulness of a mizzen in adjusting balance of a sail plan, on paper and in practice. It was also useful when riding at anchor in calm conditions and had the seldom achieved but much cherished potential of setting a mizzen staysail. The rig was popular for cruising as it had been at times for rule cheating purposes in both inshore and offshore racing yachts.

Strange's designs further popularised the yawl rig for small cruisers, though he was not its originator for this purpose, as small cruising yawls existed at least by the 1840s and probably earlier, while after the 1860s numbers were built and cruised widely. But Albert Strange's yacht designs were being created in a sailing world which supported several weekly or monthly journals giving news and views on craft and people and which were exchanged nationally and to some extent internationally.

To Strange, this liking for the yawl rig followed his earlier experiences afloat, at first on the Thames, and then with the Humber Yawl Club. In his small cruising yacht designs, it shortened the main boom and made the mainsail easier to handle than that of a comparable cutter. The yawl may also be a pretty rig and Strange made the most of it, complementing his well proportioned canoe and counter sterned hulls. However, he seems not to have used the rig in many of his transom sterned designs but there is an example in Design No 146. He also designed several cutters of which the 42 ft counter sterned INNISFALLEN (15 tons) was a good example. She was built by Dickie of Tarbert, Scotland, in 1910, a yard which built many Albert Strange designs. Unusually for him, she was designed for racing off Cape Town, South Africa, one of the world's keenest racing areas. The greater windward efficiency of the cutter rig overrode all other considerations of rig. If this shocks some devotees, we must remember that Albert Strange also designed the 6 metre racing yacht DESIRE and Mystic Designs 1.690, 1.696, 1.707, 1.708 and several racing canoes and he also contributed to the various yacht rating rules debates in YACHTING MONTHLY and took a keen interest in the development of racing boats (and in model yacht racing too.) We must not forget either AFREET and FLAPPER — non-extreme racing boat designs.

Commissions for larger cruising yachts grew. The full bodied cruising cutter TERN III was designed for Dr Claud Worth, who had very fixed ideas on the type of craft he wanted (FIGS 8 & 9). Worth wrote of the TERN III as though the design was solely his, commenting in his book YACHT CRUISING "... by about 1912 the plans seemed so perfect that the vessel simply had to be built. I sent the 'lines' to my old friend the late Mr Albert Strange who re-drew them for me on tracing cloth." This seems an odd comment. No doubt Worth drew all his plans on cartridge paper and probably could not trace accurately in ink. So it may be that Albert Strange was merely asked to trace the lines. But it is more likely that Worth, who was much more inexperienced than Strange when it came to yacht design, wanted a second opinion and possibly a check on whatever he had done to estimate and calculate weights and centres for the design. More than that cannot now be surmised but it is certain that Strange contributed to this yacht in the design stage.

As the Edwardian age unfolded, Albert Strange continued to enhance his reputation as the designer of attractive cruising yachts, particularly those with canoe sterns and yawl rig, a style which drew criticism from some because of the stern shape. Such a stern is not so effective in increasing the area of the waterplane and thus stability, when the craft is heeled under sail, as does a counter, though it is obviously more effective than a transom stern on a craft of the same waterline length. Also, its confined shape often made both its building and the stepping of a mizzen mast very difficult. The mizzen could only be satisfactorily sheeted to a short bumkin, which Strange designed to curve downwards and be stayed to the stern timber in imitation of the short bowsprit he favoured on many of his yawls, particularly those having a single headsail. Such headsails were dangerously large for changing in a seaway or strong wind in those days, before *efficient* roller reefing of the present type, although Strange employed roller-reefing headsail gear on several of his single-handed rigs. Like many of his contemporaries, Strange arranged the mizzen boom too close to the after deck and in most of his designs, the mizzen would have set better as a triangular or bermudian sail, besides permitting a lighter mast, reducing rigging weight and windage. Examples of Albert Strange's yachts with the overhanging canoe stern, included his own CHERUB III and the SHEILA II of 1911, a 7 ton yawl designed for Robert E. Groves, who owned the original, smaller SHEILA.

Strange wrote of the design of the CHERUB III and SHEILA II in the HUMBER YAWL CLUB YEARBOOK of 1911 — "CHERUB III was launched last summer and proved a very comfortable ship in all respects. The cabin arrangement, rather unusual in so small a vessel, was adopted in order that a lady member of the crew could have somewhere to withdraw to when the society of the male members grew oppressive, and has answered its purpose well. The berth is comfortable and snug, and the provision of places wherein might be kept those numerous and perplexing objects of attire and toilet affected by the gentler sex, found favour. The establishment of the kitchen in the after part of the 'saloon' was found to be far more convenient than the usual arrangement in the forecastle.

"The little boat turned out to be handy, extremely stiff and not at all slow regarded from a cruising point of view. With part of the jib rolled up, and the sheet a little to weather, she laid to perfectly. She runs very fast, and on all points of sailing her wave making is extremely slight. She will turn to windward through any channel 25 yards wide, and handles well under jib and mizzen, and was often rowed at a good rate of speed with the small paddles from the dinghy. Her light draught was not found detrimental to good windward work. In headroom, ease of handling, room on deck and in the cockpit, she fitted her crew's requirements capitally, and her bold side and businesslike look were much admired. CHERUB III was originally designed with a square stern, but the plan was departed from in obedience to a general outcry on the part of many admirers of the canoe stern. This departure, having been successfully overcome from the financial side, has not been regretted by the owner, and certainly adds much to the appearance and general efficiency of the yacht, which was built in the yard of Mr Archibald Dickie of Tarbert, who carried out the plan with the care, thoroughness and honesty for which he is justly famed. Messrs Cranfield and Carter of Burnham on Crouch supplied the rigging and her beautifully made suit of sails.

"Mr R.E. Groves, whose extended and adventurous cruises in the Irish Sea and on the west coast of Scotland are so well known to the cruising world, commissioned the designer of SHEILA and CHERUB III to prepare plans for a similar, but somewhat larger yacht than CHERUB III. His requirements as to accommodation, headroom and draught necessitated a somewhat different arrangement, giving a much more powerful boat. The plans shown here will explain in what directions the departures have been made, and though the beam, draught and displacement of CHERUB III have been largely exceeded, the sail plan is not much larger in proportion; as in single handed, or short handed sailing it is felt that is not so much the size of hull as the size of sails which counts. The arrangement of lavatory and companion (hatch) ensures complete shutting off from the saloon, while the size of the forecastle, unencumbered by cooking apparatus, gives a good extra cabin and berth available when company is on board. It should be noticed however that CHERUB III affords 4 separate berths, a number not attainable when a separate compartment for lavatory etc is demanded, although this number is rarely necessary or desirable on so small a yacht. As a cutter, much more sail could be given her, but long experience in cruising on all sorts of coasts and under all conditions has conclusively proved to the owner and designer the many advantages of the yawl rig for this size of yacht for the purpose required. She is now being built at Tarbert, Loch Fyne by the builder of CHERUB III and should be launched early in July. It will be noticed that in both boats there is room aft for the installation of a small motor if wanted."

The comparative particulars of the yachts were:—

	CHERUB III	SHEILA II
Length over all	28′ 6″	31′ 7″
Length, LWL	22′ 11″	24′ 0″
Beam, extreme	8′ 2″	8′ 6″
Beam, LWL	7′ 9″	8′ 3″
Draught, extreme	3′ 9½″	4′ 11″
Displacement	4 tons 12 cwt	6 tons 2 cwt
Sail Area	483 sq ft	545 sq ft
Iron keel	1 ton 12 cwt	2 tons 10 cwt
Inside lead, approx	12 cwt	6 cwt
Headroom, clear	5′ 6″	5′ 9½″
Least freeboard	2′ 3″	2′ 1½″

The design for the SHEILA II is thought to be the apogee of Albert Strange's endeavour with cruising yacht design and to have one of the best hull forms he produced. To this author, the hull body sections are very fair and attractive, as is the form of the after body and the canoe stern. However, the bow profile and the forward waterline endings and the inner forward bowline are not pleasing and could be improved by easing the profile curve below the waterline and allowing it to flow in a fair line above. This criticism is made in the knowledge that to some it may sound irreverent. However, I believe that Strange may have been too concerned with balancing the above water profile of the ends of many of his canoe sterned yachts, such as SHEILA II, to the extent of snubbing the bow (a then widespread fashion in yachts of all sizes and rigs) so as to use a short bowsprit, which in profile, balanced the short bumkin aft. The SHEILA II might have been improved in her handling at sea if the bow had been prolonged to its natural ending and the tack of the foresail had been taken to the stem head.

Be that as it may, the SHEILA II was a successful and much admired yacht, beloved of Robert Groves, her owner for many years. After the 1939-45 war she became well known as the heroine of the book SHEILA IN THE WIND, in which Adrian Hayter described his voyage in her from England to New Zealand, where she is still sailed from Auckland, but is presently being restored, after being partially wrecked when she broke her mooring in a gale.

The yawl JOVANNA was built in Italy in 1913 from the plans of SHEILA II and there were other yachts which Strange designed having the same characteristics as Groves' successful cruiser.

Albert Strange kept himself abreast of those parts of naval architectural theory relating to the design of sailing yachts, and amongst his reading were the works of Froude. He used Froude's wave line theory in the design of the 30 footer TUI but whilst the hull was appealing, the overall design seemed to lack the wholeness of Strange's other work. Perhaps the owner's insistence on a sloop rig for the canoe sterned hull made her appear odd compared with the yawls which had the same stern, though many other designers had produced sloops of that hull form.

It is interesting that the last boat Strange designed for himself, the CHERUB III, was given a transom stern. It was to this design that the ARIEL was built in 1925. However, Strange altered this to a canoe stern before placing the order with Dickie at Tarbert. The CHERUB III was built in 1910. Although only 22 ft on the waterline, a separate sleeping cabin was arranged for Julia Strange, partitioned off from the main cabin. A focsle having reasonable space for stowage of gear and equipment was a useful feature and as built, did not have any pipe cots. The CHERUB III is still sailing from Falmouth under the name REDWING.

Altogether, Albert Strange produced approximately 140-150 designs as far as is known, a considerable output for someone who really regarded it as a hobby, though an absorbing and well studied one which brought him lasting recognition.

CHAPTER 7

My Last Cruise in Cherub II

Albert Strange had a gift for what might be styled, 'companionable writing'; the ability to take the reader with him, in imagination, on his voyaging reminiscences. One of these experiences is related here, a cruise in the CHERUB II, "My most beloved boat" as Strange described her in the article, which first appeared in YACHTING MONTHLY in 1911.

We join the little yawl in the Solent, then set off up the Channel to round the Foreland and enter the mouth of the Thames, then into the Medway. Strange recalled his youthful pleasures on board the Gravesend sailing bawleys, one of the most revealing passages in his writings and one which is all the more interesting in that he had made a stowboating trip after sprats, in winter, which says much for his determination to see something of fishing under sail and its hardships. But why delay enjoyment? Let Strange tell the story.

"When a man has owned and parted with a good many different boats, each one leaves in the memory its own particular stories which are never forgotten. To turn over their old logs brings back vivid recollections of the days and nights spent happily in them at sea, and no ship that I have ever owned has left more or happier memories than the little Humber yawl, whose doings in the North Sea have already been chronicled in these pages.

She was a good, dependable little creature, such a sea-boat for her inches, and, if you did not want to walk about below, gave such comfort and ease when the toils of the day were over, that the affection she compelled has never been obliterated by her successors, and whatever allowances one has to make for the glamour of past days, in which all discomforts are forgotten and only the shining hours remembered, there is no doubt in my mind that she thoroughly earned my affection and has thoroughly kept it.

I still wonder how I brought myself to part with her, even though my work compelled me to spend several successive long vacations on shore and away from the call of the sea. I suppose the truth was that I could not endure the idea of chartering her, and equally disliked the thought that she would have to spend several years in a shed, drying her life out, if I didn't, so she had to go, and not being of the same disposition as the Arab in the poem, who sold his steed and then sold the purchaser by running off with steed and purchase money too, I tore myself away from her charms and some other fellow made himself happy in her company.

On this occasion, being bound to "the Wight," and the winds of heaven being light and from the westward — time also being precious — we sailed from Greenhithe (where CHERUB had spent the winter in the Pier Master's shed) to the London Docks, and hoisted

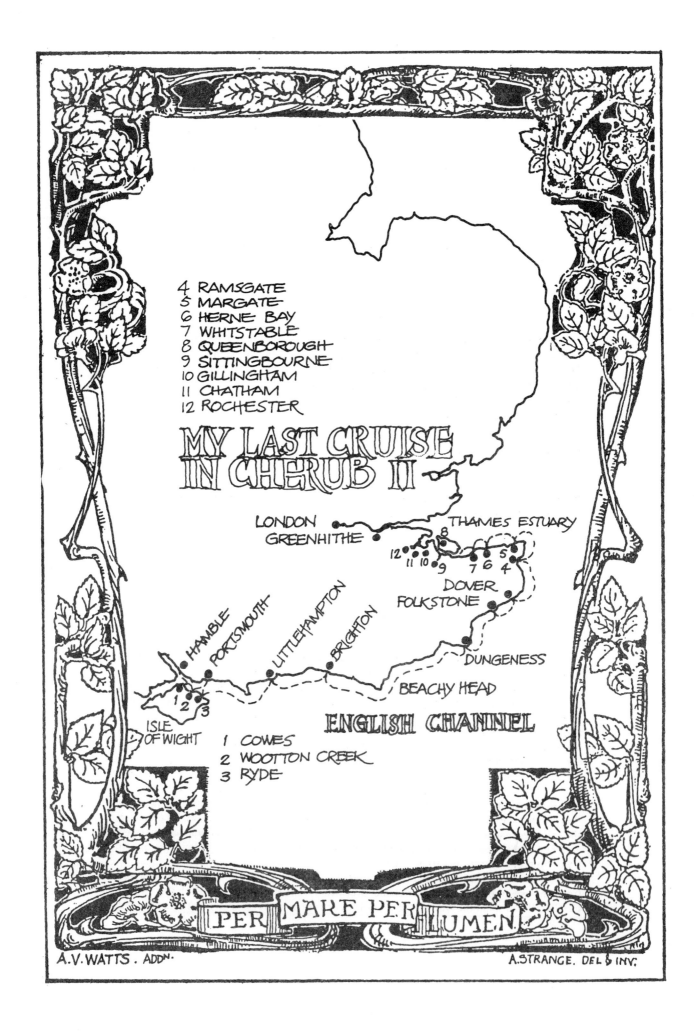

4 RAMSGATE
5 MARGATE
6 HERNE BAY
7 WHITSTABLE
8 QUEENBOROUGH
9 SITTINGBOURNE
10 GILLINGHAM
11 CHATHAM
12 ROCHESTER

MY LAST CRUISE IN CHERUB II

LONDON
GREENHITHE

THAMES ESTUARY

12 11 10 9 8 7 6 5 4

DOVER
FOLKSTONE

HAMBLE PORTSMOUTH LITTLEHAMPTON BRIGHTON

DUNGENESS

BEACHY HEAD

1 2 3

ISLE OF WIGHT

ENGLISH CHANNEL

1 COWES
2 WOOTTON CREEK
3 RYDE

PER MARE PER LUMEN

A.V. WATTS . ADDN.   A. STRANGE. DEL & INV.

her on board the LADY MARTIN, bound for Ireland, but touching at Portsmouth on her way. Here we were put "over side," and as her ladyship's captain was in a vast hurry, all CHERUB's ballast and belongings were dumped hastily on board, and we were left made fast to a buoy in a state of exasperating confusion which took some time to reduce to order.

As I had a real good shipmate for a 'deckie' who was thoroughly *au fait* in all the details of canoe yawl work (did he not own one himself?) an hour or so put us all square, and with a light wind and a good ebb tide we were not long in getting over to Wootton Creek, where the B.C.A., now moribund, I think, if not quite dead, were camping and holding their annual meet.

We had been promised moorings, but they were not ready for us, so we put the yawl on shore on a sort of slipway. As she possessed legs she sat up quite comfortably and remained there for a couple of tides until we could get our mooring. There is no doubt that in cruising in out-of-the-way places legs pay for their carriage, and enable one to attempt all sorts of spots in comfort that would otherwise not prove good berths. There were lots of little boats of a cruising type at this meet, as well as some that could only be called cruisers by stretching the truth to breaking point.

One in particular, a canoe called the YANKEE, had exactly the same accommodation as a large meat dish — no more and no less. The happy owner sat outside the boat on the end of a long plank when he was sailing, and with great agility shifted plank and himself to the other side of the canoe when she went about. The trick did not always come off, especially before the wind, and then the crew came off instead and performed other tricks of quite a protracted nature in the water before the voyage could be resumed.

I believe this sort of craft is now extinct, but it could sail at extraordinary speed so long as the skipper could keep himself on board. This gentleman, an American of most engaging speech and manners, lived in a tiny tent on shore. The canoe lived in a shed, and was much better housed than her owner. They were not often afloat, and though I was kindly offered the use of the YANKEE for a spin outside, I must frankly confess I funked it, and refrained from gaining a new experience.

Before we left the slip we had the startling experience of a fire on board CHERUB. Having carefully prepared a stew (I used to be famous for my stews) and left it on the stove peacefully bubbling, we went off to pay our call on the Officers of the Camp, forgetful of the evil nature of the stove, and also of the fact that a bottle of whisky, which, by some extraordinary means known only to itself had found its way on board, was concealed in close proximity to the stove.

Directly we had 'turned the corner,' so to speak, the stove must have indulged in one of its 'flare-ups' and the heat caused that wretched bottle of destruction to burst and set its hiding place on fire!

Fortunately, the boy who attended to the Club dinghy was near by, and being a youth of bright intelligence, managed to put the blaze out before running to tell us. We hurried to the spot, our hearts in our mouths, to find a blackened and charred stove locker, a burst bottle, and the stew pot simmering composedly, with its contents perfectly cooked. Small damage was done but what a warning!

We ate our dinner amid a strong smell of burnt wood, but could not make up our minds as to the apportionment of the blame. Were *we* to blame for leaving the stove unattended, was the stove to blame, or was the whole affair due to the wanton person who brought that bottle on board? The point has never been settled; but I have not, since then, left a stove going by itself.

After a few days cruising to Cowes, Ryde, Hamble, and the upper part of Portsmouth Harbour in the search for picturesque relics of the past, in the shape of old hulks of battleships etc., we had a race amongst the Association boats, at the conclusion of which CHERUB arrived home in pride of place, but did not win a prize, as she had to give time to all except YANKEE, who was delayed by 'tricks coming off' when about half way round.

There was only a nice whole-sail breeze, and could YANKEE have been kept upright she would have beaten all by very many minutes, and had there been more wind CHERUB would have collared the cup, as she always did best in a hard wind and with reefed canvas.

After the races the meet broke up, and we began to think about getting home to the

Thames. So we went along to Ryde and lay at anchor to the westward of the Pier to wait for a slant. The weather had been very broken, with strong S.W. winds and plenty of rain, and a good many coasters were sheltering inside the Mother Bank. We dined on shore that night, and brought our filled-up water tins with us when we came on board, and next morning, on looking out early, we found the wind a little north of west. So we made an early start on the last of the ebb, and with a single reef sail soon drew out past the Warner on our course for the Looe Channel. Clear of the Island there was a large confused sea, not breaking, but very lumpy and irregular, and we went bundling along very happily, but with plenty of motion.

Astern of us was a small sloop of about 5 tons, which did not catch us (CHERUB was hard to catch on this point of sailing), and remained about half-a-mile astern until we were not far from the entrance to the Looe.

Looking ahead, we were astonished to see right across the Channel, and beyond the Pullar Buoy, one long line of roaring, breaking seas, with no visible passage through. We were quite certain of our position, as both the channel buoys were visible with the binoculars. It is true that 'King's Channel Pilot' states that the west entrance to the Looe is 'barred by turbulent overfalls.' But as it goes on to say that it can only be used by small vessels (and we were small enough in all conscience) the warning had not impressed us sufficiently.

As there was no way round, except by way of the Owers Lightship, and as the strong tide (at least 5 knots) was sweeping us very rapidly towards the breakers, we had to make up our minds quickly and adopt the only course that seemed practical, which was to lower the mainsail almost completely, so as to check the boat's speed and yet give steerage way, and let her go bow on to the seas towards which the tide was setting us at a greatly accelerated pace. She cleared the first line of breakers with a big leap, plunged bow under the second lot, which swept her fore and aft, though not much came into the well, smashed again in the next ridge of foam, rose and shook herself free, then staggered through the remaining curlers half smothered with foam, and suddenly shot into comparatively smooth water!

There seemed to be six or eight definite lines of breaking waves about seven feet high, very thin in the crests, and having no buoyancy in them. It was then about two hours flood, and may have been the hottest part of the tide, and the long confused Channel heave perhaps helped to make things unusually bad, but one would not have gathered from the sailing directions that quite such dangerous overfalls were to be encountered. The whole affair was over in what seemed to be quite a short time, and there being no more breakers in sight we again set our sail properly and turned our heads to see how our friend, the little sloop astern, was going to manage the passage.

Evidently alarmed at the breakers, and unwilling to face them, her skipper hauled his wind and stood in towards the 'Dries' to the northward, the tide taking him bodily to leeward. The 'Dries' is a very nasty shoal a mile from the shore, with many rocky heads and gravel patches, which at this time of tide would hardly be covered. It was not long before we saw the little yacht strike the ground, and then down came her mainsail. She lay on her broadside, rolling horribly, with her headsail still set and driving her up the shoal.

Nothing is more depressing than to see a crew and vessel left helpless to their fate, and although the strong lee-going tide and the westerly wind were quite against our power to assist them, it seemed dreadful to sail away without making some attempt to help. At this moment we saw a fine sturdy cutter yacht of some five and twenty tons turning to windward in the slack of the Boulder Bank, and being ourselves somewhat to windward of her we reached off and hailed her skipper, telling him of the accident, which he must have observed, as one of the hands was standing on the weather sheer pole with binoculars to his eyes.

I asked him to stand in as near as he could and send his boat in, to which request he replied that he couldn't get near them with his yacht. He added that the crew of the stranded sloop had left in their own small boat, he thought, and that in all likelihood assistance would be sent from the shore. He then went about and stretched away to the S.W., evidently intending to use one of the three or four swatchways that intersect the Boulder Bank, but which are unmarked by buoys and only known to the native.

We lingered about, vainly trying to turn over the tide to a position from which we could see better what was going on, but as we made good to windward less than nothing at all, and were by now abreast of the Mixon Beacon, we reluctantly bore up and went on our way. After a time, looking astern through our glass, we saw what appeared to be the little sloop standing off the land to the south, still under single headsail only, bound for goodness knows where.

As we munched our biscuits and cheese we agreed that the events of the morning had been sufficiently exciting for one day, and decided that we would go to Littlehampton instead of to Shoreham, as we had at first intended.

But before we reached port we were to have one more unusual experience. Half-a-mile off Littlehampton pier end we were struck by a curious revolving sort of squall, into which the boat was luffed sharply. She luffed right round a complete circle, her lee deck well under, and then for a few moments was left almost becalmed.

Something odd and uncanny was evidently abroad today, so we took extra care when we sailed up the narrow entrance of the harbour to avoid the effect of the strong cross tide which runs athwart the piers. We were successful in getting comfortably up to a berth on the east side of the harbour, and as we were making fast a man on the wharf above said: "Did yer fall in with the whirlwind?"

On being told of the squall outside, he remarked: "'Ad it werry 'ard 'ere. It blowed the end of that there barn in." We looked towards the place he pointed to, and sure enough, just across the harbour, there stood a sort of warehouse with one end completely gone, and all its interior visible.

We felt very glad that we hadn't had it quite so "'ard" as that, for had it struck us with the same force, our ability to withstand it seemed doubtful. We might have been blown clean out of the water, and like that holy man of old, carried up to Heaven in that same whirlwind.

As the stove, since its attempt to burn the boat out, had been very troublesome, we sought out a tinker who we thought might perhaps be able to put it into a better frame of mind and spirit. But although when, after much difficulty found at home, he worked his will on it to the extent of three-and-sixpence, its moral betterment was very slight, though its outward appearance was much improved. It went no better, and my deckie, who regarded it with an amount of suspicion bordering on hatred, always alluded to it as 'that devil'.

Littlehampton we voted was rather dull. I daresay it is much improved nowadays. The only object of real interest in the port was the Pollywog, which lay just below us and had somehow found her way here from Milford Haven. She was beginning to show her ways, too.

"Wunnerful fast boat she is," we were told. "Beats all the yachts along this 'ere coast." Very likely she did, but somehow we didn't feel inclined to swop.

We half expected to see the little sloop, whose adventures we had watched in the Looe, come into harbour before dark; but nothing like her appeared, nor could we ascertain anything about her. Her fate remains a mystery to this day.

We turned into bed that night with some assurance from the look of the sky, that we should be able to resume our passage up Channel next day — which would be Sunday, a day I have invariably found an excellent one for making a passage.

Very early next morning we were out and about, and found a calm, and the ebb tide so far spent as to make it urgent to clear out as soon as possible. We found plenty of water over the bar, however, and we put her head eastward, crawling along over the ebb by the aid of a light air of wind from the N., which remained faint and fickle until we had almost reached abreast of Brighton after the flood had bent. Here it gradually backed and slowly strengthened into a fine hearty breeze from the S.W., which drove our little ship along merrily. The fair wind and tide soon brought us up to Beachy Head, whence we laid course for Dungeness and soon began to leave the land.

Never have the crew of CHERUB had a more glorious sail than this grand run up Channel. Clear and deep blue was the sky overhead, with warm tinted companies of marching clouds steadily travelling eastward. The sea, dark toned with Homer's purple, broke here and there into small crisp curls of foam. When the west going tide strengthened, a steady growing heave made itself felt, and the boat climbed the long slopes of the waves and clove through the tops with a rush. She seemed a brown-winged seabird, so easily did she run, with hardly a spray on deck, and her wake as clean as a knife-cut. Half-way across the bay the wind freshened still more, and she began to over-run the seas, almost half her length forward seemed clear of the water when she lifted above the curling crests. So it was 'snug down' to two reefs whilst there was time, yet still she ran fast and dry. The land now looked far off and we passed many craft, like ourselves under shortened canvas, turning to windward. We were in a world of our own — a world of deep blue, and wine-tinted purple, flecked with flashing whites of foam and ruby red sails, through which poured the vigour of the glorious wind, bringing strength and laden with life. How such a day stamps itself on the mind! Years have passed, yet this day still lives in my memory with as clear a vision as if it were yesterday.

Towards evening we drew close to Dungeness, running close in to the shore, where there was less sea. Just outside us, but still close in, there passed a naval cruiser, swiftly tearing through the sea on her way eastward. She was making extremely wet weather of it, spray flying aft in a continuous stream. The officer on duty peered at us through his glass, and her oilskin-clad crew gazed with grins — I daresay envying us our drier ship, yet in all likelihood wondering why men went to sea for pleasure in a craft no bigger than a jolly boat.

We luffed round the Ness into smoother water, and spoke a solitary barge brought up under its shelter. Bargee 'allowed' it wasn't far off low water and advised Folkestone for us for the night. We had half thought of making Dover, but my deckie was tired and I was getting tired too, and Dover was voted too far off. So we ran on again, seeming to go slower in the gathering gloom, and it was after dark when we luffed round the end of Folkestone Pier and made fast to a buoy to wait for water to go inside, and meanwhile to prepare our evening meal.

The stove was amiable and the oxtail soup grateful, though no amount of fenders or highly decorative language from the deckie kept CHERUB from thumping against the buoy in the uneasy ground swell. About 10 p.m. we groped our way inside in dense darkness, made fast to a species of barge, and gladly lay down to rest after a really wonderful run of 75 miles in 15 hours. Not so bad for a boat under 18 ft waterline and with 10 hours foul tide against her.

I had been inside Folkestone harbour before, but only as a steamboat passenger, so the place was quite unknown to me. Towards morning, about dawn, the wind freshened very much, and I was awakened by the violent trembling of the boat in the strong gusts. Looking out I was horrified to find that we were on a big wooden grid-iron, the boat being delicately poised on one of the timbers where her legs fortunately rested. The fore and aft parts of the boat were quite unsupported.

On the gridiron Folkestone

There was nothing at all that could be done — movement was out of the question — and I could only gently wake the sleeping deckie and warn him that if he snored at all violently the boat would fall off her perch and be smashed up.

I spent the time until 9 o'clock in a futile endeavour to sleep, the deckie still slumbering on peacefully. When the tide flowed around her again we set about getting breakfast, then shifted our berth, but not before offering up praise and thanks to the particular marine Deity that had watched over us whilst we slumbered, and had seen to it that our legs had rested on the exact and proper spot. If they had failed to do this, what would have happened was too horrible to contemplate!

That day it blew a gale, and with the wind from that quarter (S.W.) we found Folkestone Harbour a most uncomfortable place. There was a heavy range all over the part in which we were moored, and before grounding the boat ran up and down the hard shingle of the bottom in a most alarming manner. We feared that small stones would work in between the centreplate and the keel and so jam fast.

Steamers lying against the piers ground their fenders to pieces with horrid squeaks and groans, and every craft in the place seemed to have shore ropes out in all possible directions and to every available bollard. In a gale of wind S.W. Folkestone is not an ideal harbour for small craft, and we had no peace until the tide had ebbed a long way.

But we made the best of it — thoroughly cleaned up below, wrote our letters, and wandered through the town. By nightfall the wind had lessened considerably, and the sky had cleared here and there in deep blue patches spangled with stars, giving promise of a fine day's passage on the morrow if the still vexed sea had been sufficiently run down by the strong tides of this part of the Channel.

We left Folkestone as soon as our tide permitted next morning, and when the gentle south-westerly breeze took us clear of the harbour we found a very nasty sea still running, which gave us a rare shaking up all the way to the South Foreland. When we had passed this headland and were up towards the Downs, we found smoother water and rippled along gaily.

Many small coasting vessels were still riding there after the gale, and we had an opportunity of observing the behaviour of the gally-punts which were plying the Downs. CHERUB, although possessed of excellent reaching powers, could not hold her own with these long craft, in which the extraordinary lifting and driving power of the dipping lug was made clearly manifest. They held a remarkably good wind when close hauled too, though on this point our centre-plate put us more on an equality with them. Their crews viewed our little craft with interest, and we held some conversation with the hardy race of men who manned these fine boats.

What a pity it is that changing conditions and the 'march of progress' seem to combine to deprive this fine race of boatmen of their occupation. Hard as this occupation undoubtedly is, it is a school that produces men of a very splendid type, who have performed deeds in these small open boats unsurpassed in the annuls of endurance and bravery. Probably the day is not far off when the motor will be utilised to do what sails and oars and human strength and determination alone have hitherto accomplished.

It is never safe to prophesy, but if civilisation is worth a brass farthing, the new conditions ought to produce new types equally fit for their work. At least that is what one hopes: — though the hopes are tempered by inward and secret misgivings, perhaps only natural to a somewhat old-fashioned person like the present writer, who remembers the vanished fleet of sailing coasters which covered the North Sea, and flocked into the Thames and Medway when he was a boy, and the wonderful feats of seamanship performed by their crews.

We sailed on with a fair wind and tide, past Ramsgate and up through the thronged fairway until we hauled our wind and squeezed past the Longnose buoy, and, the wind heading us, stretched right off towards the Tongue before tacking into Margate, where sail was lowered and the deckie was put on shore to buy bread and beef, and to post the letters he had written during his smooth passage through the Downs.

The journey on shore took longer than anticipated, and it was rather late on the flood when we left Margate. Unless the wind backed there seemed little chance of making the Swale before the ebb met us. So we 'gave her' everything we could set, and did our best to make a good long leg along the land. The evening was fine and promised a fine night, so it would be no hardship even if we had to bring up off shore for a tide. It would not be the first time by many that nightfall had found us far from port, and was not the Thames our native place?

So we went on towards the sunset, carrying our flood up to Herne Bay. Then the wind veered still more and we had to stretch off a good way on the slack high water, and soon we were slowly but surely made aware that our tide was done.

Now, to attempt to turn to windward in a small craft, over a lee going tide, is very much like making a second marriage — it is a triumph of hope over experience. This we knew perfectly well, but still kept 'at it,' on the chance that night would bring a breeze off the land. The chance was turned into a certainty for a brief space, and we had worked up somewhere near the Whitstable Street buoy when darkness and the wind fell together. We could not quite discover the exact position of the buoy, but we had a shrewd idea of its whereabouts and we could see the Girdler light twinkling away in the North.

So, as there wasn't the remotest chance of getting any further we brought up in four and a half fathoms, and went below to make ourselves as happy as circumstances and a hot supper would permit; the skipper volunteering to keep the first watch, though there was hardly any necessity for watching, our anchorage being out of the track of any vessels who would ignore our riding light. So I sat below whilst my deckie slumbered and the little boat rolled gently on the tidal swell — thinking of the summer days and winter nights spent on these Kentish flats in company with the old fisherman who, in my boyhood, owned the bawley Eliza, and who tried to teach me some fraction of all the lore of the river which he possessed.

Many were the tales he told me of old smuggling feats: — of the mad fisherman who spent weeks and months in trawling for the golden kettle he believed to be lying on the sea floor near the Spaniard sand: — of how this 'old Nelson' swam two miles with his little son on his back when his bawley had been sunk by a steamer, and was picked up alive by a bargeman, his dead child still clinging to him; but his mind clouded and darkened for ever. And of the great gains he once made in a hatch-boat about the year '54, by gathering the carcases of many dead bullocks, washed overboard from a cattle steamer from Holstein, which was wrecked on the Shivering Sand. "Forty six bullocks we got — a pound a bullock, in two tides."

And I lived over again that wild December night when we were caught in a heavy south-west gale riding to our 'stowboat' net in the Barrow Deeps — and sailed again the long struggle to windward under a close-reefed mainsail, the bawley deep laden with sprats. All these old vanished days, came back to me, and perhaps I dozed a little, for suddenly my hazy mind was roused by a feeling of chilly surprise that the dawn had come so soon, and brought with it a clipping westerly breeze.

So to make amends for my failure of duty I quickly set the lug and got the anchor without waking my sleeping shipmate, and sailed the boat over to Shellness, where we rode out the rest of the ebb and part of the next flood, close in under the lea of the point.

After breakfast we cleaned up the ship, and suffered a great loss. Our bedding, being out to air in the strong breeze and not being properly secured, the wind whisked overboard and lost forever my favourite down pillow, bought at Dordrecht. This was a great grief to me, for, although I can sleep with my body on a bare board, I must have a soft pillow for my head — a weakness that in earlier days earned me many a bit of chaff from my fisherman friend and mentor, the master of the bawley Eliza of blessed memory.

When we had thoroughly put all in order below (and shed a tear over the departed pillow), we set a double-reefed sail and began to turn our way through the Swale. With a fair tide, smooth water, and a slashing breeze we were not long in getting half-way through, to Sittingbourne Creek, by high water; and then having the ebb with us we worked our way down to the Railway Bridge above Queenborough, lowered our mast a little to get through, and brought up between the steamboat pier and the causeway on the North side of the river.

For those who like inland tidal waterways, giving shelter anywhere, the Swale offers good cruising ground. There is no depth in the middle portion at low water, and there are mud flats and mussel beds and shoaly places to beware of. A barge yacht or a light draught boat with a centreplate is the best craft for work of this sort, as the plate is a good pilot, and in many parts short boards are necessary when turning to windward. But it is a quiet cruising ground — at least, it was at the time of which I write — with nothing more harmful than a few barges and bawleys, and, near Whitstable, the oyster fleet.

Ashore there are few indications of life or activity such as are seen on the Thames. Here and there a mysterious looking factory settles itself on the bank and builds a wharf, alongside of which an odd barge or two or a small coaster may be seen reclining in somnolent idleness. Beyond the mud flats are the marsh and the sky, sombre tinted and full of the calls of birds, which emphasise the solitude and perfect its peace.

Not many, probably, would call this a good cruising ground, but to those who feel, as do the crew of the CHERUB, that they get their best holiday away from the sight and sound of man, his ways, works, and enjoyments, it is a desirable little space of water.

That evening as we lay at Queensborough we visited a neighbouring bawley man, who, being engaged in smelt fishing, used his big boat as a home and worked his nets in a 'doble' — a sharp sterned rowing and sailing boat like CHERUB, fitted with a fish well.

Bawleys Boiling Shrimps

I suppose my early training as a supernumerary bawley boy gained us our welcome, and we spent a jolly time comparing notes of the river and its fisheries with the owner. He and his mate made a comfortable living, I should think; but they complained gently of Dutch competition in the smelt business.

The bawley was quite a big boat, about 36 ft by 12 ft. Her owner assured me that she only drew a trifle over 3 feet of water, yet, probably owing to her flat floor and hard bilge, she was quite good enough to windward for all his purposes. He said she cost complete about £140, which seemed an incredibly small price, as she was a fine roomy ship, with a big forecastle and vast spaces below. As she had no fish well I suppose she was specially built for the particular class of work in which she was engaged. I could not help thinking what a fine sketching boat she would have made for work about the Thames.

Very early next morning we were awakened by a series of thumps, followed by vigorous slappings. We had received a gift of flat-fish from the bawley man, which was tossed into our cockpit on his way home from his labours. The freemasonry of the river made these a generous present, which was greatly appreciated a few hours later.

After breakfast, in a hard south-westerly breeze, again under double-reefed lug, we thrashed our way up the Medway, having fine races with the barges, some of which we passed, but only some, for the modern barge is a fast craft in a breeze when not overladen. Two racing looking boats, rather smaller than CHERUB, essayed to turn up to Chatham as well, but were soon over-powered and ran back.

Arrived at Chatham, somewhat damp, but quite pleased with ourselves, we went on shore for letters and provisions. The letters brought bad news, which took my deckie home post haste, and I was left alone for some days, which I spent in sketching above and below bridge. The Medway offers many subjects for the brush. The curious looking cement works which array themselves in smoke and haze by day, and pale mysterious flames by night: the innumerable barges and boats of all kinds; and the old town of Rochester are full of artistic motives; Upnor, Chatham Reach, and Gillingham — all are interesting; so I was not idle.

At night Chatham High Street was full of incident. The bustling crowds of humble people who do so much of the rough work of this world are always worth observing. With all their outer roughness of manner, their great good humour and cheerfulness never fail to teach me the lessons of the 'liveableness of life,' as R.L.S. so finely puts it. There was no end of sketching to be done everywhere. For this work the CHERUB was most happily fashioned. With three minutes exertion one could be underway, dodging about amongst the barges, taking up any position necessary. She was much admired by many 'bargees' who seemed specially flattered when they discovered for what purpose the little brown boat with the brown sails was hovering about their course. Often I would ask the skipper of an anchored barge if I might hang alongside, and the request was always courteously granted. Sometimes 'bargee' would inspect my little ship below, and never failed to ask if I knew Mr Wyllie, who amongst modern artists seems to be almost the only one who can depict accurately the spirit, as well as the outer semblance of the barge.

When I had to admit that I had not the honour of that gentleman's personal acquaintance, they all said the same thing in almost the same words. "Well, that's a pity, he's a *werry nice* gentleman," which says a good deal for Mr Wyllie's popularity on the river at that time.

What few 'doblemen' are left on the Medway nowadays I know not, but quite a dozen of their boats then lay about the neighbourhood of Strood Pier. These men positively adored the CHERUB, she being in their eyes a very fine lady amongst the doble family, and they were forever alongside when I was sketching. When I told them of my various adventures and of our voyage from Scarborough (though few, I think, knew exactly where that place was), they always took it as a sort of tribute to the sea-going powers of dobles generally, and they too, would relate what their own boats had done on various occasions and in various gales of wind. They would finger the small, neat gear, wonder at the size of the battened lug, gently stroke her shining mahogany sides, and murmur to each other — "Ain't she a little beauty?"

They were all capital fellows, never letting me want for fresh fish (smelts included), and were not too proud or too shy to share a meal or a pipe when occasion gave the chance to invite them.

I must say I like bargemen, doblemen, bawleymen, and the river fishermen in general. They are almost always capital fellows, and the bargees and bawleymen are real artists in boat handling. It is a pleasure to see them under way — they always do the right thing at the right time, and come out of 'tight places' marvellously. The better class barge is extraordinarily well kept and cared for, and is handled much more cleverly than are some cruising yachts. But the Thames and Medway are their proper places. It is a piteous sight to see a barge in a North Sea or Channel gale, whether she be light or loaded.

When at last I welcomed back my deckie it was towards the end of September, and about time to think of getting home again. So the day after his return, late in the afternoon and with a very hard breeze of wind behind us, we set off down the river for Queenborough, under a lowering and portentous sunset sky, and with more canvas than we really wanted with our double-reefed lug. The barges were all wearing close brailed mainsails and 'rucked' top-sails.

Below Gillingham the wind piped up so much that the whole surface of the river was covered with spindrift, and we put one more reef in. On setting down the tack the strain proved too much for the eye-bolt, which broke off in the neck and nearly let me go overboard. Fortunately there was another eye-bolt in the deck and that held all right. The battened lug worked well in this mishap: an ordinary standing lug without battens would have played 'Old Harry' with a burst tack-bolt!

There was so much broken water to leeward that instead of going on to Queenboro' we decided to try to work into Stoke Creek, once, I fancy, the inlet that made the Isle of Grain really an island by joining the Thames at Yantlet. The boat turned in all right, the water being smooth, and we had decided to use the 'big' anchor on the chain as there was still a power of wind. Probably the awful wildness of the darkening sky made the skipper somewhat inattentive to mundane things; but the sad fact must be told that he let go without seeing the end of the chain fast, and the whole lot ran overboard—end and all! His thoughts came back to earth in time to save the situation by promptly letting go the 10-lb anchor on the warp; which *mirabile dictu* held us safely all night!

An inquiry into the skipper's conduct was held on the spot. He was found in default, deprived of his grog for the space of two hours, and condemned in costs, which were to go to the coastguard's boys, who promised to 'creep' for the lost property, which was restored safe and sound next morning when we found that the gale had moderated into half a gale, this time from the N.N.E., making quite a respectable sea in the tideway outside, when we got under way for our last day's sail. The boat did very little good to windward under close reefs, so we shook out one, when she performed again with her accustomed success and soon brought us down to Grain Swatchway, through which, with a free wind now, we ran over the strong ebb. We squeezed over to Hole Haven, a weather shore for luncheon; then on the young spring flood made our way up the river.

The little boat seemed to be in a great hurry, and early in the afternoon she was at Greenhithe. We went on to Erith in company with a yawl belonging to a friend, anchored for a little while until the ebb bent, and then turned back to Greenhithe where we brought up and spent the last night on board our good little ship. Perhaps not the *last* night, for I hear that she has now come back to her native country and is living in the South, and some day, perhaps, I may greet her again and once more enjoy the pleasure of a sail in my most beloved boat."

CHAPTER 8

Albert Strange on the
Cruising Yacht's Stern

Albert Strange is also remembered for a form of pointed stern which has become associated with his designs, as well as favouring yawl-rigged small yachts. We have seen the influence of his early experiences on the Thames, particularly with the ex-peter boat DAUNTLESS, with her pointed stern. His membership of the Humber Yawl Club and his connection with the canoe yawl centre-boarders in its formative years, all influenced his later design ideals. However, the craft with which he was concerned and in which we can see the input from both these origins, had the 'conventional' style of pointed stern with a straight or only slightly curved sternpost, perhaps set at a slight rake and having the rudder hung on it. In Chapter 6 we have seen that the style of stern adopted by Albert Strange for many of his designs had been discussed with one of his pupils, L.N. Sanderson. It appears to have been conceived by Strange some years earlier — independently of the similar form in designs by others, including his American friend, W.P. Stephens. This style of stern became one of the hallmarks of Strange's work.

It appears that Strange first used this type of stern in a projected design for a single-handed cruiser put forward in a paper to members of the Royal Yorkshire Yacht Club in 1891 (FIG 42). This boat, a gaff rigged ketch, was 18 ft length overall, 16 ft waterline length, 5 ft 8 in beam and 1 ft 8 hull draught. A centreplate extended the draught to 2 ft 8 in. Displacement was 33 cubic feet (slightly under 1 ton) and a total ballast weight of between 1120-1176 pounds was allowed for, half as a keel and the remainder as internal ballast. The total sail area was 169 sq ft in jib, brailing mainsail and mizzen. The centreplate only increased the draught by about 12 inches and was costly to install. However, it was a typical British-style centreplate in a small cruising boat of that time. Craft with plates of this type will sail to windward satisfactorily in shallow water but are naturally slower in a seaway than those with plates of greater draught. What is interesting, is that the stern appears to be fully formed in the canoe style Strange was to adopt in many later designs. The rudder was necessarily elongated because of the shallow draught and was therefore an inefficient shape. The whole design is very different from that of the transom sterned WREN. Although still amateurish, it shows much more original thought.

However, not all admired this type of stern, and in the course of controversy as to its merits, Albert Strange and his critics revealed something of the design philosophy behind it. This is an interesting insight into the serious way in which he approached yacht design and strove for a technical basis for it, which is unusual in many artists and even some yacht designers.

A letter by H.H. Bristow in the YACHTING MONTHLY for March 1913 initiated the controversy. He referred to comments made by the editor on entries in a

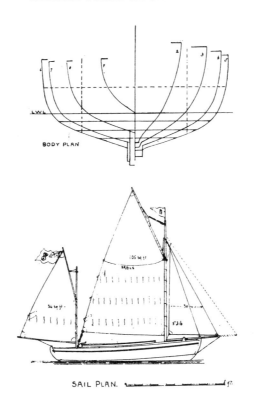

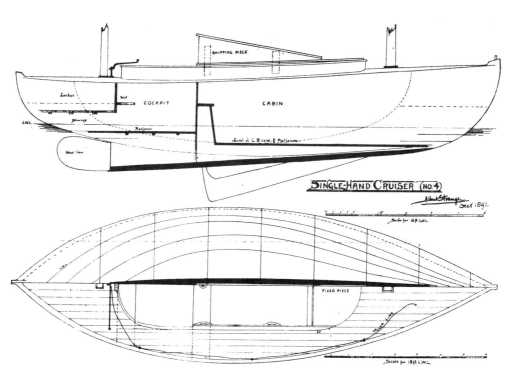

Single hander cruiser design in/a/paper by Albert Strange to R.Y.Y.C. 1891

FIG 42

design competition, December 1912. "I should like to see a discussion based on actual experience of canoe and counter sterns in sailing yachts of small size. My own experience is directly contrary to the statement you make that 'in its favour the counter has some extra deck space but nothing more'. Besides extra power and buoyancy, the counter tends to easier steering in a following sea. This is the conclusion I have come to from sailing a yawl on the lines of MAY (FIGS 43 & 44) but smaller, and another with full counter. The former, besides being tender, has an uncontrollable tendency to sheer, and the latter steers as sweetly in a following sea as in a head sea. The lines are similar, although the canoe-stern yawl is much smaller than the counter-stern boat. The experience of other yachtsmen with similar boats would be interesting reading."

Dr Harrison Butler responded in the next issue, ". . . the question of sterns is one eminently open to argument. From the designer's point of view there can be no doubt that canoe sections in the stern balance a slightly spoon bow better than a counter stern with flat sections. It is easier to obtain a form in which the centre of the wedges of emersion and immersion approximate to each other. In other words, a counter with flat sections and an ordinary transom postulate a hull which has a tendency to bore by the head when inclined, and which, as a necessary corollary, will gripe in strong breezes, although the relationships between the centres of effort and lateral resistance may be theoretically correct. From this point of view the double-ended mule bat (a Yorkshire coble with whale-boat stern — J.L.) is even better; with such a stern it may be possible to get an exact balance without resorting to an immoderate spoon bow. The very worst combination is a straight stem with forward sections without flare, associated with a broad transom and heavy quarters. Such boats are exemplified by the Plymouth hookers, and by the (Falmouth) quay punts in a lesser

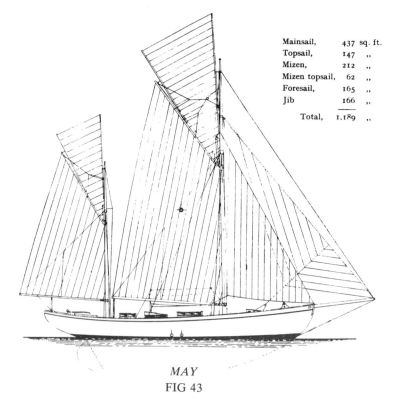

Mainsail,	437	sq. ft.
Topsail,	147	,,
Mizen,	212	,,
Mizen topsail,	62	,,
Foresail,	165	,,
Jib	166	,,
Total,	1,189	,,

MAY

FIG 43

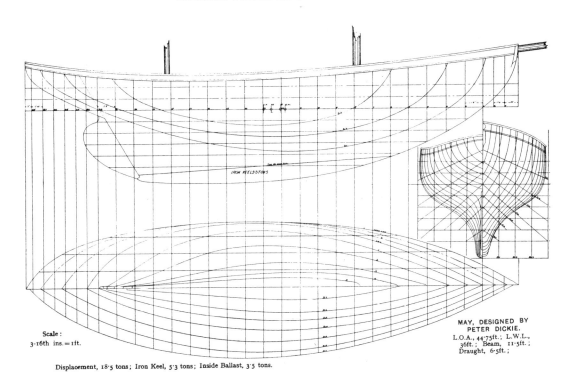

Scale :
3-16th ins. = 1ft.

MAY, DESIGNED BY
PETER DICKIE.
L.O.A., 44·75ft.; L.W.L.,
36ft.; Beam, 11·5ft.;
Draught, 6·5ft.;

Displacement, 18·5 tons; Iron Keel, 5·3 tons; Inside Ballast, 3·5 tons.

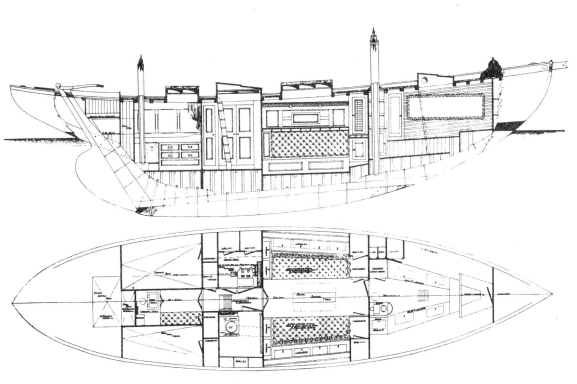

ACCOMMODATION PLAN OF MAY.   Scale : 3-16ths in. = 1ft.

FIG 44

degree, for the latter have finer quarters. The mule stern and the canoe stern have two great disadvantages in yachts as opposed to canoe yawls; they are exceedingly ugly, and they contract the deck space aft, and make a ketch's mizzen as difficult to reef as a cutter's mainsail, and also make it difficult to get a good lead for the mizzen sheet unless a bumkin be fitted, which is still more inartistic. All the good qualities of the canoe-stern can be obtained if the counter be designed, not with flat sections, but with vee sections. Such a counter will be seen on the single-handed cruiser which I designed for Mr Worth, which appears in YACHT CRUISING. This type of stern, if kept short and well out of the water, is far better looking than the canoe-stern, is probably cheaper to build and gives excellent deck room to handle the sheets. For a canoe yawl of the Humber type, with shallow draught and good beam, the 'Strange' stern is the best and most natural termination, and, I think, the most artistic. On a big yacht it still looks, to say the least, peculiar. The transom and sharp mule stern have one important advantage which is always overlooked in the discussion on sterns. A short overall length means in practice light spars and a small sail area. Sail area is largely apportioned by eye and increases on the square of the base. A few feet saved in overall length means a large diminution of sail area. A main boom which looks handy on a countered yacht, would look very much the reverse on a plumb stemmed transomed boat. One hears that these boats are so easy in a seaway, and the reason is obvious. They have a small sail plan and light spars, and yet the owner is satisfied because they look well rigged. Take a boat 20 ft overall, with no overhangs. 300 sq ft will cover her well — in fact it may look a little too much. Add a snout and a counter to the same boat, making her 26 ft overall and then put 300 sq ft over it. The effect would be ridiculous! 400 would be necessary.''

Here was an amateur designer's view, ignoring the strict requirement of sail area needed to propel efficiently the yacht of known below water form, resistance and displacement (assumed to be the 300 sq ft quoted), in favour of following fashion in appearance, which would add a further one third to the necessary area, resulting in a 400 sq ft sail area. This might overpower her more quickly in strong winds, resulting in earlier reefing and possible danger in bad weather with a small crew.

A contemporary advocate of the canoe stern was C.W. Adderton, owner of the attractive Strange designed ketch QUEST II, which had a fine example. He noted, ". . . such of us who have adopted the canoe stern would not return to the counter.'' And "The loss of deck space, so frequently bemoaned, is so small that in a boat up to 25 tons it is not worth consideration. I suppose a racing boat designed to lie far over in smooth water does make some use of her long counter, or it would not be there; but who would wish to own a cruiser that requires her lee rail under before she gets up her speed?

"When I am asked why I went in for the canoe stern when I built (sic) QUEST II, I gave three reasons — i) it is stronger in construction, the planking finishes in a proper rebate, like the stem, and it offers no flimsy edges and corners . . . ii) it helps in the making of a better sea boat, lifts one high and buoyant over a following sea, shows no inclination to poop when overtaken by a breaking crest, and does not slap and pound into every swell when one comes to anchor in bay or roadstead. And iii) . . . it is more beautiful.

"To produce an entirely satisfactory stern the overhang should not be too short but somewhere about 1/6 of the waterline length. The outline should leave the WL in a perfectly straight line and continue so for quite 1/3 of the length, then gradually grow into an ever steepening curve to a just perceptible amount of perpendicular at the finish.''

Albert Strange's response to these various views on the canoe stern was comprehensive.

"Whatever may be the faults of the canoe-stern I do not think those mentioned by Mr Bristow are amongst them. The causes of yawing and uneasy steering proceed from underwater defects of design, and can by no possibility spring from above-water form of hull, though, of course, position of mast may help. Short, round boats have a tendency to wriggle about whatever may be their form of stern; rockered keels, short keels and very deep bilges produce uneasy steering on a reach or running. The only cure for some of these evils is to lengthen the boat — a remedy worse than the disease.

"The curve mentioned by Mr Adderton is either a parabola or the hyperbola. Either has a beautiful outline, the aesthetic charm of which was discovered ages ago by the Greeks. In the finest periods of Grecian architecture the outlines of all mouldings were parabolic, hyperbolic or some other form of conic section. . . . Parabolic curves have played and do still play an important part in yacht design. Nystrom invented a complete system of ship design based on the principles underlying the geometric construction of the parabola; but like all rigid systems which exclude art, it never became popular, nor do I remember that any successful yacht was ever built under its laws." (This reference to Nystrom is most interesting since his work would be known to few professional yacht designers, yet Strange, an amateur, was familiar with it and had determined its limitations for his purposes. His reading of naval architecture would appear to have been remarkably wide.)

"Many of Dr Harrison Butler's remarks are perfectly true — it is incontestable that the very flat sectioned counter and no forward overhang make a very boring boat. It is also perfectly true that one of the reasons for the transom stern boats' good behaviour is the moderate sail area generally compelled by limited overall length. But, having owned a 'mule-sterned' boat (the FULMAR — J.L.) in the shape of a Loch Fyne type of cutter, I have very live memories of the way in which she took weather helm when pressed. After a good deal of thought I have come to the conclusion that the much belauded Loch Fyne type is, for a yacht, the very worst that can be chosen. If one cannot have a counter or a canoe stern there is nothing better than a transom stern, if it is a well designed one. I have seen the little Clyde 17-19's go through weather and sea that were astounding. They would have gone better still with canoe-sterns, I believe, but don't tell me that the transom stern is a bad stern, because I have seen them hard-pressed and sailed in them in very bad weather and they have played no tricks.

"I have ventured to include a few sketches showing purely parabolic profiles of canoe sterns. (Figs. 'A', 'B', and 'C'.)

'A' is the sort that grows naturally out of a flat, hollow midsection, and on this point I might say that as the relative depth of bilge in a 60 ft WL boat is less than that of a 30 ft WL boat, it is really easier to design a handsome long canoe stern for a big yacht, than for a medium sized one of the cruising type with full mid-section. 'B' is the general kind of profile obtainable on a beamy cruiser with moderately full mid-section, while 'C' is the sort of curve available with high freeboard, big mid-section, great beam, and very short allowance of overhang aft. On this same section I have contrasted the kind of counter favoured by Dr Harrison Butler, with a canoe stern. There will never be total agreement as to what constitutes beauty, and few short overhangs can be very beautiful; there must be a certain minimum length to get a good curve. But, seeing the two together under the same conditions, I wonder how many men would prefer the steep angle of the counter to the more gracious round of the parabolic curve?''

Albert Strange's views were soon challenged. Frank Gilliland, an experienced cruising yachtsman, wrote in reply, "So far as I am aware Mr Strange is the first designer to condemn the Loch Fyne type for a yacht, and if its supporters in the past have been mistaken, they, at least, can claim to have erred in good company. An article in one of the recent editions of 'Dixon Kemp' (written, I believe, by Mr Alfred Mylne) spoke in terms of approbation of them, as did Mr Warington Smyth in MAST AND SAIL, and finally you, Sir, [to Herbert Reiach, then Editor of YACHTING MONTHLY] commended the type when you awarded the prize, in one of your early designing competitions, to THETA. It would thus appear that fairly strong arguments should be forthcoming to alter these conclusions. So far as I can judge from a letter received lately, Mr Strange bases his deductions largely on his experiences in a Loch Fyne type boat called FULMAR. Seeing, however that Mr Strange admits she was somewhat badly designed, I do not think he should condemn the type because of the faults of one boat, although I feel sure he has seen many of them in Loch Fyne. After all, if the sharp stern of the Loch Fyne type is wrong, what a number of other sharp sterned craft must share the same fate! MAST AND SAIL affords many examples including the famous Norwegian life-boats, and judging by the sketches their quarters are pretty full.

"I may, however, be told that a yacht is different from a Penzance lugger or Norwegian pilot boat, and there will always be people who dislike yachts built on fishing boat lines, in spite of their good points. Personally I have always admitted that the round quarters sometimes found in Loch Fyne type yachts are a distinct drawback. I have noticed it frequently in my own boat, but this surely is due to faulty

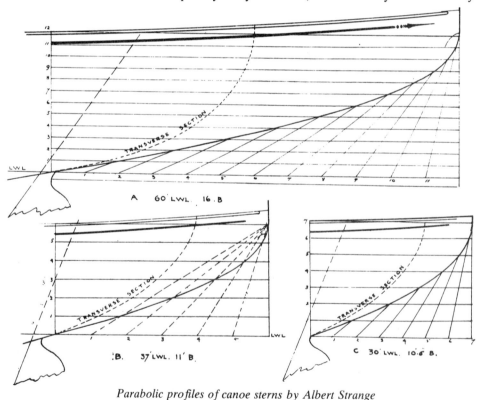

Parabolic profiles of canoe sterns by Albert Strange

FIG 45

design, and from an attempt to provide exceptional room for the tonnage, an effort which has been successful, though at the loss of some power when going fast. The good points of the boat, handiness generally, seaworthiness and accommodation, seem to me to more than compensate for this one defect, which is common to many short, beamy craft, besides Loch Fyne boats. While making this defence I cannot deny the attractions of a neat canoe stern, if for no other reason than to secure additional deck room and remove the bare look of a pointed stern. On the other hand, Dr Harrison Butler's point that a short overall length practically means light spars and a small sail area, deserves careful consideration. The question of the attributes of an ideal cruiser are nearly insoluble; men's tastes differ so much."

This was wise comment.

Harrison Butler was quickly up in arms. "I really must protest against the abominably ugly counter that Mr Strange says I favour. Such a counter would be about the most unsightly ending a boat could have, even more so than the canoe stern. My idea of a short counter with all the advantages of the canoe stern is embodied in the design. This is naturally a little longer than a canoe stern would be, but it is not the unsightly monstrosity that Mr Strange has fathered upon me in his letter."

Albert finally responded to his critics:—

"I fully expected to find my conclusions as to the relative values of Loch Fyne, transom and canoe or counter stern dissented from by those who, like Mr Frank Gilliland, possess excellent and able vessels of the Loch Fyne type. It is not a question of condemnation (I haven't the heart to condemn any kind or sort of boat); but it is a question of relative efficiency, and, so far as power is concerned, everything that conduces to power in a cruising yacht is of value. The Loch Fyne is the least powerful stern of the three, and owing to the sharp upward turn of the buttock lines, is potentially less speedy, as giving a relatively shorter body on the same LWL as a transom stern.

"Judging from early types of herring boats found on the western coast of Scotland (which were square sterned boats of great power and displacement) the present type was not produced to give greater efficiency under canvas, but the round stern, and the comparatively light displacement, were adopted so that the boats could be propelled by oars more easily. It was the change from drift net fishing to 'trawling' or 'ringing' (ring netting) that was the root of the matter. Doubtless in 'pre motor' days it was a great convenience, enabling the boats to work in pairs, and to get into their market under oars in the usual calm weather of the western Scottish lochs during the herring season. It cannot be denied that for their purpose the boats are efficient; but their purpose is not the yachtsman's purpose. In almost every case the adoption of 'local types' of fishing boats has been caused by quite other things than absolute efficiency as a sailing craft. Even safety is sacrificed, as in the coble, which is one of the most unsafe types under canvas, and which is, notwithstanding this fact, sometimes senselessly copied for cruising purposes.

"FULMAR was a fair average sort of Loch Fyne type yacht, but she no more resembles the genuine fishing boat type than does MAY. (Not the MAY referred to earlier in this chapter but a Loch Fyne type yacht, designed by Alex Robertson of Sandbank — J.L.) She was deeper and heavier, and as she was not required to get along under 'oar power' was quite rightly so. But the short full run, due to the pointed stern, spoiled her. That was the fault in the design of the hull; whilst the cabin plan was popular, but futile — a big saloon with no headroom, a tiny forecastle and a steering well of about 6 ft (sic) area, only big enough for one person, though two were necessary to handle sheets and steer. Had she had a transom stern her run would have been longer and her after-body easier on the same midship section — with an actual gain of power when heeled. She was as safe and as seaworthy a boat as one could wish to have, but the wasteful after-end always annoyed me. Fishermen are intelligent conservatives, and I often discuss with them the reasons for the types they use. The most frequently offered excuse for the sharp stern is the necessity of close packing the boats in small harbours, and the real fact that the sharp stern receives less damage than a square stern or a counter when late-entering vessels endeavour to squeeze a way into a rank of boats already moored. But the canoe stern also has this advantage as well as others connected with seaworthiness and speed. And some of the larger east coast Zulu types have so elongated their pointed sterns that they are practically canoe sterns with the rudder hung underneath. In nearly all ports where there is ample room and a good depth of water, the square stern will be found generally to be used by fishermen viz: Falmouth, Plymouth, Poole, Southampton and the Thames. Fashion may play some part in the matter, but not as much as necessity of work or nature of port. Therefore I think that my contention is fairly proved that if you cannot afford overhang and don't want to specialise in fishing, the transom stern is better than the pointed stern. If Dr Harrison Butler is so shocked at the short counter of which I gave a sketch when illustrating the difference between it and the canoe stern, I wonder how he can survive the sight of them in reality. For they are far from uncommon, especially on the south coast. But he cheerfully admits that they are ugly — 'worse than a canoe stern' — when they are so short, so a point has been gained. I see no cause why the counter with which his letter is illustrated is 'naturally' a little longer than a canoe stern would be. There is no reason to make a canoe stern shorter than a counter. But when it *has* to be made short, by reason of economy or preference of owner — then it is really a much better and more efficient ending aft than any counter can possibly be. But the lifting power of the stern he shows is greatly less than that of a canoe stern of the same length and therefore '*all* the advantages of a canoe stern' are not in it, though, as a counter, it is meritorious enough.''

These exchanges seem to set out thoroughly Albert Strange's views on the relative merits of stern shapes for small cruising yachts, differences which are sometimes still debated almost eighty years later. The canoe stern remained his favourite, and it is interesting that his friend, Dr Harrison Butler, in designing the yacht SINAH in the 1930s, chose to incorporate the overhanging canoe stern as being conducive to good hull balance under sail and continued to embody it in several subsequent designs for that reason.

CHAPTER 9

A Sketching Cruise on the Irish Coast

Albert Strange's love of art, which was his life's work, seems to have equalled his fondness for small boats. For holidays he sought to mix the two. In Victorian and Edwardian times and sometimes since, some artists have made 'sketching cruises', just as others have made 'sketching tours' ashore, often with one companion, sometimes more.

The cruise described here by Strange was made in 1906 in the 13 ton yawl QUEST, built at Port St Mary, Isle of Man, in 1903 to a design by a Mr Hamilton. She was owned by C.W. Adderton who lived near Derby, was a former pupil of Strange at the art school and was fond of cruising in the Irish Sea and around the Western Isles of Scotland. The two men seem to have been congenial companions and were competent seamen under sail. They were aided on this cruise by the yacht's professional hand, Collister, who, in the manner of his calling, would do most of the maintenance and cleaning on deck and below, most of the cooking, and stand his watch as required. So, with a good sailor to help, the friends could make the most of their holiday. As Adderton later had the 44ft ketch QUEST II built for him by Dickie of Tarbert, to designs by Albert Strange and launched her in 1907, it seems likely that this cruise was also an opportunity for the two to discuss the design for a new yacht.

This account is interesting in many ways. The whole of Ireland was then still part of the United Kingdom but yachts were unusual on some parts of the coast, as Strange remarks. There were then few detailed pilotage directions for small craft in those waters and in the manner of amateur yachtsmen of the time, Strange and the owner drew several charts for the guidance of others who might visit the anchorages they found so attractive.

There is a freshness in Albert Strange's account of this cruise which remains undiminished after more than eighty years. It reminds us that besides the shallower, tide ridden surroundings in which much of his sailing was done, he also enjoyed the deep waters and different conditions of the Irish Sea and the Scottish West Coast.

"To be an artist is, in most people's opinion, to be a dawdler; and if dawdling means the absence of haste, hurry, or bustle, and the presence of a leisurely, contemplative mind — tasting the delights where the non-artistic man finds nothing delightful, gleaning enjoyment from sights and sounds which bring no pleasure to others — then most people are right, and the artist is without doubt, a dawdler. When two artists are joined together in the contemplative life then I suppose the dawdling is doubly intensified; and as there were two of us on this particular cruise, the seeker after tales of wild delights and adventures in gales and storms, of nerve-wracking record-breaking, and of long miles hurriedly ploughed through stormy seas is

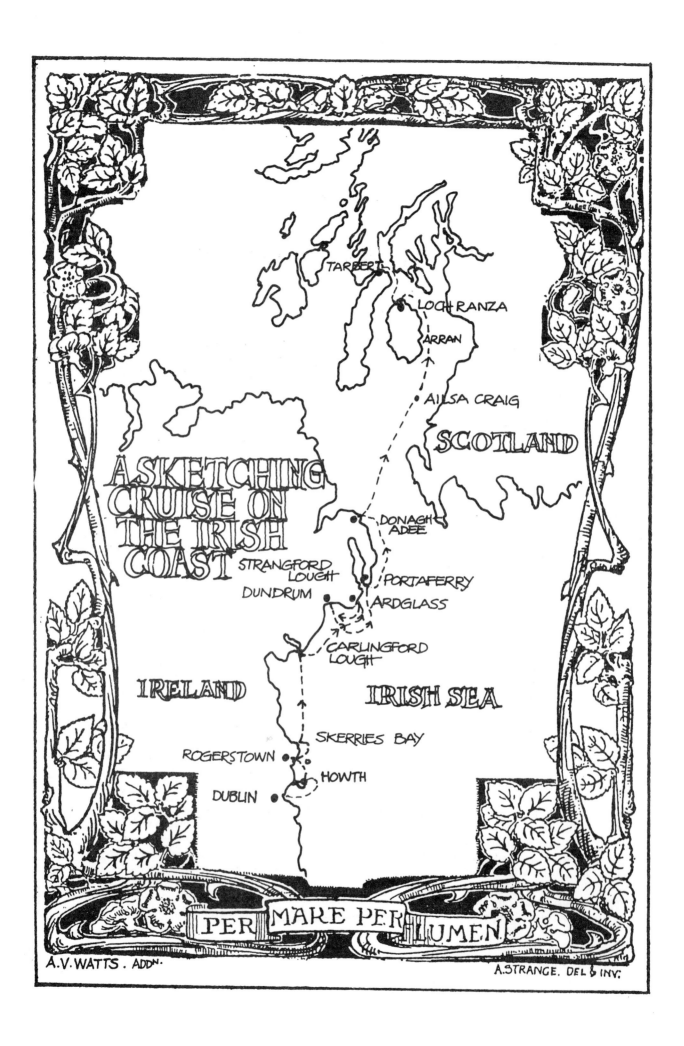

A SKETCHING
CRUISE ON
THE IRISH
COAST

SCOTLAND

TARBERT

LOCH RANZA

ARRAN

AILSA CRAIG

DONAGH ADEE

STRANGFORD LOUGH

PORTAFERRY

DUNDRUM

ARDGLASS

CARLINGFORD LOUGH

IRELAND

IRISH SEA

SKERRIES BAY

ROGERSTOWN

HOWTH

DUBLIN

PER MARE PER LUMEN

A.V. WATTS. ADDN.

A. STRANGE. DEL & INV.

respectfully warned off the perusal of this very plain tale, which contains nothing of the kind, and will not bring a throb of excitement to the breast of even the most inexperienced seafarer.

But it may perhaps reveal some new ground to our friends of the Emerald Isle and of the land of the thistle, because in one or two of the trade-forgotten ports we visited the advent of a yacht was in the nature of a new and startling event to the inhabitants. We were occasionally treated with as much kindness, respect and suspicion as if we had sailed from Mars in an air-ship, and it may be that the astounding eagerness of the men on the 'white yacht' to obtain and devour shell-fish of all kinds is even yet a subject of wondering conversation amongst the kindly natives who once took an interest in us, watched our queer doings, and gravely contemplated the waste of energy on the part of our paid hand when he made the brasswork twinkle and flash in the morning sunlight.

It was a cheering sight to the tired traveller, who had spent about twenty hours in trains and steamboats, to see the smart little white yawl, QUEST I, at anchor in Kingstown Harbour, and still more cheering was it to find owner and crew waiting to carry off the voyager to a much-needed breakfast, even though the hour was but 5 a.m. And although such very early meals have their drawbacks, they certainly do leave a huge piece of leisure for after-breakfast conversation, and also produce just the requisite amount of lassitude for the enjoyment of the after-luncheon repose.

As everybody knows Kingstown Harbour I do not intend to describe it — nor more than mention that we spent several days, or parts of days, in exploring 'dear, delightful, dirty Dublin' with great profit and amusement. We noted, with mixed feelings of awe and admiration, that Ireland had really a language and an alphabet of her own, in which the names of the streets and squares were inscribed in letters of gold, much resembling Greek. To prevent the complete undoing of the stranger within their gates, the authorities have most thoughtfully added other inscriptions in the commonplace Roman letters beloved of the prosaic Saxon, so that no man need lose his way about the city. This one touch of originality alone, apart from many other minor ones, provides the agreable feeling of being in a new land, which adds so much to the enjoyment of cruising.

When in the snug confidence of after-dinner talk we hauled out the charts to assist ideas, we found that all along the coast to the north there were little harbours and inlets that looked fit places for the exercise of the brush, and we selected Howth, Rogerstown Inlet and Rush as the first to which we should point our bowsprit. One fine morning we ran out of Kingstown on our way to Howth, which port we reached without any incident of an exciting sort, and let go our anchor in the only spot that seemed to be out of the way of the big crowd of herring boats on the one hand, and the equally large number of small yachts on the other. The harbour is a big-looking place at high water, but ebb tide reveals a continent of sand and mud and stones, which fills the centre leaving two narrow, shallow gutters following the piers running west and south. We took a berth near the red buoy at the entrance, hoping we should find water enough for our six feet and a little over, but we took the ground at low water, and, as the tide neared springs, we lay down at a very uneasy angle, though our bilge was water-borne for an hour or two about low water. But we were nicely out of the way, and could get away much sooner and easier than we could have done had we taken a quay berth and shipped our legs; and it was not low water all the time.

There was much to see at Howth, and we thought there might be much to paint. The craft were of all kinds — black-hulled, 'cod-head and mackerel-tail' Arklow boats, outworn Manx boats, luggers from up and down the coast — all raggedly picturesque. They lay close packed along the west pier, baking and blistering in the sunshine. It was a poor season for herring, but every evening they lumbered out of the harbour, bumping along the sides of their fellows and against the quays, the crews shouting, singing, laughing just as merrily as if they expected to bring in many barrels of herrings in the morning. Then the yachts were not idle; races in the evening, races on Saturdays, cruises with loads of pretty sisters, mothers, and fathers — all jolly and light-hearted. The only solemn people we saw were the young priests, a whole seminary having apparently descended upon Howth. These walked always two together, sometimes more, but never alone. Possibly they were happy too, for they were young; but the contrast was striking — the sombre dress, the downcast eye, the silent pacing along the piers, thronged with gaily dressed boys and girls and jolly, blustering hairy fishermen — and it was difficult not to feel sorry for them.

Amongst the crowd of small yachts we found an old acquaintance in the owner of MARIE, whom we had previously met in the Isle of Man. With the delightfully frank hospitality which is so fine a quality in Irishmen he took charge of us, and in little less than no time we were 'talking boat' in the most intimate fashion with the whole family. MARIE is a sturdy, wholesome, ketch-rigged canoe-yacht of about 6 tons, and her owner and his wife were living on board, whilst the younger people kept house on the hill above, where the strangers were made welcome to the family dinner or the afternoon tea in a manner that left no doubt whatever of the real kindness of the entertainers. Neither of us will soon forget the delight of the evenings spent ashore with our kind host and hostess and his equally kind offspring, and the memory of these adds a charm to Howth over and above its natural beauties.

But this could not last forever. There were ports to call at and paint. Malahide seemed charming and was well known, but the somewhat sinister and suggestive combination of a lunatic asylum and extensive golf links detracted from its attraction, and a little creek just north of it, called Rogerstown Inlet, seemed to offer more advantages and less opportunity for cynicism. Alas! when we enquired about Rogerstown nobody seemed to know anything about it. Malahide they knew, and Skerries they knew; but Rogerstown might have been in India, so vague were all the people of Howth on the subject. Our chart was an old one, with quite impossible landscape drawings giving the leading marks. There was a nice big 'middle-sand' apparently just at the mouth, and the usual limekiln so beloved of cartographers of the year 1836. No yachts had ever been there that we could discover, and not even the oldest fisherman could tell us anything about it, except that "it wasn't a place to take a nice yacht like yours to." The mystery only impelled us more and as we could get no one to take us there we thought we would go and spy out the land for ourselves, taking train to the nearest station, and walking the rest of the way to the coast. We found it still there; only the limekiln had turned itself into its very opposite — a coal shed! — and the leading marks long since gone; but the middle-sand still swelled high in all its pride. A few decaying smacks lay high and dry on the beach, with bleached masts and bulging decks; but they were bigger than the QUEST, and if they could get in we could. Moreover we learned from a sort of imbecile who looked after the transformed limekiln that steamers came with coal once in a while. So we stayed till the tide ebbed enough to enable us to make a rough chart of the entrance, and the next day we were down off the bar waiting for water in. Of course, the wind was dead out of the place, and the channel not wide enough to turn in, so we made her very flat and sailed in the wind's eye; poled and pushed and sounded until the boathook got no bottom and we knew we were beyond the middle-sand and in the deep channel of the river, up which the flood tide was humming at a rare pace. We anchored abreast of the little pier with the transformed limekiln in line, and at high water hauled alongside, made fast our warps, put on the legs, and settled down into what we saw was a snug harbour and a very paintable place with no surfeit of inhabitants. We felt pleased at having come in without a touch, though with only a few inches to spare in the narrow channel at the north side of the middle-sand.

We were soon visited by a few of the inhabitants. One old lady was charmed at once by our request that letters might be left by the postman at her cottage. "Sure, an' yer honour's very welcome! And might I send ye a little salad to take wid yer tay?" The salad promptly arrived by the hands of a bare-legged little boy, who hesitated at accepting the modest tip offered to him for his trouble, and after tea we sallied forth and made our evening sketch.

To those who imagine the Irish peasantry are, without exception, idle and thriftless, Rogerstown would prove an 'eye-opener'. These poor people made a hard living by the cultivation of market vegetables on land which was veritably nothing but sandhills, the soil sweetened and made to some extent productive by the application of seaweed. Early and late were they at work, rain or shine; digging, sowing and gathering; and we could hear their carts rattling over the sand at 2 a.m. on their way to Dublin market, laden with the produce of their toil.

Everybody, young and old, took a share in the work, clad in the most nondescript clothing. They were not so poor as they looked, for on Sundays the girls went off to mass in the most fashionable and variegated costumes and hats imaginable. We believe that their charms were the cause of our dinghy being stolen one night, for the young men from the other side of the river arrived in twos and threes, and stayed so late that the ferryman went home to bed and left them to get back the best way they could — hence the disappearance of the dinghy, which was reposing on a sandhill, newly varnished, and thus away from the care of the large yacht and its crew. It was not brought back, and only discovered by the aid of binoculars next morning lying on a sandbank across the river, and our paid hand made a perilous journey across to bring her back, in a sort of floating box which belonged to the coastguard. As there was nothing to steal but the bare boat, nothing was stolen; but these young men were of a different sort from the people on our side. A few nights afterwards we were aroused from our slumbers by loud requests to "lind us your yawl". This was about midnight; and on giving a prompt refusal we were loudly cursed and threatened. Apart from the oaths, the worst thing was that we were informed that we could never get away, "No pilot will take ye out", "Y're boycotted sure", etc. This was almost amusing, seeing that we had got in unaided, but not so amusing as the hasty scamper off which was produced by the sight of a gun! Although it was only a rook rifle, and unloaded, the glint of the moon along the barrel and the click of the hammer acted like magic. We were never again awakened from our slumbers by any demand for the loan of our yawl, nor were we boycotted by our good neighbours on our side of the river, who professed themselves much scandalised by such blackguardism, and sent us propitiatory offerings of more and more salads, refusing any payment. We were also taken out mullet fishing; at least I suppose we were mullet fishing, for it was only mullet we caught in our nets, though there were anxious wonderings whether there was a salmon in every time we hauled the seine. And though we had no salmon for breakfast, good grey mullet are not to be despised.

Altogether we found Rogerstown Inlet a very jolly and amusing place, and we were sorry to leave, when we had taken the cream of the subjects. So that no mishap might befall us in going out, one member of the crew made a chart of the entrance and got the leading marks across the bar on the back of an envelope. Quite a crowd assembled to see us off. My old lady came rushing up the quay, asking, "Where's himself — where's himself?" with a tear rolling down her honest, withered, weather-beaten cheek. I fled to the cabin, but was hauled out and handed over to her embraces. And the QUEST, with only headsails and mizzen, sped down the river over the last of the flood, bound for Skerries. On our way there we had an illustration of the handiness of the yawl rig for cruising. Halfway across the bay the wind, already strong, freshened considerably, and a cutter, about our own size, under a double-reefed sail, had very much more than she wanted, and was hove almost flat in the squalls. We still kept under headsails and mizzen, and were smoking along comfortably, dry and fast, running over the strong eddies inside the Skerries rocks and turning into Skerries Bay under the same canvas. We were there first, had our anchor down, and everything stowed before that overpowered cutter arrived, ship and crew drenched and streaming. Of course they may have liked that sort of thing; but after the first flush of youthful innocence has passed most people only want to be wetted all over once a day, and that the first thing in the morning.

Skerries, promising-looking on the chart, did not prove a very detaining place, and we left next morning, with a very light breeze, bound for Ardglass. The day dragged slowly on until evening found us off Carlingford Lough, lying idly on a glassy sea. We could hear far away the grunt of the whistling buoy and muffled thud, thud, thud of the steamers bound into the Lough. It was a long, foggy night, and we took turns to watch and perform solos on the foghorn whenever we heard the thump of an approaching steamer; but the watch below slept peacefully until the dawn turned the fog into a pinky halo and sunrise brought a smart breeze off the land, which, strengthening every half-hour, soon brought us abreast of Ardglass — sparkling in the morning sunlight, and packed full of herring boats all tucked away behind the protecting arm of the pier, their crews busily engaged in shaking herrings out of their nets. Our morning tub, surrounded as we were by a large crowd of masculine spectators, produced a kind of stupefaction. These hardy mariners seemed amazed to find anyone insane enough to endure the delightful sensation produced by deluges of nice cold salt water poured from full buckets at that early hour. With one consent all hands knocked off 'shaking out' and gazed. And when we had gone below to dress, someone, doubtless feeling that this was a form of entertainment deserving reward, sent us a present of fine fresh herrings and one or two shad.

Well, we knew Ardglass pretty intimately — everyone who cruises on this part of the Irish coast does — and we wanted to get information as to the possibilities of Dundrum, which looked eminently picturesque on the chart. The sailing directions were of the usual terrifying nature, which only made us the more anxious to see it. The local mariners were not more reassuring than the sailing directions. They spoke with awe of the strong tide and the two big 'bulls' (anglice 'sands') which barred the entrance. At last we found a man who said there was a pilot who lived at Dundrum, and that a wire to Paddy McGuire, for that was his name, would secure him. So we wired, and next day were off to Dundrum bell buoy some time before half flood. Paddy came out in his long yawl, and had dinner in the forecastle whilst the tide made. His boots had the most awful nails in them, and he had to be provided with slippers before he was allowed at large on the deck. Slowly we sailed in, discovering that, after all, the place was easy when you had once seen inside; like so many other harbours.

Sand boats at Dundrum

Paddy was mightly curious to know what we were and what we wanted at Dundrum. He could not make us out at all, and came to the flattering conclusion that we were 'lords', partly because we seemed to have no occupation other than sailing about in a pretty little yawl, but more so from the remarkable likeness of the owner of QUEST I to Lord Arthur Hill, well known there, and, as Paddy declared "The very image of yer honour". Paddy anchored us in what he said was the best spot for lying afloat in, assuring us that there was always 8 ft of water at low tide. But he was wrong, for we took the ground every low water, and the tides being so strong we generally dragged our anchors (though we were moored) on the last of the ebb, as the yacht swung on her keel broadside to tide and the bottom was not good holding ground. This was a nuisance, as we had to be about at 'tide-time', but the climax arrived with a heavy N.W. gale. She hung on all right on the ebb for some reason, and after breakfast we were congratulating ourselves on having got through the night without a mess, when suddenly we felt her keel give a big bump, and we knew she was ashore. We bolted on deck, hardly able to see through the mixture of rain, spray, and sand which the tide tore up from land and sea, and as the tide was flowing we decided to try to get the shelter of the pier half a mile to windward. There was no difficulty in getting the anchors, as both of them were huge bunches of weed, and with reefed foresail and mizzen only we positively tore though the water with the strong flood under us and shot her up into the wind alongside an old dredger, where there happened to be just water for us. This was another occasion when the yawl-rig was a godsend, for there was so much wind that I doubt if the yacht would have carried even a reefed trysail. As it was, she lay down to deck edge under not much more than 150 sq ft of sail, yet she handled splendidly. Of course, in so small a space there was no sea to speak of; but the force of the wind was such that many trees were blown down and a large military encampment in the sandhills was simply flattened out, some of the tents being blown half a mile from their moorings, and the Tommies were much demoralised. We took this visitation as a judgement on them, as one individual, under the innocent demeanour of an interested lover of the fine arts, bagged my best No 10 sable, which had cost me 5s 6d and was just in the very prime of life, neither new nor old. Why a cockney Thomas Atkins should want to steal my sable brush remains a deep mystery to me to this day; but so he did, and Providence was displeased.

We liked Dundrum very much; there was so much to see and to paint, and the people were most entrancingly interesting. The chief officer of the Coastguard, or Customs, could not make us out any more than the pilot could. "I see you sittin' about drawin'," he said one day; "but what's your real business here?" We assured him that we had landed a valuable cargo of contraband on the night of our arrival, and that he was much too late to make a haul now. He departed, more puzzled than ever.

Then there was the noble Marquis, owner of Dundrum and all that was therein and roundabout for many miles. He also was a character, disguising himself as the third engineer of a tramp steamer and fraternising with the crew of his yacht in an ultrademocratic manner, not supposed to be at all usual with marquises. When we had at last pierced his disguise and separated him from the rest of his crew, he proved to be most affable and kindly, and I fished his river with impunity and some success.

Then the little farmers who lived across the Lough, and who on market days consumed rather more of the light wine of the country than was compatible with a law-abiding spirit, were very amusing. It seems that in this part of Ireland it is forbidden to sing certain songs, such as 'The Wearin' o' the Green,' or to consign His Holiness the Pope to a warmer climate than that of Italy, under pain of the law. On market days they wanted to do one or the other of these things most intensely, and quarrels arose in consequence. They would meander down to the quay, behaving pretty well whilst the stern eyes of the constabulary were fixed upon them, but so soon as they were deposited in the ferry-boat and safely afloat they sang the forbidden songs very bravely and loud, fell over-board, were rescued, embraced one another, and fought immediately afterwards in the most diverting manner possible, and in the end nobody seemed a penny the worse. Even the fighting was good-humoured and, in a way, light-hearted and friendly!

Dundrum Lough is at high tide a splendid sheet of water, several miles long from north to south, and pretty wide. It is only available for sailing in a light draught centreboard boat from two hours before high water to two hours after, and is even then rather a tricky place. At half ebb it is a sandy desert, with shallow streams here and there. Many a good sail did we have in our 10 ft centre board dinghy. The views of Mourne Mountains from all parts are extremely fine, and there are heaps of all kinds of fish, from the lordly salmon right down to humble cockle, which here attains aldermanic proportions. The channel from the bar to the quay offers sailing opportunities according to the tide and wind all day long as there is about 2 ft at dead low water in the shallowest part. But the tide is a caution and wants watching in this part, though in the great lake-like expansion it is hardly felt. Then there is a delicious old castle, unique in some respects, and dating from the earliest part of the thirteenth century; still in many parts well preserved, and conjuring up endless visions of the early civilisation of Ireland to the imaginative mind.

Altogether we spent a very enjoyable time here and only the feeling that such a place was too good to use up all at once, but deserved several other visits, led us to put to sea once more, this time bound for Strangford Lough, another of the places that, according to the sailing directions, afford every opportunity of getting wrecked, and are impossible for the stranger to attempt to take without the aid of a pilot. This is pure nonsense, provided that one has a handy vessel and ordinary plain common nautical sense. The great precaution to take is to be off the entrance about high water by the shore, keeping well clear of St Patrick's Rock (marked by a perch) and also to choose the east channel in preference to the west. And as there is a strong indraught into the Lough for about one and a half hours after nominal high water one cannot help, even in the lightest weather, being carried in. There is nothing to 'pick you up' that is not very clearly marked by beacons. The Meadows Rocks may be neglected at this time of tide, as there is 9 ft of water on them at low water. About half way up the narrows are some whirlpools on the east side which would take charge of a vessel; but they may easily be avoided even in a turning wind, as the place is much wider than it looks on the chart, and there is plenty of room to work by keeping to the west side clear of all dangers that are not marked by beacons. When you arrive at Portaferry, after having overcome the difficulties (mainly imaginary) of the entrance, you will probably be hailed by pilots. These may be neglected, and you will make your way peacefully round the corner to the southward, and bring up in 2 or 3 fathoms L.W. in the safe shelter of Audley Roads.

The danger, which is not made enough of by the pilot-book, is to attempt to leave Strangford when the wind is even only moderate from any point with south in it, for the lightest air from this direction makes the ebb overfalls at the entrance quite a boiling, irregular sea. When QUEST left there was a mere air from the south-east, yet the yacht could not be sailed, and several big lumps broke over her exceptionally high bow. I fancy the worst of this could be avoided by keeping well to the north-east; but the bay here is rocky and foul, and care would have to be exercised if the craft drew more than 4 ft or so.

Audley Roads is a snug anchorage, out of the tide, and convenient in all ways. From it one can explore a fraction of the huge expanse of Strangford Lough (for it would take a season to do the whole of it thoroughly) in the dinghy, or take exercise ashore in the beautiful demesne of Lord Bangor. The Lough itself is entirely different from any other place I have ever visited, being absolutely full of rocks and islands, some merely tiny places, others of considerable size. Very little traffic is carried on between Portaferry and the small villages around the shore of the Lough, and I should think it unlikely that any living being knows his way about the whole of this great sheet of water. There are recognised routes, of course, to the different villages; but navigation at night must be very risky, as there are not only rocks above water, but below (and not so far below) as well. There is a dreariness quite inexpressible about the place, whose lonely shores and islands seem to have the power of impressing their sadness on the soul. A haunting sense that at one time the Lough supported a large population, which had died out from the mere sadness of their surroundings, was on my mind all the time, though there is no evidence in history for such an idea, and, from all I could hear or could gather, the few people about the district are not more melancholy, but, on the contrary, are quite as cheerful as all the rest of the peasantry and fisherfolk one meets in this part of Ireland. Yet to stand on the edge of the narrows at dusk and listen to the mysterious murmurs and clapping of the tide as it rushed in or out of the Lough is an experience few would forget. These vast solitudes would certainly afford a lot of exploring to a man (or two men preferably — it is a far more uncanny place than the wildest sea-shore) in a light draught canoe-yawl with a tent. They would need to be well provisioned, for though the place has plenty of fishes, the supply of loaves is neither great nor frequent.

The most cheerful spots in the whole place are certainly near humanity. At Audley Roads and thereabouts a few yachts are moored, and an odd fishing boat or two, whose owners never seem to fish, may be seen. Occasionally a coaster or a coal-laden steam-lighter comes to Portaferry; but on the whole there is curiously little life about the Lough, and if any place in the three kingdoms is 'out of the world' to the same extent I have yet to see it. It was not without a sort of sense of relief, and with sketch-books not very well replenished, that we slipped down on the brief space of time which cannot be truthfully called 'slack water', QUEST seeming glad too to get once more on the open sea. The rush of tide coming on soon carried us clear of everything, though we filled our decks at the overfalls at the mouth. We sailed on northward, past a low, somewhat mournful looking coast, dotted with rocky islets and indented by little rock-guarded bays, with here and there a tiny fishing port, only revealed to the passer-by by the tops of the masts of the fishing craft peeping over the rocks. On some of the little isles are burying grounds; indeed one is marked as Burial Isle on the chart. Clearly the aborigines held the old and almost universal superstition that the spirits of the departed could not cross water, and so selected a convenient island as a bourne from which no ghostly traveller might return.

As we sped along with a fair tide and a light quartering wind we passed a wreck high up on the inner South Rocks, and yet another ashore near Clogher. Both were large steamers, and it seems odd that with so wide a space as this part of the Irish Sea presents for vagaries on the part of steamship captains that so many should be lost hereabouts. At Strangford Lough lives one who seems to make a prosperous living by salvage operations, for there was a sort of knackers-yard, with several vessels in process of being demolished. The lightships — South Rock and Skulmartin — are good and well off the land, and the soundings are not difficult. It must be the power of the tide, aided by the other powers — darkness and carelessness — that brings so many ships ashore on this dangerous bit of coast.

The afternoon was still young when we were off Donaghadee, and we could fetch in easily. Seeing us from afar, a boatman came off, and was greatly disappointed when we told him we knew our way in. However we gave him a tow, the while he sat in the stern sheets of his nice looking little yawl and mopped his weary and dripping brow, for the weather was warm and he had had a long pull. He earned a trifle by taking our stern warps on shore, and we rode quietly, as is the custom here, to our own anchor ahead, with two ropes to the quay aft. The owner of QUEST, who had been in this harbour in a gale, does not speak with much confidence of it as a shelter in time of trouble; but whilst we were there all was peace, with a few fights on the quay as diversion in the evenings. We intended to make no long stay at Donaghadee, but really went in to meet the first owner of MIST, who came on board and was our guest for an evening, and who photographed us successfully as we slipped out through the piers on our way to the land that was calling us — Scotland.

No sooner were we clear of the harbour than a slight, but very clinging, fog came on, the breeze still holding fair from the SE enabling us just to lay our course for Ailsa. The little ship, with all set and drawing beautifully, slipped along at her best pace, and we sailed on hour after hour in an opalescent world, with no horizon, no sound, and only the gentlest of motion. It was a long stretch across conflicting and strong tides, and when her time was up, as calculated, we still were in a small, silent world of our own, with no sight or sound to guide us. Then a trader crossed our bows quite close, and at last high up in the sky loomed the white, scarred head of Ailsa Craig. We were dead on our course, and felt proud of our exact navigation, and squared away for Arran, as we were bound for Loch Ranza for the night.

What perverse demon persuaded us to take the east side of Arran instead of going up Kilbrennan Sound will never be known; but after debate we chose this course, which proved to be what is commonly called in horsy circles a 'wrong 'un'. All went well until we were off Sannox, and the evening light made Goat Fell glorious. Then we sailed slap out of our nice little breeze into a flat calm, and Loch Ranza was miles away. Reluctantly we got out the sweeps, and swept and swept in turn, the while the moon rose in the east, and yet no night breeze came to aid us. Round us rode many fishing skiffs vainly searching for herring, and long after we had expected to be sound asleep we rounded the north-east corner of Arran, when a tiny flaw from the south sent the boom gently over to starboard, and we rested from our labours and watched the tiny phosphorescent ripples spread from the bows. Then the air died away, and once more we swept with aching arms, for fourteen tons of boat and ballast are not light to row even when they are moulded into a pretty form. Again the air wafted from the hills, sweet with the scent of heather, and we stole round into the bay, to receive a knock-down slam that laid our deck in directly we headed for our anchorage. But we went there, head to wind and anchor down, in a moment, and the QUEST and her tired crew slumbered in the deep shadows of the hills until long after the sun had roused the gulls and filled the whole bay with his glory.

We made a leisurely run from Loch Ranza when next we weighed anchor, after a week of delicious warm September weather, still and fine, most propitious for sketching; and entering our home port — Tarbert, Loch Fyne — regretfully packed traps, bade the owner goodbye, and, feeling that one more glorious summer had been placed on the right side of the ledger of life, boarded the Columba bound for home, via Glasgow.

QUEST I was sold that winter, and QUEST II, of ampler proportions, was designed and built for the next summer's jaunt; but I shall always remember her good qualities and the many happy days at sea spent in the little yawl in company with her genial owner and her good crew — Collister — whom the sea has taken, but whose merry eye and cheery whistle are not forgotten."

CHAPTER 10

An Album of Albert Strange Designs . . . 2

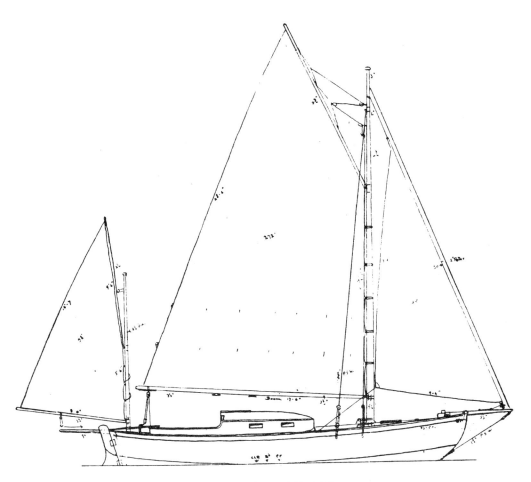

Psyche (No 122/1911)

The 27ft yawl PSYCHE was designed for Lieut Norman Jones, RNVR, and was built in 1912. She was of Strange's shallow draught, Humber Yawl style cruiser and has the single headsail and lug mizzen of the type. The hull sections are shapely, but with moderate beam and a hull draught of 2′ 11″ she would heel readily under the full sail area of 425 sq ft. The L shaped centreplate is pivoted at the ballast keel and the top of the case is open at the deck, with the lifting tackle made fast to the mast. The only advantage of this arrangement of plate is that if blocked by stones or clay the slot could easily be cleared from above.

FIG 46

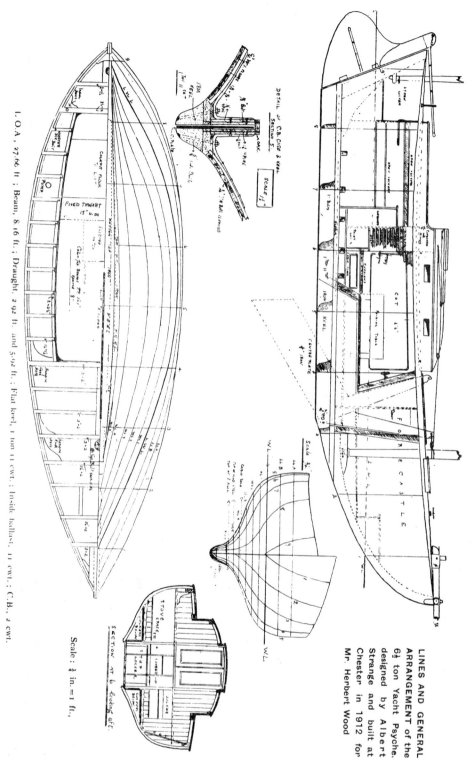

LINES AND GENERAL
ARRANGEMENT of the
6½ ton Yacht Psyche,
designed by Albert
Strange and built at
Chester in 1912 for
Mr. Herbert Wood

L.O.A., 27.66 ft.; Beam, 8.16 ft.; Draught, 2.92 ft. and 5.92 ft.; Flat keel, 4 ton 1 cwt.; Inside ballast, 14 cwt.; C.B., 2 cwt.

Scale: ¼ in. = 1 ft.,

FIG 47

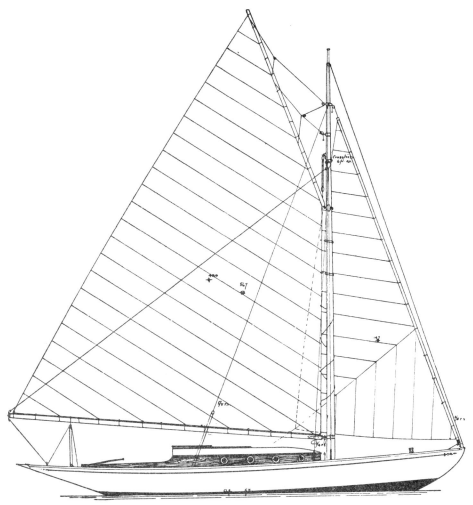

SAIL PLAN OF THE 7-TON AUXILIARY SLOOP: AREA 567 SQ. FT.

7 ton Auxiliary Sloop (1911)

This auxiliary yacht shows another aspect of Strange's designs. She was a fast cruiser with a stemhead sloop rig and a nicely formed hull for the type and period (the Mystic plans include a sketch for a gaff yawl rig). The lines have a suggestion of influence from the I.Y.R.U. classes, then current. She would be a fast yacht but would be improved by being rigged as a cutter and better still as a bermudian yawl. The design emphasises the versatility of Albert Strange as a yacht designer.

FIG 48

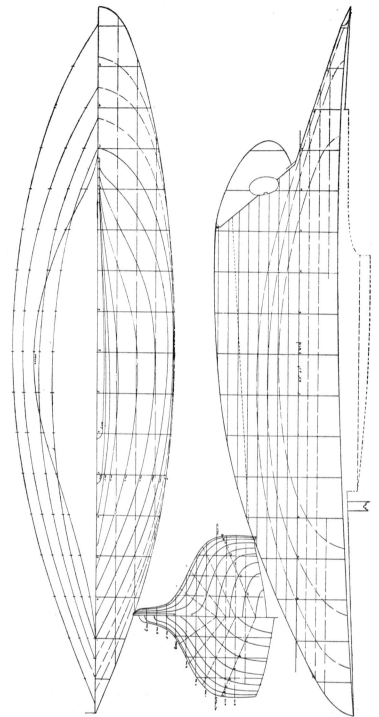

7-TON AUXILIARY SLOOP DESIGNED BY ALBERT STRANGE. SCALE, ¼ IN. = 1 FT.

L.O.A., 34·65 FT.; L.W.L., 24 FT.; BEAM, 7·92 FT.; DRAUGHT, 4·25 FT.; DISPLACEMENT, 5·1 TONS.

FIG 49

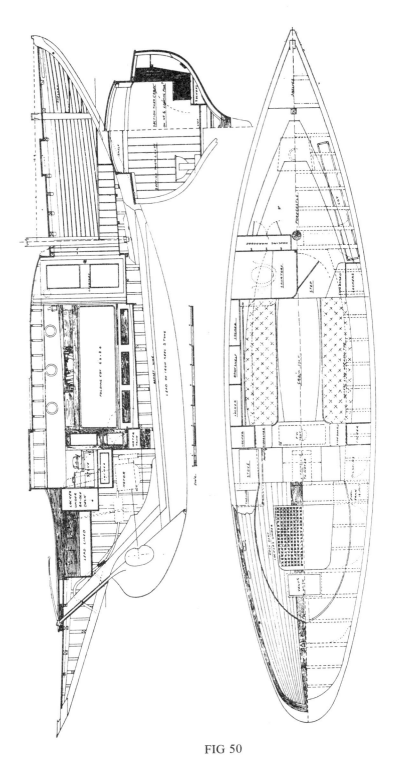

ACCOMMODATION AND GENERAL ARRANGEMENT PLANS OF THE 7-TON AUXILIARY SLOOP.

FIG 50

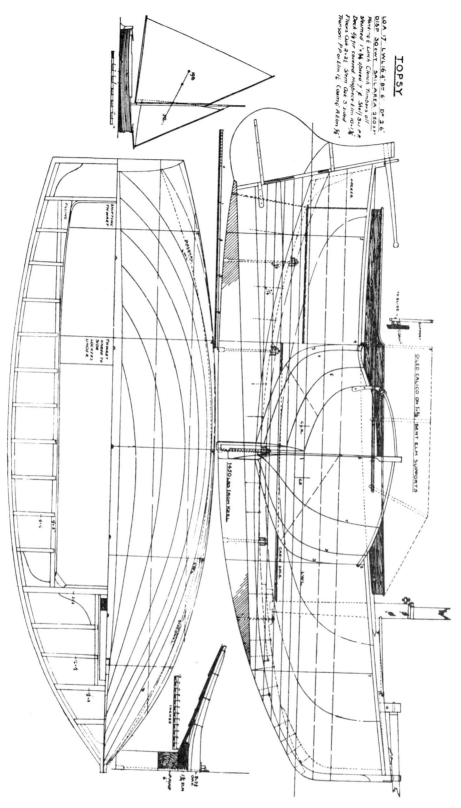

Topsy (1912)

The TOPSY was a small, clinker planked keel dayboat with a gaff sloop rig. The lines are again
spoiled by a plumb stem instead of a slightly rounded one. The mainsail is lofty and well
peaked. She would be initially stiff but would need to be reefed progressively in strong winds.
The hull sections show she would not lie comfortably on a drying mooring but the canvas tilt
suggests overnight cruises in enjoyable spartan conditions, for the young.

FIG 51

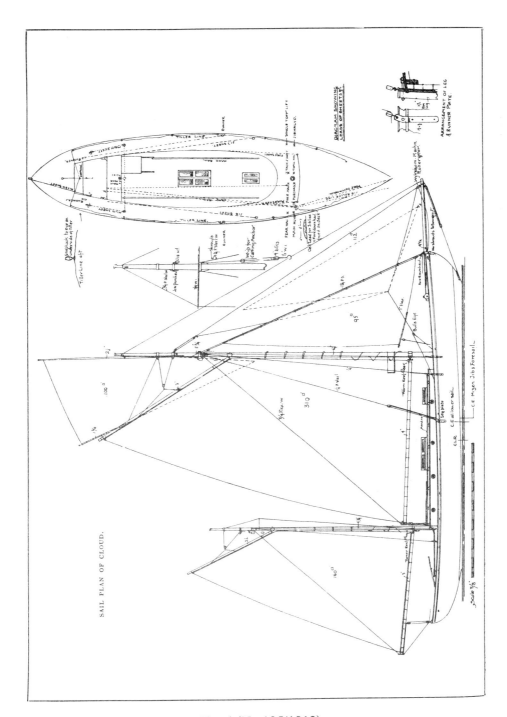

Cloud (No 125/1912)

The ketch CLOUD was Albert Strange's winning entry in a YACHTING MONTHLY designing competition of 1908 for a cruising yacht, though it was a difficult decision for the judges, such was the quality of many entries. The hull form is particularly pleasing, though the stern sections err towards a flatnes suggestive of a counter. The sail plan is lofty and has a useful mizzen, and a yard topsail for lighter breezes. Running backstays are shown but would be a nuisance when short-handed at sea. A large balloon or reaching jib would have been a useful addition to the sail wardrobe. Accommodation was typical for the time but the bridge deck was unusual in Britain. It makes a yacht snug below because of the more secure hatchway, which also keeps out unwanted draughts.

Dimensions:— LOA 38.75ft LWL 30ft Beam 9.58ft Draught 5ft Sail Area 846 sq ft (originally 777 sq ft).

FIG 52

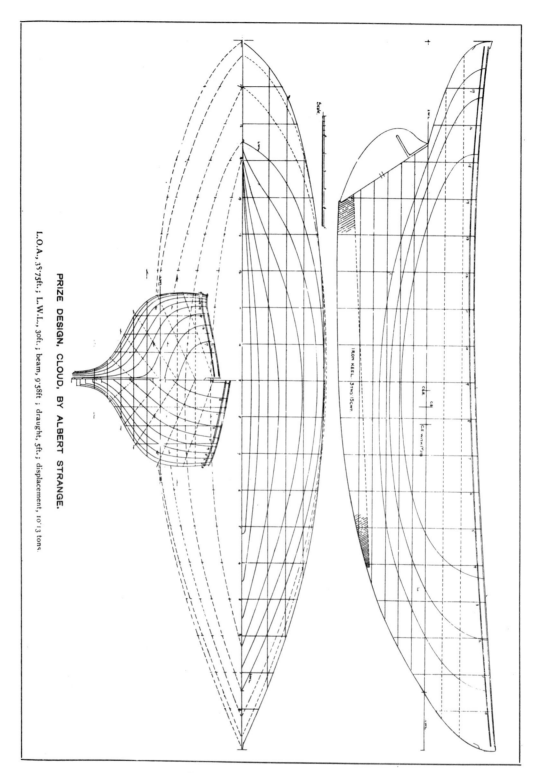

PRIZE DESIGN, CLOUD, BY ALBERT STRANGE.

L.O.A., 38·75ft.; L.W.L., 30ft.; beam, 9·58ft; draught, 5ft.; displacement, 10·13 tons

FIG 53

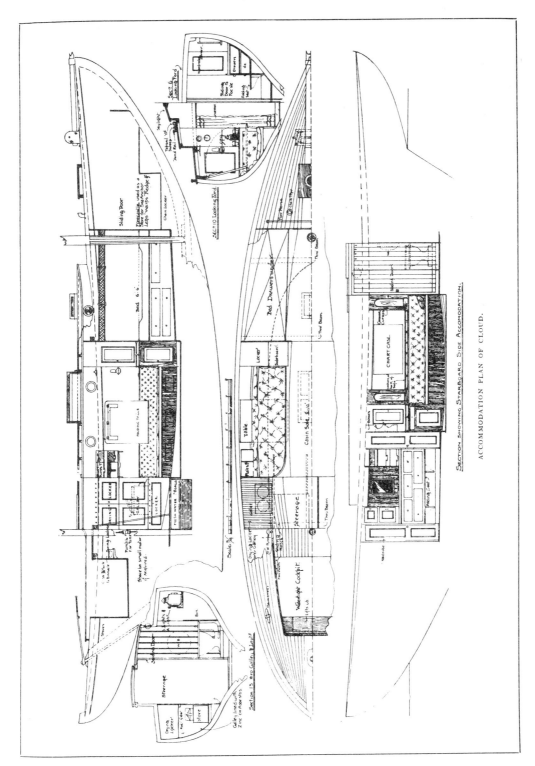

FIG 54

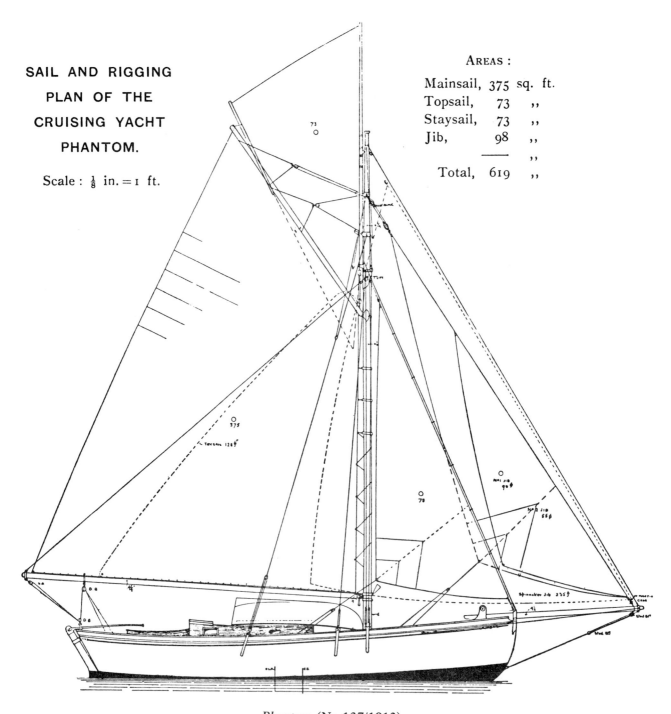

SAIL AND RIGGING PLAN OF THE CRUISING YACHT PHANTOM.

Scale : $\frac{1}{8}$ in. = 1 ft.

AREAS :

Mainsail,	375	sq. ft.
Topsail,	73	,,
Staysail,	73	,,
Jib,	98	,,
	——	,,
Total,	619	,,

Phantom (No 137/1913)

Strange described this little cutter as 'a tubby little thing built around a cabin plan'. However, she is a size and type of small cruiser well suited to passage-making, and to cruising coasts where she would not need to take the ground. The owner was a single-hander and the cooking arrangements were such that he could attend to them at the hatch whilst the yacht kept her course for a short time. The folding table to starboard was also used for chartwork and the 6ft headroom under the coachroof was specified by the tall owner.

The plans reproduced are basic ones and Strange seems to have usually prepared only lines, offsett tables and general arrangement.

FIG 55

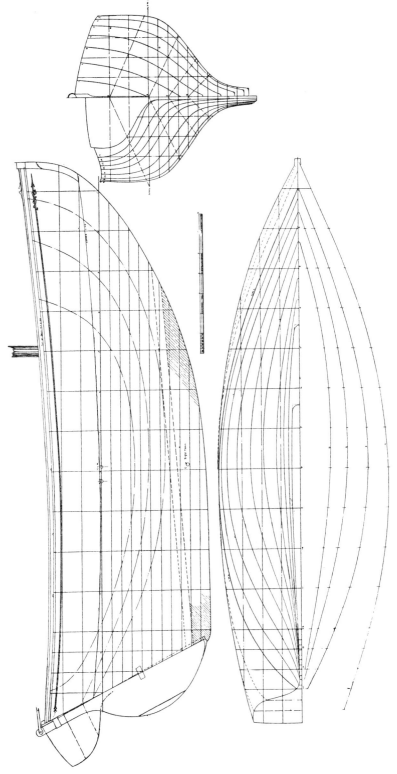

LINES OF THE 7½-TON CRUISING YACHT PHANTOM DESIGNED BY ALBERT STRANGE FOR MR. J. S. TRENCH.

FIG 56

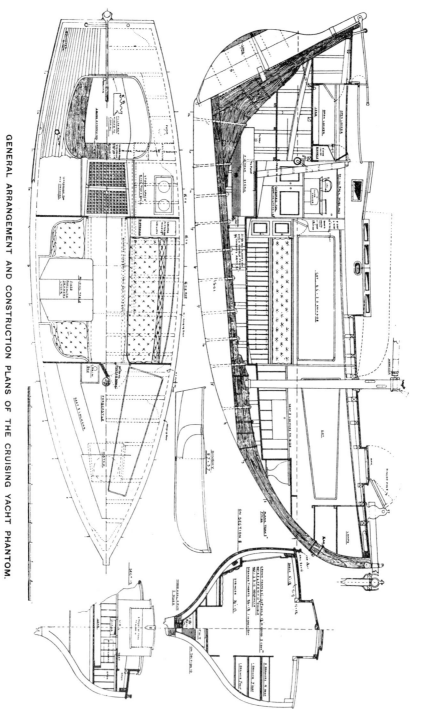

GENERAL ARRANGEMENT AND CONSTRUCTION PLANS OF THE CRUISING YACHT PHANTOM.

FIG 57

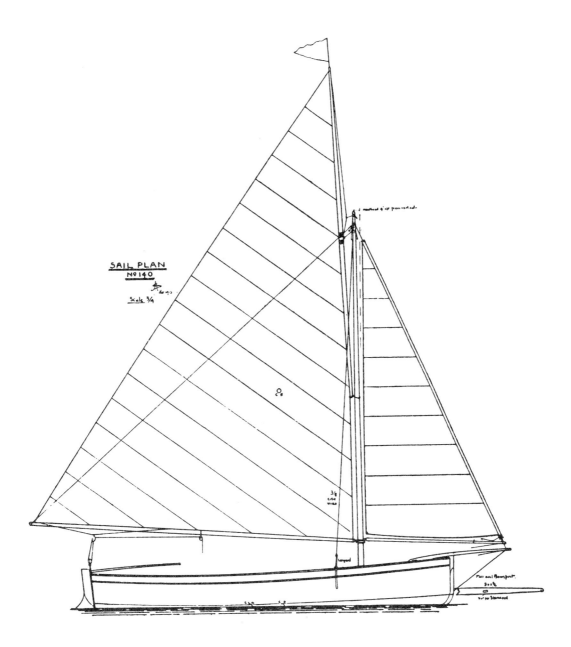

Sailing dinghy (No 140/1913)

Strange designed several sailing dinghies including this example which had too great a rise of
floor and fineness of forward waterlines and diagonals to have been a stiff boat in strong winds
under the generous gunter sloop rig. The plumb stem resulted in exaggerated fineness forward
and she would be improved with a rounded forefoot and a drop plate rudder.

FIG 58

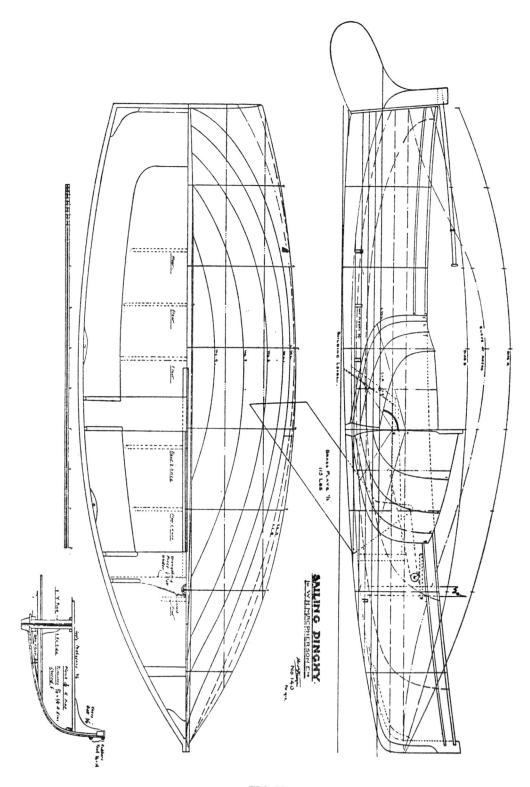

FIG 59

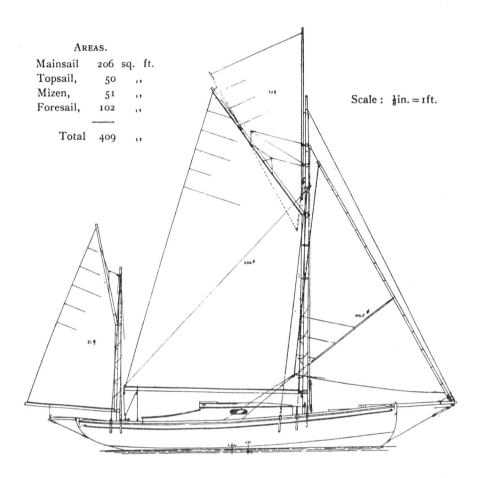

AREAS.

Mainsail	206	sq. ft.
Topsail,	50	,,
Mizen,	51	,,
Foresail,	102	,,
Total	409	,,

Scale : ⅛in. = 1ft.

Sail and Rigging Plan of the Single-handed Canoe-Yacht Theresa II.

Theresa II (No 139/1913)

The 25ft 6in yawl THERESA II was designed as a two berth cruiser with the useful draught of 3ft 7in. The shallow cockpit was apparently self-draining but would have been more comfortable if the sole had been lower. The single headsail would need powerful sheeting in strong winds. Altogether an attractive looking little yacht and one of the most practical designs for present day use.

Dimensions:— LOA 25ft 6in LWL 20ft 6in Beam 7ft 6in Draught 3ft 7in Sail Area 409 sq ft.

FIG 60

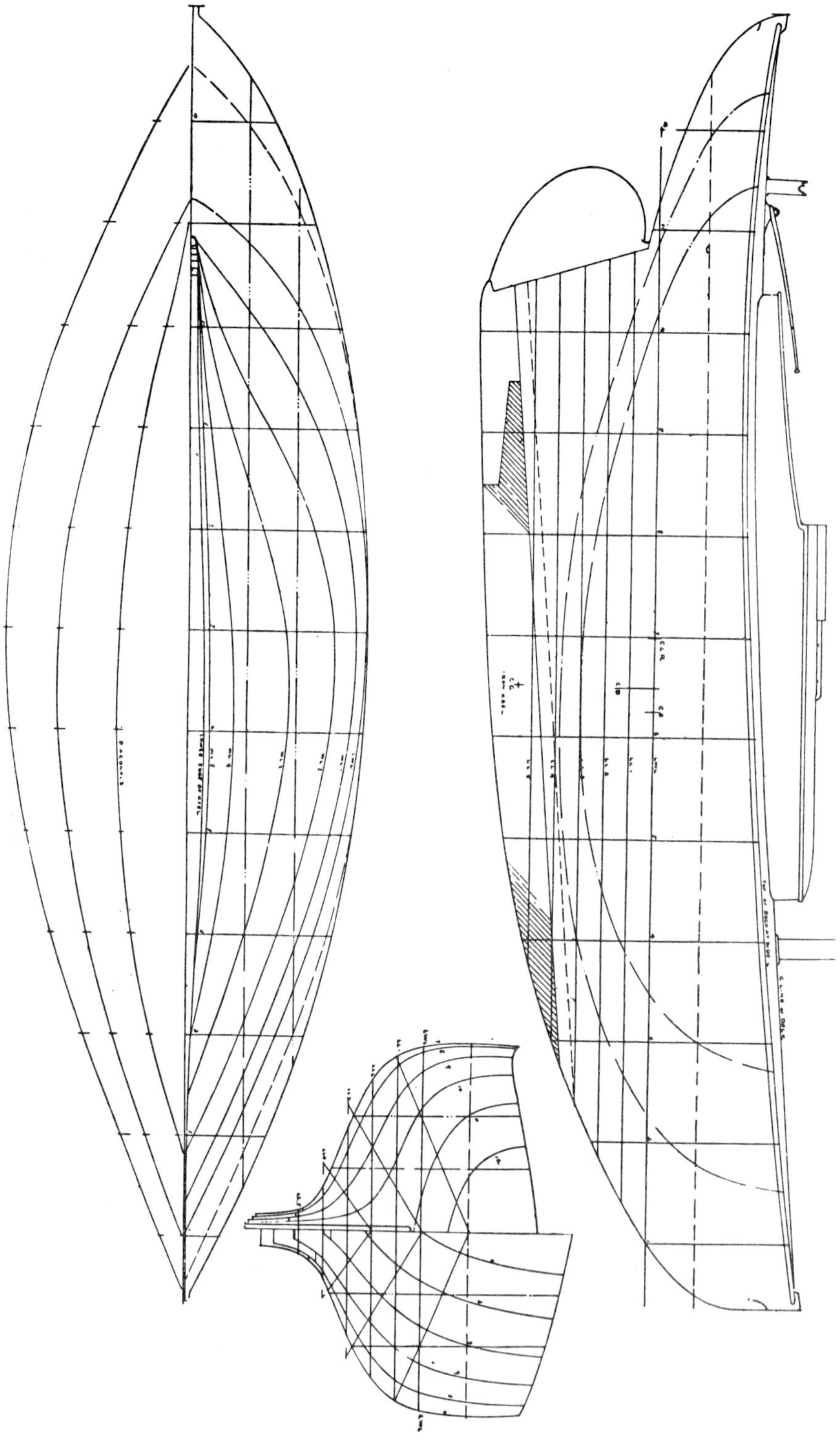

LINES OF THE 4-TON SINGLE-HANDED CANOE-YACHT THERESA II, DESIGNED BY ALBERT STRANGE FOR MR. C. WALTON.

L.O.A., 25.5ft. ; L.W.L., 20.5ft. ; Beam, 7.5ft. ; Draught, 3.62ft.   Scale : ¼in.= 1ft.

FIG 61

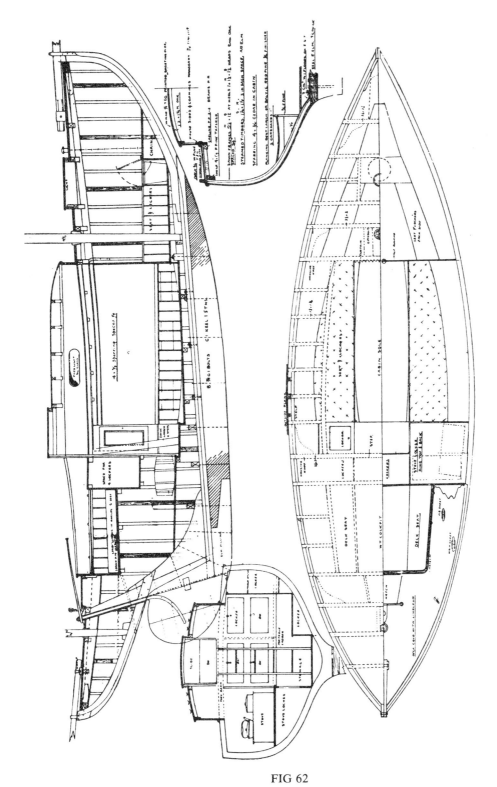

CONSTRUCTION AND GENERAL ARRANGEMENT PLANS OF THE 4-TON SINGLE-HANDED CANOE-YACHT THERESA II.   Scale: ¼in. = 1ft.

FIG 62

Mainsail, 439 sq. ft
Mizen, 82 ,,
Topsail, 83 ,,
Jib, 119 ,,
Foresail, 88 ,,
———
Total, 811 ,,

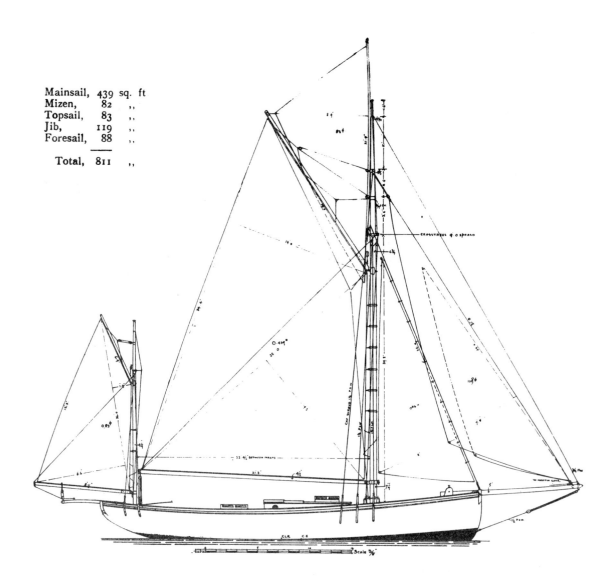

SAIL PLAN OF THE 10-TON AUXILIARY YAWL TERN.

Tern (No 133/1913)

This auxiliary yawl was required to be a strong and a good sea boat with accommodation for four in the owner's party and a professional hand and a boy forward. The aft cabin was sometimes to be used by ladies in conjunction with the WC and lobby at the hatchway, to provide dressing space for their Edwardian toilettes. A 7½ horsepower engine was tucked away inaccessibly right aft. It provided about 4¾ knots in smooth water but there would be little rest in the after cabin when it was running.

FIG 63

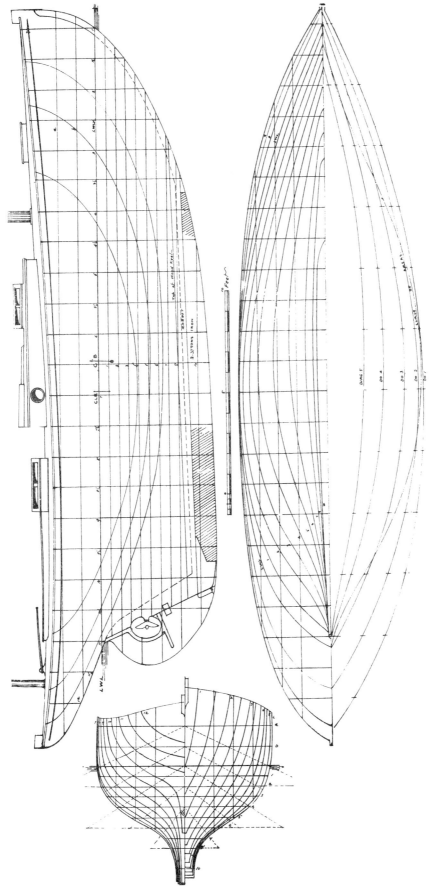

LINES OF THE 10-TON AUXILIARY YAWL TERN. DESIGNED BY ALBERT STRANGE AND NOW BEING BUILT BY THOMAS OF FALMOUTH FOR MR. HERBERT R. COOPER.

L.O.A., 36.3ft.; L.W.L., 30.5ft.; Beam, 9ft.; Draught, 5.9ft.; Power,

BODY PLAN OF TERN.
To same Scale as Lines.

FIG 64

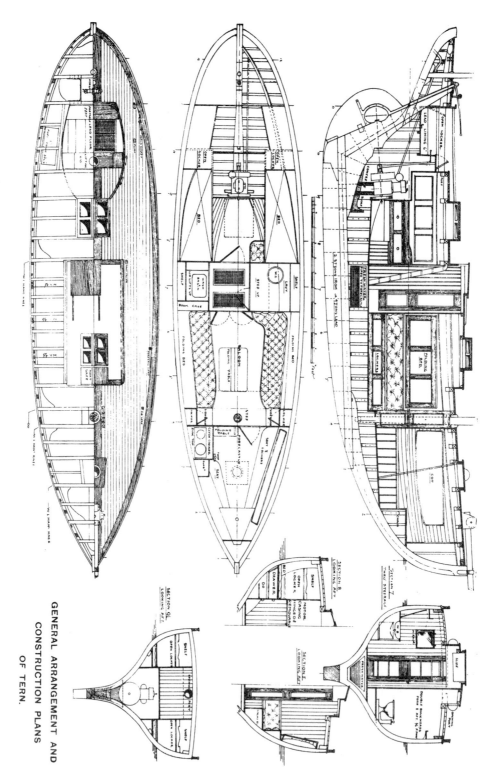

GENERAL ARRANGEMENT AND
CONSTRUCTION PLANS
OF TERN.

FIG 65

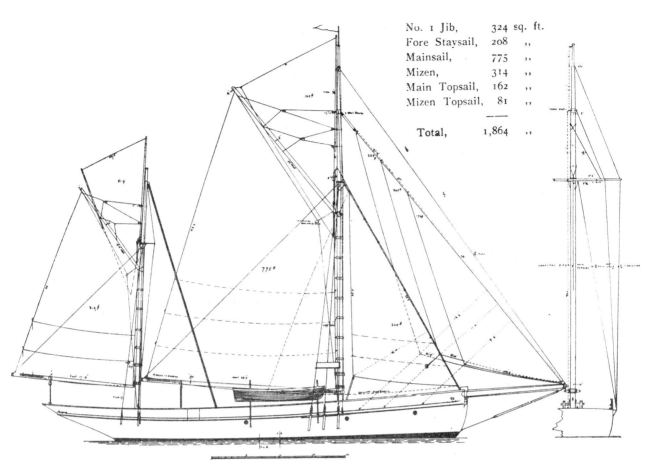

No. 1 Jib,	324	sq. ft.
Fore Staysail,	208	,,
Mainsail,	775	,,
Mizen,	314	,,
Main Topsail,	162	,,
Mizen Topsail,	81	,,
Total,	1,864	,,

SAIL AND RIGGING PLAN OF THE AUXILIARY KETCH BETTY II.

Betty II (No 138/1913)

The auxiliary ketch BETTY II was one of the largest yachts designed by Albert Strange and
followed the same owner's cutter BETTY, also a Strange design. Increased size dictated a
ketch rig, similar to that of a sailing trawler. She was built by Stow and Son at Shoreham,
Sussex to their usual high standard and as she was built under the Special Survey of Lloyd's
Register of Shipping, a structural midship section showing scantlings had to be provided. This
shows typical yacht practice of the time.

The owner's stipulations included strength, seaworthiness, and economy of working. She was
intended to be sailed reasonably fast and be capable of voyaging to ports which could be
reached from England in the duration of a summer's cruise. The accommodation had to be
comfortable for the owner, his guests and the crew.

She was one of the most seaworthy yachts designed by Strange. A four cylinder Thornycroft
paraffin motor was installed, driving the centreline propellor shaft via a chain reducing gear to
attain 5½ knots under power. The BETTY II was launched, incomplete, at the beginning of
the 1914-18 War.

FIG 66

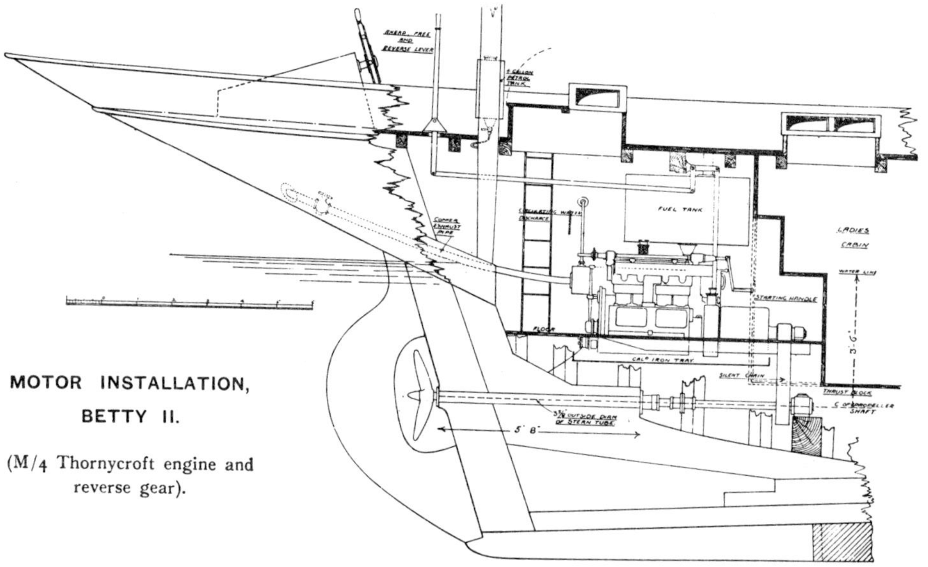
FUEL TANK
LADIES CABIN
FLOOR
STARTING HANDLE
5' 8"

MOTOR INSTALLATION, BETTY II.

(M/4 Thornycroft engine and reverse gear).

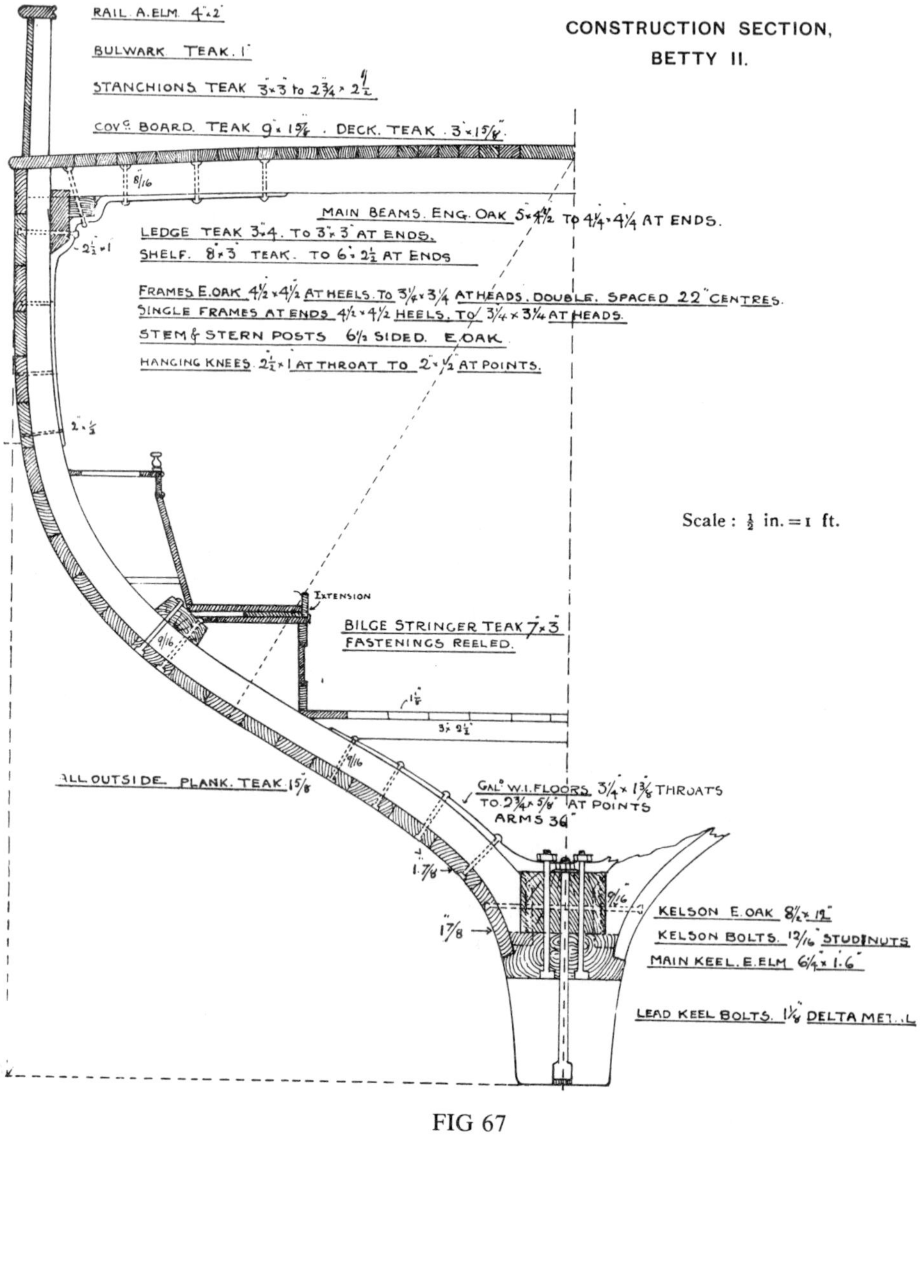
RAIL. A. ELM. 4" x 2"
BULWARK TEAK. 1"
STANCHIONS TEAK 3" x 3" to 2¾ x 2½
COVG. BOARD. TEAK 9" x 1⅝ . DECK. TEAK . 3" x 1⅝"
MAIN BEAMS. ENG. OAK 5 x 4½ TO 4¼ x 4¼ AT ENDS.
LEDGE TEAK 3 x 4. TO 3" x 3" AT ENDS.
SHELF. 8" x 3" TEAK. TO 6" x 2½ AT ENDS
FRAMES E. OAK 4½ x 4½ AT HEELS. TO 3¼ x 3¼ AT HEADS. DOUBLE. SPACED 22" CENTRES.
SINGLE FRAMES AT ENDS 4½ x 4½ HEELS. TO 3¼ x 3¼ AT HEADS.
STEM & STERN POSTS 6½ SIDED. E. OAK
HANGING KNEES 2½ x 1 AT THROAT TO 2" x ½ AT POINTS.
EXTENSION
BILGE STRINGER TEAK 7 x 3
FASTENINGS REELED.
ALL OUTSIDE PLANK. TEAK 1⅝
GALV W.I. FLOORS 3/4 x 1⅜ THROATS TO 2¾ x ⅝" AT POINTS ARMS 36"
KELSON E. OAK 8½ x 12"
KELSON BOLTS. 12/16" STUD & NUTS
MAIN KEEL. E. ELM 6¼ x 1.6"
LEAD KEEL BOLTS. 1⅛" DELTA METAL

CONSTRUCTION SECTION, BETTY II.

Scale: ½ in. = 1 ft.

FIG 67

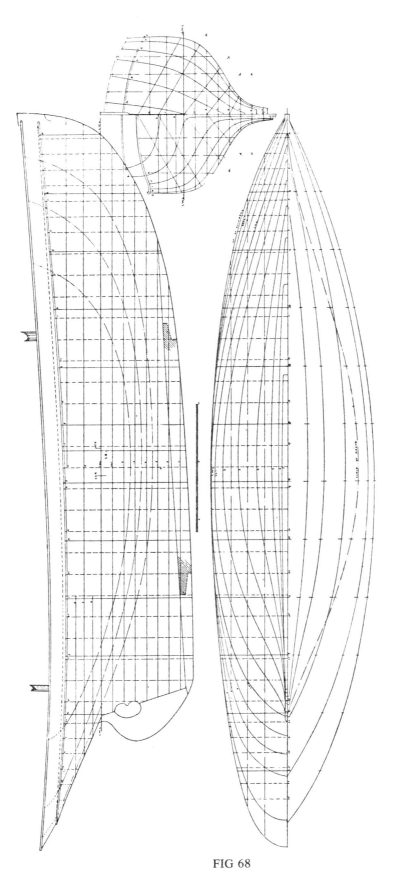

LINES OF THE AUXILIARY KETCH BETTY II, DESIGNED BY ALBERT STRANGE FOR MR. CHARLES HELLYER.

L.O.A., 63.75 ft.; L.W.L., 50.25 ft.; Beam, 13.5 ft.; Draught, 8.16 ft.

FIG 68

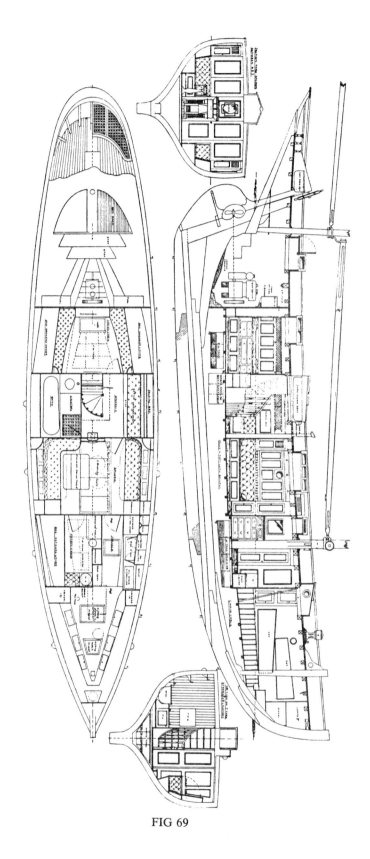

GENERAL ARRANGEMENT AND ACCOMMODATION PLANS OF THE AUXILIARY KETCH BETTY II.

FIG 69

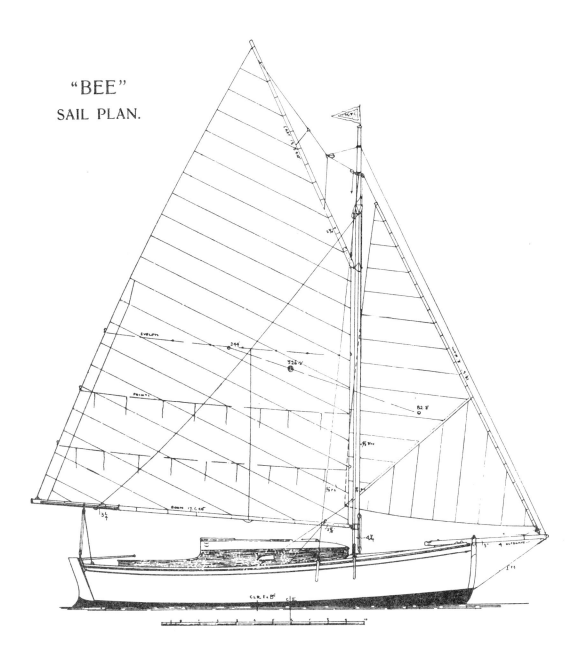

"BEE"
SAIL PLAN.

Bee (No 142/1914)

This small gaff sloop was designed by Strange for his own use, but was never built. Her after body is well formed but the forward body is too elongated and fine. The boat would lack power under the generous sail area of 327 sq ft and would be a handful for a single-hander, though the headsail furling arrangement is a gesture to ease handling. She would have been easier to sail as a cutter. It is doubtful that the peak halyard and span would set as drawn. A vertically sliding centreplate is shown with its case at the forward end of the cabin. This could be subject to damage in taking the ground as no lateral movement was allowed. It was no doubt so arranged to suit the accommodation layout.

FIG 70

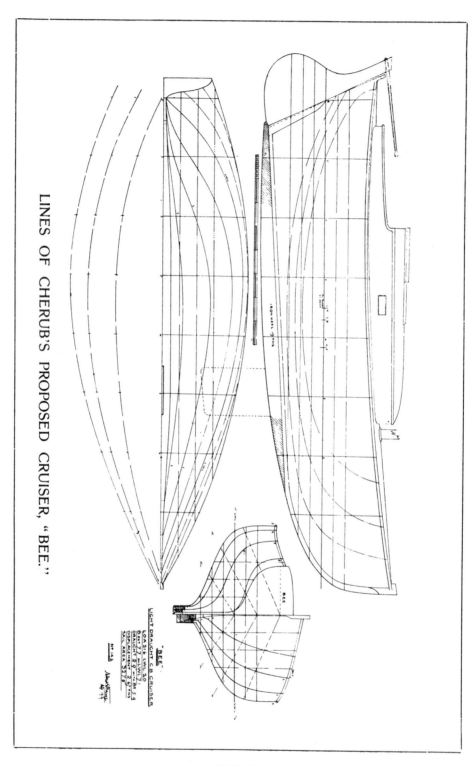

LINES OF CHERUB'S PROPOSED CRUISER, "BEE."

FIG 71

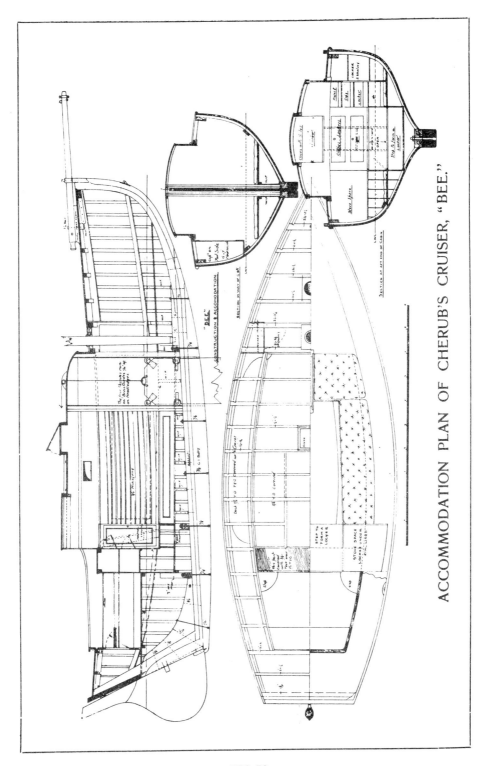

ACCOMMODATION PLAN OF CHERUB'S CRUISER, "BEE."

FIG 72

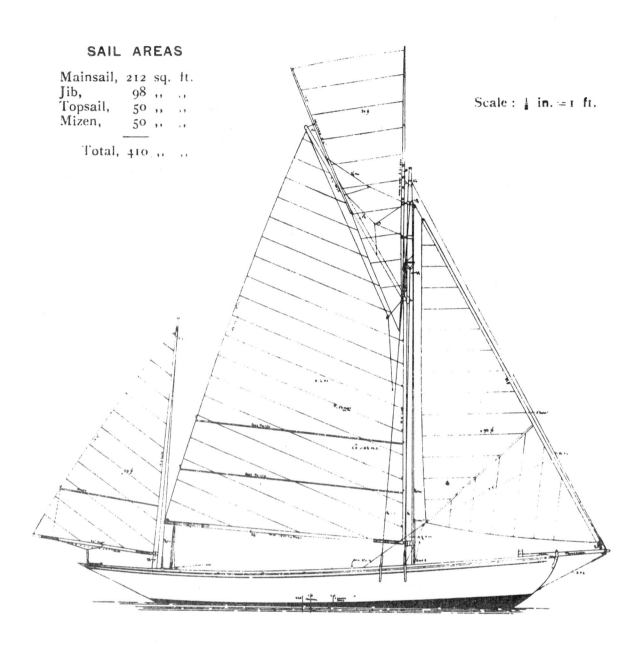

SAIL AREAS

Mainsail, 212 sq. ft.
Jib, 98 ,, ,,
Topsail, 50 ,, ,,
Mizen, 50 ,, ,,

Total, 410 ,, ,,

Scale : ⅛ in. = 1 ft.

4 ton Cruiser (Venture) (1917)

Strange thought this 4 ton yawl fit for extended cruising. The sail area was considered modest by contemporary standards and because of this the displacement was limited to 4.3 tons. The hull is interesting as it has a well proportioned counter stern which allows the mizzen to be sheeted to it. Despite the proposed use for offshore sailing Strange clung to a single headsail, relying on the integrity of bowsprit and bobstay to stay the mast longitudinally in whatever rough conditions might be faced. She would have been abler with 2 headsails and a forestay to the hounds. This design was incomplete at the time of Albert Strange's death.

FIG 73

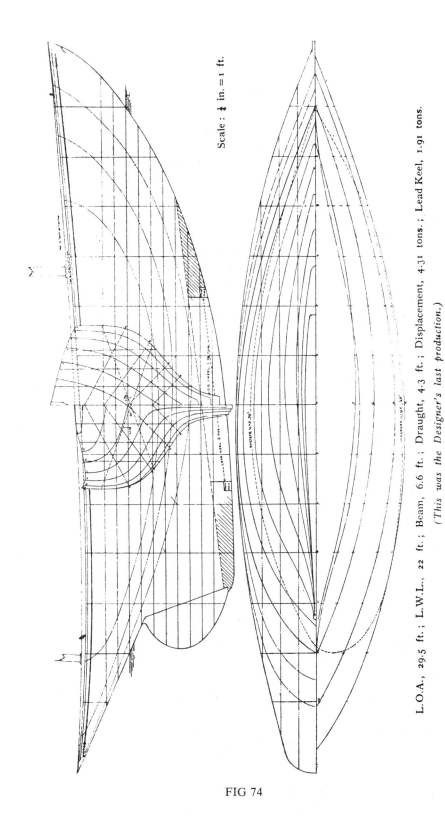

Scale : ¼ in. = 1 ft.

L.O.A., 29.5 ft.; L.W.L.. 22 ft.; Beam, 6.6 ft.; Draught, 4.3 ft.; Displacement, 4.31 tons.; Lead Keel, 1.91 tons.

(*This was the Designer's last production.*)

FIG 74

CHAPTER 11

Albert Strange as an Artist
by Tony Watts and Sheila Willis

It is perhaps inevitable that in this appreciation of Albert Strange he should be considered primarily as a marine artist. It is true that he painted landscape and townscape frequently and with facility, but it is the marine paintings that have the quality and immediacy that stem from an exceptional knowledge of and love for his subject. Perhaps more so than in any other field of art, marine painting poses many problems for the untutored artist. The sea is a fluid and restless element, subject to the ever changing play of light and is a real challenge to those who seek to represent it through painting. Similarly, the relationship of a vessel to the sea is complex, it is in and of the sea and not just upon it, and it is the ability to capture this that identifies the true artist and frequently also, if not the true sailor, then certainly one who has a real interest in, and love for the sea. Numerous marine artists have started out in life on board ship and the combination of familiarity, opportunity and of course talent, has produced the likes of Nicholas Pocock (1740-1820), George Chambers of Whitby (1803-1840), Captain Richard Beechy (1808-1895) and later Frank Mason (1876-1965) — Albert's pupil and friend. Time at sea is obviously not a necessary qualification for commendable marine painting but it is perhaps true to say that those with marine connections do produce work of a freedom and vitality which stems from an innate knowledge of the subject. As in much painting, what is left out of the composition is often as important as what is retained; to suggest rigging and blocks with a couple of brush strokes, rather than painting every detail, is often more effective and telling. Strange certainly had the knowledge and the ability to do this and although not by any means an Impressionist, his fluid and assured style marked him as a distinctive master of his art.

To put his work into context, it is perhaps initially helpful to reiterate briefly the history of British marine painting until his entry upon the scene and secondly, to evaluate his contemporaries and their effect on him and vice-versa.

It is generally accepted that marine painting in Britain as it is now recognised started with the arrival of two Dutchmen — Wilhem Van der Velde and his son (also Wilhem) in 1672. Fleeing from the invasion of Holland by Louis XIV, they were patronised by Charles II and gave impetus to what was at the time a somewhat dormant aspect of British painting, although there were of course artists at work, such as Isaac Sailmaker (1633-1721) in London and Francis Place (1647-1728) in Scarborough. Later, Samuel Scott (1701-1772), introduced a new direction into marine painting by including shorescapes and esturial scenes into 'sea' pictures, creating the English Tradition which has continued to the present day and J.M.W. Turner (1755-1851) revolutionised not only marine painting but the whole art establishment by his innovative technique and his use of vibrant colour and dramatic

St Valery

PLATE 4

BILL JAMES

Scarborough Harbour; Scottish fishing boats becalmed

PLATE 5

STEPHEN RILEY

perspective as components of his compositions. His influence was to affect most who followed him and his atmospheric portrayal of the sea, sky and ships introduced new elements into marine painting which hitherto had been excessively realistic.

One of several schools of painting that was not strongly influenced by Turner was that at Hull; John Ward (1798-1849), Thomas Binks (1799-1852), Thomas Brooks (1818-1892), Henry Redmore (1820-1887), William Settle and others were in the earlier tradition of ship and harbour painters and were exact in their attention to detail, perhaps only Redmore on occasion breaking the mould with more flamboyant essays.

Conversely, the Whitby/Scarborough School of the same period (more properly a part of the English School) which included George Chambers, H.B. Carter (1803-1868) and the Weatherill family, favoured the atmospheric effects of Turner and their seascapes and coastal subjects are wreathed in spray and mists and embody dramatic viewpoints and ethereal colours. One individual talent of this period, who was to have a lasting effect on marine painting out of all proportion to the span of his brief life, was Richard Parkes Bonington (1801-1828). His muted palette, impressionistic style and free brushwork brought a freshness and lightness that was to command widespread admiration, and it is obvious from a study of Strange's work that here is an influence that can be recognised and that he would no doubt have acknowledged. The same may be said in relation to the work of David Cox (1783-1854) of the Norwich School, whose simple treatment of fishing boats and the sea is exemplified in his *Entrance to Calais Harbour* of c. 1827 which both in composition and colour has similarities to Strange's many studies of the fishing fleet off Scarborough.

Near contemporaries of Albert (born 1855), included the influential Charles Napier Hemy (1841-1917), initially inspired by the Pre-Raphaelites, who developed an exact and individual style revelling in the use of strong colour and depicting coastal, river and fishing scenes; James McNeil Whistler (1834-1903), the flamboyant American, famous for his twilight and evening scenes or 'Nocturnes' as he described them; Atkinson Grimshaw (1836-1893), who went further than Whistler by painting many full moonlight pictures; William Lionel Wyllie (1851-1931) whose free watercolour style, dramatic compositions and strong lighting frequently included yacht subjects (as in his *Yachts at Anchor* c. 1900) and Philip Wilson Steer (1860-1942), perhaps the foremost Impressionist sea painter of his period.

Strange's move to Scarborough (1882) coincided with the establishment of schools of painting at Cockburnspath (1883), Staithes (1884) and Newlyn (1899) although Stanhope Forbes had painted at Newlyn with others as early as 1884. These schools were to popularise marine and coastal painting in a way that gave the genre a new impetus and style, significantly encouraging amateur painters whose numbers increased dramatically in late Victorian times. Many of Strange's friends and pupils became involved, particularly with the Staithes School, and the presence locally of such diverse talents as those of Frederick Mayall, Charles Mackey and Laura Knight, must have been an inspiration to the students of the Scarborough College of Art and their Headmaster.

The influences that contribute to an artist's style are many and varied; they involve time and place, tuition and experience, contemporaries and companions, and of course, fashion and history. Ability to some degree must be inherent, technique can be taught but technique without imagination and initiative is lifeless — it can produce paintings but not art. Albert Strange had but two years of formal tuition, first at a

Fishing boats beating to windward
PLATE 6

Berwick on Tweed
PLATE 7

local class in Gravesend and then at the Slade School before deciding that study and experience in France, the accepted mecca for aspiring artists, was the course he wished to follow and indeed he remained there for some five years, until 1880. Although there is no extensive record of his life in France, it is known that initially he lived on his boat and sailed along the coast of Brittany, an area beloved of the French Impressionists some of whom undoubtedly he must have met. The coast and coastal towns provided a rich source of material for his painting and it is likely that he supplemented his allowance from his father by the normal method of the impoverished student at that time — paying for the necessities of life with paintings and sketches. Two paintings from this time are in the Scarborough Art Gallery; *St Vulfrain Abbeville* (c. 1880) in an exceptionally mature traditional watercolour of the church in its setting, well composed, using strong colour and heavy shadow whilst *St Valery* (PLATE 4) is an equally assured atmospheric seascape, showing local craft under sail in calm waters off the port.

On his return from France, he was appointed Second Master of the Liverpool College of Art, a position he held for two years before the move to Scarborough and the Headship of the new School of Art in 1882. Although he had already exhibited his work at the Royal Society of British Artists and the Walker Gallery, Liverpool, this year was also to see his first acceptance at the Royal Academy (*Deserted* No 957) and this, at the age of 27 must have been the highlight of his career up to that time and an indication of recognition by the establishment of his professional talent. He was to exhibit ten paintings at the Royal Academy over a sixteen year period.

CRESCENT MUSEUMS SCARBOROUGH AND SCARBOROUGH ART GALLERY

W. Bevan   P. Hall   A. E. Horsley   F. Richardson   C. Wanless   H. Watson
H. Wanless   F. Appleyard   A. Strange   E. Edwards   F. Yewdale

Group portrait; School of Art, Scarborough – c.1900

PLATE 8

The herring fleet, Scarborough

PLATE 9

His appointment to the position of Head of the new Government School of Art in Scarborough (photograph, PLATE 8), indicates that he had gained a reputation as both artist and teacher and also that he had the confidence to accept the post; undoubtedly his artistic ability was not in question but to take on such a responsibility after only two years experience at Liverpool shows resolve of a high order. He must have matured quickly after the student life he himself had only just given up and perhaps his marriage to Julia in the same year was another significant factor. The curriculum of the School was extensive — as well as painting, sculpture and drawing, it reflected the current interest in arts and crafts, with graphic design, book illustration, wallpaper, furniture design and pottery all being included. Although his own bias was towards watercolour painting, at least two of his pupils became nationally known as painters in oils — Harry Watson and J. Henry Inskip. Other pupils included Frank Mason, whose strong colours and free manner of painting remained distinctive throughout his long life and Charles Pears (1873-1958), a 'Realist' painter of considerable repute and a founder member and first president of the Society of Marine Artists. With the success of his first acceptance at the Royal Academy, his own work was becoming more widely known and over the next few years was to become looser in character, more painterly and less graphic, although never fully accepting the tenets of the then currently fashionable Impressionists.

He combined in many of his sea pictures an accurate portrayal of a particular vessel and allied it to an atmospheric background and sky — it is as if the sailor in him could not accept that the suggestion of, say, the Scottish herring fleet off Scarborough, was enough, the boats had to be accurately shown whereas the lighthouse, quays and castle could be a simple but effective indication.

Scarborough fishing fleet
PLATE 10

STEPHEN RILEY

Dutch estuary scene
PLATE 11

To discuss his paintings chronologically is difficult, as many were undated, and to establish themes and changes in his work is virtually impossible as there is no comprehensive collection of his work in any one place — indeed the whereabouts of most of his output is unknown. The Art Gallery at Scarborough has some sixteen works, many of which are small sketches, presumably done for teaching purposes and the remainder of the known paintings are dispersed widely, as Appendix 3 shows. Given this situation it is only possible to generalise in attempting an assessment of his work as it is in considering his standing with, and relationship to, his contemporaries.

A frequently recurring subject was the fishing fleets so frequently seen at the time. The Scottish Fleet, following the herring, was an annual and colourful event at Scarborough, augmenting the numerous local craft. In *Scarborough Harbour: Scottish Fishing Boats Becalmed* (PLATE 5), the light and reflections are Turneresque in quality and the sense of calm and quiet tangible; the same subject painted in watercolour as an illustration for J. S. Fletcher's, PICTURESQUE HISTORY OF YORKSHIRE entitled *The Herring Fleet, Scarborough* (PLATE 9) is perhaps more typical with greater detail in the boats, movement in the water and the suggestion of activity in the harbour. *Scarborough Fishing Fleet*, watercolour, Bootham School Collection (PLATE 10) is reminiscent of Bonington's work as is *Fishing Boats*, watercolour, both paintings employing a subdued and restricted palette, the foreground vessels being strongly emphasised against a light background and the sea being painted freely and expressively.

Fishing Boats Beating To Windward, watercolour, Humber Yawl Club Collection (PLATE 6), is a dramatic study of heavy weather with the figures of the crew unusually forming in an essential part of the composition. *Huzzah Rocks*, watercolour, is another wild seascape with a foreground and distant rocks providing the interest and the reefed down yawl giving scale. These watercolours are all painted with great fluency and show an ability to paint the sea in all of its moods, capturing

Lake and trees
PLATE 12

DAISY on the Zuiderzee 1893

PLATE 13

either calm or storm with the minimum of brushwork and an enviable lightness of touch. Skies are generally achieved by the 'wet into wet' watercolour technique, are subservient to the seas and being light in tone, provide contrast to the darker hues of hulls and sails.

In the watercolour *Berwick-on-Tweed* 1888 (PLATE 7), the composition of boats, bridge and buildings is particularly assured and the handling of light and water achieved with that facility that was becoming the hallmark of his marine painting. The same quality is present in his landscape painting at this time and ensured that the sombre landscapes of Scotland that were a favourite subject were never dull, the browns and purples of bracken and heather always caught a shaft of light to make the colours glow and the surface of a loch would shimmer with the reflection of a luminous sky. *Entrance to Loch Carron*, watercolour, G. William Johnston Collection, has all these qualities as do the strongly painted watercolours in Bill James' Collection *Across Kilbrennan Sound* and *Ferry House and Pier, Loch Fyne*. In contrast, an untitled painting of a Lake and Trees (Chris Rowntree Collection PLATE 12), is a masterpiece of understatement, achieving considerable effect through careful composition, simple treatment and a restricted use of colour and *View from Across Fields* believed to have been painted as a demonstration at the School of Art in 30 minutes and now in the Scarborough Collection, is in the same vein.

Two sources of reference, and invaluable ones when the scarcity of his work is taken into account, are the Year Books of the Humber Yawl Club from 1892 to 1905 and issues of YACHTING MONTHLY from the early part of the century. The Year Books contain reproductions of watercolours, an oil painting and pen sketches illustrating contemporary cruises, and the quality of the work is such that with the exception of the pen sketches, they were probably painted for exhibition or by commission and only incidentally but conveniently used as illustrations. *Dutch Estuary Scene* (PLATE 11) and *Daisy on The Zuider Zee* (PLATE 13) both watercolours, are in the 1894 Book and refer to his cruise in Holland in 1893. The painting of DAISY in particular is full of life and movement and invokes the thrill of open boat sailing in boisterous conditions. The 1895 Book has *A Weighty Problem*, a narrative painting of an incident when CHERUB had to be manhandled around a defunct lock and *A Passing Squall – Grimsby* (PLATE 14), a limpid and atmospheric watercolour which to some extent romanticises the river and that port. The following year has an untitled watercolour of Fishing Boats off a Harbour signed in full and dated 1895, an unsigned watercolour *An Ocean Tramp* and *"Luff Boy", Cherub In a Heavy Squall off Walberswick* (PLATE 15), an oil painting of the highest quality which illustrates his mastery of that medium although his use of it was relatively infrequent. The drama in the painting is achieved by strong lighting, perspective and tonality and the subject, being caught in an unexpected heavy blow after a long passage, is familiar to all yachtsmen and evokes a feeling of sympathy for the crouching figure of the helmsman who is obviously wet and cold but who is driving his craft under a rag of sail to a safe haven. The Book of 1900 includes *North East Coast Sketches* to illustrate a brief North East Coast Pilot that he contributed that year, the sketches are pen and ink and interesting for showing the pilotage marks traditionally as silhouettes, yet also incorporating sketches of local craft.

The articles written for YACHTING MONTHLY are copiously illustrated with watercolours of the utmost fluency and highest quality and show incidents from the cruises described together with seascapes and landscapes. It is particularly noticeable in these later watercolours that the handling of the painting of the sea has a remarkable assurance and economy, resulting in a distinctive style which may fairly

A passing squall, Grimsby

PLATE 14

be said to have contributed significantly to the vocabulary of subsequent marine painting. References are readily identifiable in the work of Frank Mason, Harry Hudson Rodmell and others of the North-East Coast School. The articles reproduced earlier in this book include examples from this period which are representative; Appendix 3 shows how numerous these illustrations were.

Book illustration and graphic art were other facets of his talent although as with the paintings, evidence of his output is scarce. J.S. Fletcher's epic PICTURESQUE HISTORY OF YORKSHIRE mentioned earlier, employed many artists to illustrate its pages and Strange was commissioned to paint the coastal scenes. These paintings varied from full watercolours, including some moonlit scenes not unlike those produced contemporaneously by Atkinson Grimshaw, to light small scale wash sketches used at the beginning and end of chapters. For evidence of his interest and ability in graphic art, the Humber Yawl Club's Year Books are again a source of reference; from 1897 until 1917 he contributed cover designs, usually signed with his monogram and the abbreviation 'DEL & INV'. These designs make a fascinating study, as they give an insight into his interests and influences in a way that his paintings are unable to do. From the paintings we can see that with time, his fluency and competence increased but his style remained essentially the same throughout his career. The Impressionists, Realists and the distinctive styles of the various Schools throughout the country, passed him by or were discounted by him for his own reasons. This is not to say that there was no trace of their existence in his paintings but such influences as he absorbed were always subjugated to his own style. In the less demanding task of designing the HYC Year Book covers, however, he gave his imagination free rein and showed that he was fully aware of the 'modern' movements of the time and the popular fashion in graphic design. His first cover of 1897 is pure *Art Nouveau* (PLATE 16) with a reference to Beardsley in the black and white heading; the following year he incorporated photographs of the then club captain and of Hornsea Mere — one of the Club's waters at that time and in 1899, a photograph and watercolour sketches of the three bases of the Club — the Humber, Hornsea Mere and the River Hull. The covers for 1900, 1901 and 1902 are similar, in 1903 he produced an extremely traditional pen and ink cover showing a galleon with dolphins and stylised seaweed forms and 1904 had a sketch of a yawl with a classical architectural surround of pilasters and pediment.

1905 saw a return to *Art Nouveau*, this time with references to the linear quality of the pen work of Walter Crane and then he returned to tradition for four years until 1910 when he produced perhaps the most finely drawn cover the Book has ever seen — a mermaid blowing a conch shell horn (PLATE 17). A humorous cover design was that of 1914, where a baffled mariner contemplates his recalcitrant outboard motor whilst in 1915, Strange depicted a patriotic theme marking the onset of the Great War. His last contribution to the Year Book was the cover of 1917, the year of his death and it is some measure of his affection for the HYC and its unique publication, that even when unwell and surrounded by the troubles of world war, he found time to pen the cover. Miss Cole of Scarborough, one of his pupils, contributed many covers from 1919 onwards, as did his friends George Holmes and Robert Cole. The cover designs show that his knowledge of the arts and crafts movement, *Art Nouveau* and the illustrative styles of Beardsley and Crane was extensive and it interested him to apply them to the minor arts of graphics and design and it is perhaps surprising that there is not more of this influence in his painting.

Any attempt to classify or rate Albert Strange as an artist by reference to his peers, to the various Schools or by historical perspective is difficult and indeed

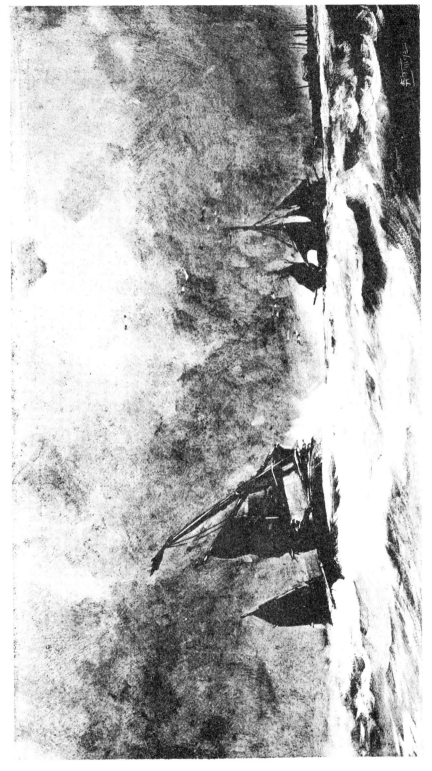

"LUFF BOY!" – CHERUB in a heavy squall off Walberswick

PLATE 15

perhaps unnecessary. There is no substantive collection of his work that may be viewed and assessed for chronological progression of talent and style and, of course, being resident in Scarborough, he was away from the mainstream of contemporary art. There is no literature, criticism or memoir that may be consulted, the paintings must speak for themselves and it may not be too fanciful to think that this is how he would have wished it from what we know of his own nature through his writing on seafaring matters where he was humorous, down-to-earth and essentially practical. Indeed it may have been sufficient for him to give pleasure to others through his paintings without concern for fashion or contemporary moods. He was undoubtedly an excellent painter, principally in watercolour, of marine subjects, who evolved a personal style early in life and then refined and developed it over many years to be as distinctive and easily recognisable as his other love and creation — the Canoe Yawl.

Humber Yawl Club Yearbook cover 1897

PLATE 16

Humber Yawl Club yearbook cover 1910

PLATE 17

Canoe Yawl SHEILA owned by Mike and Jane Burn

PLATE 18

JANE BURN

Canoe Yawl CHERUB III now REDWING owned by Jeremy Burnett

PLATE 19

L'ATELIER PHOTO, DOUARNENEZ

Counter Yawl FIREFLY owned by Jim Clay

PLATE 20

Canoe Yawl NIRVANA OF ARKLOW owned by Peter and Nancy Clay

PLATE 21

161

CHAPTER 12

Albert Strange — The Model Yachtsman and Canoeist
by Tony Watts

The design and sailing of model yachts in the late nineteenth century was both a widespread and serious pastime which was enjoyed equally by both amateur and professional sailors, and designers from 'real yachting' and those who restricted themselves to models. In 1882 there were but five model yacht clubs in the United Kingdom, by 1891 this number had grown to seventy two with the major centres of the sport such as London and Hull having several clubs each. Competition was the essence of the sport with nationally recognised classes and rules enabling Club and Inter Club racing to be held for significant and valuable trophies. Design development was continuous and designing to and within the rules produced as much controversy as in the full-scale sport, with frequent exchanges of polite but pointed letters in THE MODEL YACHTSMAN AND CANOEIST, THE FIELD and other journals as the adversaries argued their causes. Dixon Kemp, G.L. Watson and the eccentric Lieutenant Middleton were much interested as significantly was Strange, both as a prolific designer and as an enthusiastic sailor of model yachts. It is undoubtedly true that in the days before tank testing the construction and sailing of models was of considerable help to the naval architect and provided a relatively inexpensive way of trying out and developing new ideas in hull form and rig as well as of course, in self steering gear which was much advanced by the sport.

The classes generally sailed were to the '1730' Rule, 20 Tons, 15 Raters and 10 Raters which produced boats from 3 ft to 4 ft waterline length and from 20 lbs to 30 lbs displacement. Keen owners would have at least three suits of sails for light, medium and heavy airs and the rig was most often Gaff Cutter with top'sl but with many variations, including Bermudian Sloop and the carrying of spinnakers for downwind work. Steering downwind was a major problem and evoked much discussion: weighted rudders, counterbalanced rudders and tiller lines linked to main booms were all fashionable at times but boats running off their helm was a continual problem.

THE MODEL YACHTSMAN AND CANOEIST was the journal most devoted to the sport and carried details of the Clubs, matches, designs and a lively correspondence column. It was founded in Hull in 1884 and printed and published monthly by Thomas Grassam at 161 & 162 High Street with E. Marlborough & Co. of 51 Old Bailey being the London agents. The original price was twopence per copy but this rose to threepence with the 'enlarged series' of 1888. The magazine had separate editors for the model yachting and canoeing sections and George Holmes of the Humber Yawl Club became the canoeing editor in February 1891. Each section contained an editorial, 'Doings' of the Clubs' (the Humber Yawl Club retains this title in its Yearbook to this day), correspondence columns and usually one page of illustrations. Designing competitions were held and the magazine sought to act as a stimulus in matters of design development, rating and measurement, competition and social activity. It is thought that the paper was published for a period of some ten years but the only copies available at the time of writing are from 1885, 1888, 1891, 1892 and 1893.

Albert Strange was a founder member of the Scarborough Model Yacht Club which was formed in April 1887 with a Mr Sewell as promotor, Strange as Vice-Commodore and Robert Cole, his friend and fellow designer, as Secretary and with The Mere at Scarborough as the sailing water. The January 1888 edition of THE MODEL YACHTSMAN AND CANOEIST reported that "Saturday, December 3rd (1887) was extremely boisterous, insomuch that it prevented any match sailing, but it shewed the hard weather qualities of some of the craft, the waves almost making the spectators think that they were witnessing a regatta upon the sea. Our Vice-Commodore, Mr. Albert Strange, took the opportunity to launch his new model the 'Mischief,' rigged as a Bermudian Cutter; this model, over which great pains and care has been bestowed on her design, measures 36 l.w.l. × 8½, with 23¾ lbs lead on her keel. Sail area (fine weather suit) 2200 sq. inches. She is a taking looking craft, and on her trial trip under small suit proved a fast and powerful boat. A new development was noticed in her steering apparatus, which so far as that day was concerned was fully satisfactory, and if your readers care for details, Mr. Strange will place them at your service." 'Mischief' was to feature regularly as a winner in the coming seasons and was probably exhibited at the Scarborough MYC Exhibition held in the Town Hall on February 8th and 9th 1888, an event opened by the Mayor and supported by the MP, Joshua Rowntree where upwards of 100 models were presented to public view, including several from the Manchester and Hull Clubs. THE SCARBOROUGH GAZETTE particularly noted that "those models of Messrs H. Sewell, A. Strange, R. Cole . . . of the Scarborough Club are worthy of special mention."

Apart from active participation in building and sailing models Strange, who at this time was sailing CHERUB, was most interested in the two questions that preoccupied model yachtsmen at the time, models running off their helms and rating and measurement. Both were covered in his letter to THE MODEL YACHTSMAN AND CANOEIST in April 1888.

The Editor, *The Model-Yachtsman.*

Dear Sir,—The very able correspondence that has been kindly published by you has doubtless done very much to clear up the vexed question of "running off." Some of the causes are now fully known, and can be avoided by us when designing future racers. But I venture to think there are one or two points that do not seem to have been dwelt upon sufficiently by your correspondents, and I beg leave to point out those that seem to me to produce or aggravate the evil:—In the first place, if a model be sailed to windward with a weighted rudder, although she may sail truly enough at a slight angle of heel, she will very likely run off if buried by a puff, because as she lays down and loses way the rudder drops to leeward and finishes the matter by running her off. I think it a good rule that no boat should be sailed close hauled with a weighted rudder, although to my knowledge many are so sailed, and do pretty well until pressed. If the boat will not balance on a wind without lee helm she should have more head sail. Again, a low cut clew to the mainsail is a great evil, generally causing a model to run off because the boom sail drags to leeward when the boat heels, and in any case causing an immense loss of speed. The boom should always be kept well up, very much higher than seems at first yachtlike, and if the mainsail can be kept out of the water, it helps all the more to keep the boats' head up to windward. Too much sheer to the deck is another cause of running off, especially when combined with a low freeboard and high bulwarks, when heeled the water heads up on the after part of the deck, and is quite as bad as heavy quarters, or worse; because heavy quarters give great stability although not good for speed. Finally I am convinced that a very large proportion of models are over burdened with lead and sails. As you have often pointed out, moderation in these respects is eminently conducive to success, and the little "Flying Cloud" exhibited in our late exhibition, and illustrated in your last month's issue, is a proof to this effect. When models are sailed on large exposed pieces of water like our own (of 7 acres) they want to be of good displacement to hold their own to windward in anything like a breeze, but a heavy boat overdone with sail is worse even in this case than a lighter one lightly canvassed. Sails should never be reefed, it ruins them in the matter of setting flat, separate suits should be provided for different strengths of wind, and if the boat is rigged in simple manner a fresh suit can be set quicker than a reef can be taken in, and the boat can thus always be properly balanced, and sailed fairly upright, I am sure this will be found to pay in the long run. The "1730" rule has a good deal to do with boats being failures, because men naturally wish to get the greatest speed from the greatest length, this, the rule (in models anyway) prevents because so much has to be sacrificed to gain the length—For 10-ton models 38½ l.w.l. is about the limit of safe length, and certainly makes a handy sized boat easy to carry about, and large enough to give good sport. In drawing this lengthy communication to a close, I should like the opinion of yourself or your readers as to the advantages or disadvantages of adopting a rule by length on l.w.l., breadth and mean depth combined not to exceed one-half or say, ·6 of l.w.l. length, but in any proportions. If, for instance, a 36in. class were established, a man would have a large choice of dimensions as to beam or depth, as a little calculation will soon show. The merits of the rule seems to me to be simplicity and elasticity, and it does away with the exceedingly unsatisfactory measurement of sail area, which would be one continual bone of contention if ever the length and sail area rule were adopted by clubs. I think it would prevent the "monstrosities" engendered by a length rule pure and simple, but it may conceal dangers and evils that have escaped the notice of him who introduces it, and if so, they will soon be pointed out by your readers. Nobody loves the "1730" rule very much, and we are all looking for something simpler and more rational, now the Y.R.A. has come to its senses.

Faithfully yours,

ALBERT STRANGE.

This evoked a response from the Editor in the same edition.

[Respecting the establishing of a 36-inch class, with beam and depth taxed as suggested, our opinion is that it is unnecessary, that it would be no improvement on what we have, and that it would be impossible to introduce it. Our correspondent's opinion that the introduction of such a class would give a large choice of dimensions, would be correct in the beginning, but wrong in the end, as it would after reasonable experience become known exactly what amount of beam and draught was the best for 36 inches of length, and there is little room to doubt that 18 inches of allowance for beam and depth would result in 9½ inches beam and 8½ inches of depth and this would mean a length class. We may further point out that the 1730 rule was adopted as the only one that could be carried through for adoption by all; that in Model Yachts it allows very considerable scope for variety; and that the end of its possibilities have not as yet been reached. Further than this it is questionable if variety in yachts is the only desideratum. Model Sailers often attribute their defeat to their boats, when in reality it is their want of care and attention in sailing them. Ultimately, no doubt we shall have to follow the yachts in matters of classification, and it is best for many reasons that we should do so. Some simple form of applying the sail-area rule is however wanted before we can with any hope of success, recommend its adoption, and until this is evolved we may well perfect those classes we have, and no doubt shall prove that the 1730 rule is not so bad as represented, and with a slight modification could have been continued in force with every prospect of success for yachting.—ED]

A further letter from Strange in June 1888:—

MEASUREMENT.

THE EDITOR, *The Model-Yachtsman.*

Dear Sir.—I am gratified to find that my suggestion as to the measurement of model yachts was found worthy of comment by you, although that comment was unfavourable—in fact, rather crushing. The objections you urge seem to me to be founded on the assumed impossibility of getting the clubs to take it up, rather than to any inherent fault in the rule, which on your own showing would tend to produce boats of about four beams to length, which is exactly about the Length and Sail Area rule is producing, and will continue to produce. Boats of these proportions can scarcely be called length class boats as the term is understood on the Solent and in other places, for the ordinary length rule allows unlimited beam and depth. If the sail area rule be taken up by model yacht clubs I foresee immense difficulty, and constant measurement, for sails can be easily altered and enlarged, whilst hulls are not so readily manipulated and as difficulties have already arisen with the large yachts in the matter of measurement of spars and sails, what may one expect with models? Every rule tends to produce a particular type of boat, the 1730 included, only the 1730 happily from the absurdity of the type it fostered brought about its own destruction. The rule that I suggest tends towards the production of a hull that can carry sail well without undue depth, and is also one that gives wide variety of midship section, rake of keel, and depth, but does not allow one to obtain an increase of speed in the easiest manner, *i.e.* by increase of length. I do not think it can be fairly said that the '1730' rule gives one much chance of variety, except the old vicious one that proved its ruin. "A little more length, a little more depth, and a little more lead." I am looking forward to the comments of my brother model-yachtsmen, and meanwhile, I should like to add a little table of yachts, which I have compiled from Dixon Kemp's "Yacht and Boat Sailing," and which I think goes far to prove how near a shot I have made at the results that are in actual practice in some of the best types of real yachts, under all sorts of rules. In it you will see that length class boats pure and simple are "out of it" hopelessly.

Name of Yacht.	Length.	Beam.		Mean Depth.		Total B. & Mean D.	
	ft.	ft.	in.	ft.	in.	ft.	in.
"Constance"	27	5	11½	6	6	12	5½
Itchen boat "Keepsake"	30	9	8	9	0	18	8
Mr. Long's design, Itchen Boat.	30	7	0	9	0	16	0
"Buccaneer"	34·2	10	0	7	3	17	3
"Snarley Yow" (3-ton)	28	4	10	8	0	12	10
"Amy" (2-ton)	21·6	4	11¾	5	6	10	5¾

Observe in these last two beam type of boat, that my rule would give them just the extra allowance in the matter of beam, that would convert them into wholesome craft—and also, how the wide and deep "Keepsake" would have to pare down somewhere to compete with reasonable boats on fair terms. The prettiest and most satisfactory boat in the lot, the "Buccaneer," fits the rule to a few inches.—*Verb. Sap:*—There seems to be something about the rating of yachts that tends to the production of undue length both in letters and boats. I ask your indulgence, as well as that of your readers, on the ground that I am doing my best to bring about a fairer system of measurement, and consequently perfect unanimity on this point amongst model-yachtsmen.

Faithfully yours, ALBERT STRANGE.

P.S.—By "mean depth" of course I mean depth of *hull and keel*, not *draught.*

A partial retraction by the Editor followed:—

[It appears we mistook the meaning of the word *depth* in our note to Mr. Strange's letter in the April number, which caused us to give an erroneous estimate of the beam and draught that would be taken. The correction alters our opinion, and we think a good class of boats could be built under such a rule, but our opinion on the other points remain the same. We can assure our correspondent that the '1730' rule could not have been brought into universal use if it had not been the rule of measurement of the yachts, and we shall never be able to accomplish uniformity in another classification unless any alteration steers in the same direction. It is too early yet to say what the sail-area rule will produce. In speaking of length class boats we meant not the Solent lengthers but models, the most successful of which are not above 4 beams.—ED.]

This correspondence was continued at intervals with others contributing but apparently reaching no firm conclusion although allowing Albert to exercise his not inconsiderable wit and humour in print. Such good spirit and charitable debate was not always present in the correspondence columns of the journal, however, especially where Lieutenant Middleton was concerned. Middleton had been inspired by Rob Roy Macgregor's voyages to purchase the KATE, a craft similar to the Yawl ROB ROY in which to circumnavigate England and then write of his experiences in 'The Cruise of the Kate'. He also wrote and advertised widely 'Middleton's Yacht Books' which included 'Choice Winning Proportions for Racing Yachts' at 5/- supported by the claim 'Middleton's Yachts are all Aristocrats'; 'Sail Tons' at 2/6 and 'Cubic Yacht Measurement' at 3/6, all available from the good Lieutenant at Cosy Nook, Eastwood, Essex. That Strange was not over-impressed by the arguments of this particular theorist is evident by his letter of January 1891:—

THE EDITOR, *The Model-Yachtsman.*

DEAR SIR,—Will you allow me a small space in your journal to enter a protest against what Lieut. Middleton is pleased to call his "patient advocacy of pure tonnage and fair sailing."

To describe Red and Green's interesting letter in such terms as "unblushing stupidity of the most profound kind," an "advocacy of unfair sailing knowing it to be unfair," and to brand the *Falcon* as a "swindling vessel" when she was designed, built, and races under exactly the same rule as her competitors were, seems to me to be if not ridiculous—at least extremely impertinent.

Any sane person can see at once that there is nothing unfair in Red and Green taking all the advantages that the 1730 rule gives, even if his competitors refuse to do so. The rule may be bad, but the obvious fact that it has been adopted by the club to which Red and Green belongs seems to have been entirely overlooked by Lieut. Middleton.

From the occasional letters this gentleman has contributed to your paper it is not at all difficult to gather that he knows very little about Model Yachting, and were it not from the fact that he has published in "The Cruise of the Katie" a very interesting account of a single handed cruise round England, in which voyage he displayed what some people would call great pluck, (and what other people would describe very differently); I should find it difficult to believe that he was a yacht sailor, and it is evident that he does not understand the difficulties a man undertakes when he builds and races an extreme 1730 model. Practical Model Yachtsmen *do* know and require no information from him or me on this point.

As for Lieut. Middleton's panacea—"Cubical Yacht Measurement" it has long since been examined and almost contemptuously condemned by the yachting editor of *The Field* in a review which appeared in that paper on Oct. 30th, 1886. A rule which increases the *cubical* tonnage of a yacht like 'Mayflower' from 91·73 tons with her centreboard *stowed,* to 155·25 with it *down* seems to me to merit contempt, and to be many times worse than even the much abused "1730."

I have not the pleasure of Red and Green's acquaintance, but I cannot stand by without a word of protest and see a brother Model Yachtsman abused for making public his experiences of long narrow tonnage craft. Such letters are valuable contributions and are so much useful knowledge made public, but I fancy very few people will describe Lieut. Middleton's letter as such, or consider it at all likely to advance the cause of Model Yachting.

Very truly yours,

Overbeck, Scarbro'.   ALBERT STRANGE.

Needless to say, a spirited response to both 'Red & Green' and Strange was penned, the unfortunate 'Red & Green' bearing the brunt of the attack and Albert being dismissed in the last two paragraphs by the modest Lieutenant:—

No other rules but mine will admit of this precision on the proportions, and my book *"Choice winning proportions"* was purposely written out in decimals of a ton in order to shew this *wonderful force and precision in the rules* themselves, and at the same time I also shewed how easy it may become to race in decimals of a ton. Your correspondent from Scarboro cannot have read these books nor yet the second edition of the Kate, or he would be better informed.

His letter is full of inaccuracies even to his remark about the *Field* newspaper. The criticism in the *Field* was on sail tons, and not on cubic yacht measurement.

I am, faithfully,

Eastwood, Essex,   E. MIDDLETON,

Jany. 16th, 1891.

This correspondence continued over a considerable period at infrequent intervals but with no lessening of passion on either side. Middleton's formula for rating measurement was L × B × D divided by 285 and it was particularly this figure of 285 that was regarded as divine by its proponent and with contempt by Strange. In December 1892 he wrote:—

THE EDITOR, *The Model-Yachtsman.*

DEAR SIR,—I am very sorry to have caused our Lieut. some months of anxiety, and hasten to oblige him with a calm and unbiased opinion on his rule of measurement, the principle of which he was rash enough to explain in your June issue of this year.

And later in that same letter:—

No, thank you, Lieut. Middleton. I am not taking any of this "magical divisor 285" rule to-day.

When I read the remonstrance from the author of the 285 rule in the November issue of the *M. Y. & C.* I was somehow reminded (goodness only knows why, for there is not the remotest connection with the subject under discussion) of an event of my boyhood's days, which, with your permission, Sir, I will relate.

We had, amongst other household goods, a wonderful parrot, which had been brought home and presented to us by a sailor uncle. This parrot could say almost anything, and was, moreover, very proficient in swearing in several languages. Consequently it was usually removed from the room during family prayers. One evening, however, he was forgotten, and remained in the room silent and unobserved, until my father happened to make a longer pause than usual in the course of the devotions. The parrot, impatient I suppose at the silence, remarked in a rather loud voice. "Heave ahead, shipmate," which caused a titter to go round the family assembled. My father rather angrily said to me "Remove that bird." As I was leaving the room, struggling with suppressed laughter and the cage, Poll observed, "D——n my eyes! sorry I spoke."

Yours, (and the Lieut.'s) very truly,
ALBERT STRANGE.

The matter was still prompting Strange to put pen to paper in February 1893:—

THE EDITOR, *The Model-Yachtsman.*

DEAR SIR,—I have no desire to occupy your valuable space in slaying the slain, but I must say our Lieut. seems singularly ungrateful. After complaining that his letters are unnoticed, and after a sincere effort on my part to remove this complaint, he turns to, and accuses poor me of perversity, because I find I am unable, even with the extremely slender stock of mathematical knowledge he credits me with, to swallow his "magical divisor 285 rule."

Contradictions, however vehement, are not usually considered good evidence, and our Lieut. seems quite unable to *disprove* what I point out as the inevitable tendencies of his magical rule. And, as he displays such colossal ignorance of the meaning of the word displacement, and of the elements and objects of designing; to say nothing of the exceedingly astonishing assertions as to the *result* of an increased divisor on the same formula, made in the last paragraph of his letter, I feel that it will be better in future to leave the Lieut. and his "only formula" to occupy that obscurity which so much annoys him, and thus leave your pages free for the ventilation of more practicable suggestions.

Yours faithfully,
ALBERT STRANGE.

Perhaps we should leave "our Lieut" so consigned.

To revert to the building and sailing of models rather than the theory and return to 1888 when, following the successful Exhibition held in Scarborough, the Model Yacht Club continued its programme on The Mere with races on Easter Saturday and Monday reported fully in THE MODEL YACHTSMAN AND CANOEIST:—

Scarboro' M.Y.C.—Saturday, March 31st, was devoted to a 3 ft. length class race, 4 boats only competing, 'Sprite,' Mr. Benton (a new model); 'Mischief,' Mr. A. Strange; 'Alice,' Mr. Luscombe; and 'Pass-by,' Mr. Sellers. Four runs were sailed, two to windward and two to leeward. First beat to windward 'Mischief' came in well ahead of 'Sprite,' which in the run back gained considerably and came in first, 'Pass-by' second, 'Mischief' third. In the next beat-to-windward 'Sprite' first, 'Mischief' close astern, this was as pretty a beat as has yet been seen on the Mere. The race was closely sailed throughout in a fresh breeze. Score—'Sprite,' 2 3 3 3; 'Mischief,' 3 1 2 2; 'Pass-by,' 1 2 0 1; 'Alice,' 1. On Easter Monday, the first 10-ton race of the season, for a silver cup, was sailed in half a gale, which rendered sailing somewhat exciting. Ten models raised their fighting colours—'Iris,' Mr. M.J. Spyer; 'Pass-by,' Mr. Sellers; 'Sprite,' Mr. Benton; 'Mischief,' Mr. A. Strange; 'Albatross,' Mr. R. Cole; 'Eva,' Mr. Thompson; 'Genesta,' Mr. D. Maynard; 'Fancy,' Mr. F. Goodwill; 'Alice,' Mr. Luscombe; and

'Lively,' Mr. Simpson. But only some of these managed to score, for a young sea curled and broke all over the Mere, causing many of the wee craft to labour heavily. Four runs were sailed, two to windward and two to leeward. The 'Iris' distinguished herself under a snug trysail and small jib, she pegged well to windward, winning both beats, one in spite of a foul at the start. The 'Pass-by' showed good speed and weatherly qualities, and the 'Genesta' went with something like her old form, though like some others, carrying too much canvas. The race was watched with much interest by a large number of spectators who stayed until the close in spite of a heavy snow squall in the middle of the match. Score—'Iris' 8, 'Pass-by' 6, 'Albatross' 3, 'Genesta' 3, 'Eva' 2, 'Mischief' 2. The second race of 10-tonners, for the cup, took place on Saturday, April 7th. Twelve boats started, consequently it was decided to race in two heats to avoid fouling. In a nice moderate breeze the 'Atalanta' and 'Pass-by' took the lead in their respective heats, which they maintained in the final with 'Iris' following. The 'Atalanta,' owing to being over measurement, was disqualified, the result being 'Pass-by' first, 'Iris' second. On Tuesday night, April 17th, we had an interesting social gathering, at the London Inn Coffee House. Mr. Henry Sewell, commodore, presided, and there was a large attendance of members and friends. During the evening Mr. Albert Strange, vice-commodore, gave a practical address on the preliminary stages of model yacht drafting, throwing out in his lucid manner several valuable suggestions which met with hearty approval. Several songs, &c., followed, given in capital style, and refreshments were provided, the company spending a highly enjoyable as well as an instructive evening.

In June 1888, The First Annual Inter-Club Match for the East Coast Challenge Shield took place on the Kingston Model Yacht Club Lake in Hull, with teams from the Kingston and Albert Clubs in Hull and from Boston and Scarborough. The visiting teams were met at the railway station by wagonettes and conveyed to the Lakeside where unfortunately they were met by the lightest of airs but nevertheless a keen match ensued with Albert Strange and MISCHIEF being one of Scarborough's representatives. This was not to be his or his Club's day however, and eventually the Home Club triumphed. In October, the Scarborough MYC held their First Annual Meeting for the distribution of prizes and their second Social Evening at the London Inn Coffee House in Scarborough and it was reported in THE MODEL YACHTSMAN AND CANOEIST of December 1888:—

In the early part of the meeting Mr Albert Strange (Vice-Commodore) continued the second of his very interesting and valuable practical lectures on "The designing of vessels," illustrated by diagrams and models, which were much appreciated by the audience. He showed the various drawings necessary for designing any vessel, and pointed out the variations in shape required to perform different kinds of service, so as to obtain a vessel perfectly adapted for the work it might be required to do.

Albert also featured as a prize winner taking first place in the 3 ft Class with MISCHIEF and as a contributor by donating a painting as the prize for the 3 ft 6 in Class and then giving "an amusing description of a trip made recently to Holy Island in his small yacht CHERUB". To bring the evening to an end, Mr R. Cole sang an original composition "Our Model Yacht Club" accompanied by Messrs Hill and Strange. Albert's energy and enthusiasm for the Club are patently obvious and were confirmed at a meeting in December 1890 when he gave a lecture to the Club on the recently introduced Rating measurement taking the 15 Rater as the example and illustrating his talk with diagrams chalked on a blackboard. The lecture was followed by entertainment to which he contributed and he also collected the First Prize for the

10 ton Class with JULIA — surely named for his wife. Once again he gave an oil-painting, this time as the prize for the 4 ft length Class. At the AGM of the Club on 12th February 1891, Albert exhibited his new model of a 15 Rater DOLLIE and it was reported that "her graceful symmetry and splendid finish was the admiration of all".

In April 1891, THE MODEL YACHTSMAN AND CANOEIST announced the result of The Bruce Prize Designing Competition, judged by Ardagh E. Long of Jarrow on Tyne who, from the numerous entries, awarded the First Prize to Strange. Long's adjudication read:—

Cupid, 44in. × 6.·7in. × 9·4in. 25 lbs. (First Prize).

This design is a well worked out attempt to get the advantages of a long 10-tonner with a moderate displacement. The full entrance and clean tail are both conducive to steadiness, and the craft would probably prove a fairly easy vessel to handle. The fullness of the extreme fore-end of the entrance is however somewhat overdone and a *slight* reduction might with advantage be made. An increase of ¼ of an inch depth to the keel amidships, leaving the ends as they are, would both improve the stability and the appearance. With these trifling alterations the boat should prove a formidable competitor in good breezes, especially to windward. The drawings require a little fairing, and are in parts rather roughly finished, but the style is good. The lines of CUPID are shown on Page 171 (FIG 75).

The season of 1891 commenced with racing on The Mere on March 21st:—

Fourteen 10-tonners came to their starting flags. A strong northerly wind of second suit strength tested the hard weather capacity of the craft, and some keenly contested events afforded a capital afternoon's sport. The chief scoring lay with 'Snowdrop,' G. Bolder (new) 42 × 7, 29 lbs displacement, 'Julia,' A. Strange, 42 × 7, 24 lbs., 'Annie,' J. Frank (Lug) 38½ × 8, 16 lbs., and 'Sprite,' E. Benton (Lug) 36 × 8½—each made the maximum of 6 points each. 'Terror,' W. Robson, 38½ × 8, 'Freedom', R. Andrews, 38½ × 8, and 'Arrow,' D. Maynard (new) 41½ × 7, each made 5 points. 'Julia,' A. Strange, holds the cup for this year, and her owner has made a good start to keep it.

The season continued with Inter-Club Challenge Matches at Bradford on Easter Monday where Albert was in the points but not a winner and at Hull on Whit Monday on the water of the Kingston Club for the East Coast Challenge Shield, a perpetual trophy previously won by The Kingston Club (1888), Scarborough (1889) and Kingston again in 1890. On this occasion the winners were the East Hull Club and after the match, "Mr Albert Strange, Vice-Commodore of the Scarborough Club, paid a graceful tribute to the ladies in the entertainment department". In September, THE MODEL YACHTSMAN AND CANOEIST initiated another design competition for 15 Raters, with the Naval Architect G.L. Watson as the Judge and Albert contributing to the prize fund. In the same month he also acted as Starter in a

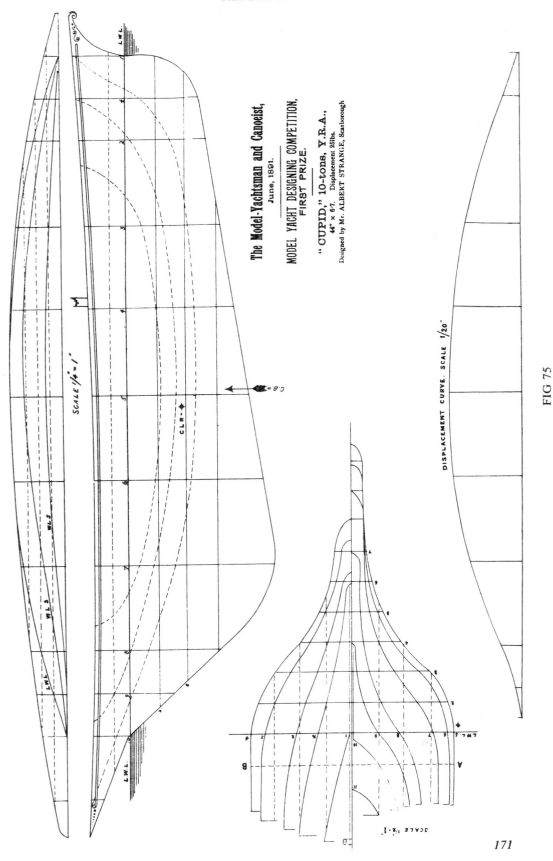

The Model-Yachtsman and Canoeist,
June, 1891.

MODEL YACHT DESIGNING COMPETITION,
FIRST PRIZE.

"CUPID," 10-tons, Y.R.A.,
44" x 6.7.   Displacement 25lbs.
Designed by Mr. ALBERT STRANGE, Scarborough

DISPLACEMENT CURVE. SCALE 1/20"

FIG 75

match between Scarborough and The Albert Model Yacht Club of Hull. In January of 1892 he spoke to the Royal Yorkshire Yacht Club on "Single Handed Cruisers and Cruising" and in the audience was George Holmes, who by this time was the editor of the canoeing section of THE MODEL YACHTSMAN AND CANOEIST and who reported the lecture in his editorial in the February edition of the magazine — it was also reprinted in THE YACHTSMAN at the time. April saw his election as Commodore of the Scarborough MYC and later that month the entry of CUPID in a race for 10 Tonners. She was built to the design that had won the Bruce Prize and he wrote of her that she "had satisfied him in every respect as to her build, fittings and finish, and that he has tried her as a very fast and weatherly boat in a strong breeze, albeit one that would require careful handling". On her first outing she gained maximum points.

It would appear that George Holmes invited or persuaded his friend to contribute to the canoeing section of THE MODEL YACHTSMAN AND CANOEIST as in the November and December issues he wrote the following:—

CANOE-YAWL OR CANOE-YACHT.

It has been pretty freely stated by men who ought to know, that in England, at any rate, the canoe-yawl is destined to increase and multiply, and the canoe proper is doomed, for the purposes of cruising. Many, who formerly were keen canoeists, have gone in for larger ships, and many, who never were canoeists at all are joining the ranks of those who either don't want, or can't afford a bigger craft than will carry themselves and their duffle around the coasts, or in and out of rivers and creeks during the summer and autumn; or at least during the months when, in our curious collection of samples of weather miscalled a climate, these seasons are supposed to be.

So far, only one account ('Deva's') of a voyage performed in a canoe-yawl proper, that is, one coming within the definitions of the R.C.C., has appeared — and that was an exceedingly curt log — merely giving a summary of events and dates (none the less valuable on that account, as a record) but unsatisfying in that no *opinions* are expressed as to the suitability or otherwise of the size of craft used on this occasion, as a river and estuary cruiser; nor any evidence to show that the authorized type of canoe-yawl — *i.e.* simply an enlarged canoe — is sufficiently commodious, handy, and comfortable for the purpose of a lengthy cruise.

Indeed, one glimpse was given of the great disadvantage of a tent, in a moment of emergency, which might have resulted seriously.

No instances of portage, running ashore to escape a dangerous sea, or of transportation by cart or rail, are mentioned; and we are left in ignorance on some of the most important points urged in favour of the R.C.C. type.

Speed and power are noted on one occasion in weather that seemed too much for an open boat of much larger dimensions. But there are open boats, and open boats, and it is now acknowledged that if extreme speed is desired, most other things pertaining to comfort or security have to be sacrificed in a canoe-yawl.

At any rate it is conceded by all hands that an absolutely open boat is an undesirable thing to cruise in, whilst at the same time a canoe-yawl of equal power and speed, is infinitely better adapted for cruising in safety, and can be built for little or no more than the cost of an open craft.

But, taking the tent episode, there seems enough to moralize on there. A dark night, a strong wind and tide, and an iron cable sawing across one's bilge, whilst the cruiser is vainly endeavouring to get on deck and see what is the matter. This does not form an enticing picture. I happen to know what a nasty spot Burnham River is to bring up in, with half a gale blowing right through, and all the oyster fleet riding just astern of one, and my sincere sympathy went out to 'Deva' when I read his short account of this event, and there rose to my mind my own unsatisfactory experiences with tents before I abolished them as unnecessary evils.

I remembered the misery experienced one night in Sea Reach, after a beat up as far as the Mucking Light, when, tired and wet, hungry and cold, I started to erect a close reefed tent in the dusk at anchor over on the Mucking Flats. Do you think that tent would permit me to erect it properly, or that the boat would ride comfortably or securely when it *was* up? no, not a bit of it, so that I finally cursed tents, and took the whole thing down, and ran back to Hole Haven, there to get something at the "Pub" and afterwards to roll my tired carcase up in the tent, and get what sleep I could that way.

Another time, in the Medway, do I remember a sudden breeze in the middle watch, when brought up just above the bridge at Rochester, having to turn out and lower the whole thing down to save being blown from my anchor, and again was sleep murdered and rheumatism involved, by that horrible institution the tent; while I wondered whether the authorities who so strongly recommend these abominations had ever experienced such games as these at its hands, to say nothing of the revilings and chaff of the barges and bawley boats at "that there (adjective adjective) horse marine's affair." But they were right, although blasphemous. It *was* a "horse marine affair" when it went cruising on open rivers, and stayed out all night on the bosom of the deep. And so I decided to have no more to do with tents, but to have something substantial, if no bigger than a rabbit hutch, wherein to creep at night.

Was it the tent, that drove poor 'Dragon' from under the land at Winterton, and on top of Hasborough sands? And was it not one of those instances in which my dear namesake was keeping his weather eye open, and fulfilling his duty of "sitting aloft to look after the life of poor Jack" by bringing that fortunate smack along in time to save the crew?

In the good old far off days of my youth, I owned something very like a large disreputable sort of canoe-yawl, certainly not a canoe-yacht. — she had been a whitebait boat in *her* far off youth. In her I wandered about Thames and Medway, Swin and Swale, mostly alone, and always to the extreme astonishment of the solitary coastguards who now and then came alongside at Hole Haven, Harty Ferry, or elsewhere.

This "packet," as the bawleymen called her, carried me two or three thousand miles during my ownership of her. Her first state with me, was the half decked state, with coamings — and a tent. — After one season she blossomed out into a "cabin," built on to the coamings by myself at a very minimum of expense; and, by the aid of a "tip" from a sailor uncle, sported a new suit of sails, sprit mainsail, foresail, and mizen, (cost £3 10!) and in this guise she gave me for years, more solid, complete, and unadulterated happiness than falls to the lot of many more ambitious yachtsmen. (See FIG 3.)

It is true the cabin was only 3 feet high at most, and not more than 6 feet long, and not particularly beautiful. But, as a merciful providence has fashioned me on the 3 beam model, (and not much length at that,) I could eat, sleep, and rest in that small space, as comfortably as if it had been a good deal bigger, and many a score of happy nights have I spent on the old 'Dauntless,' as she was somewhat boastfully named, (boys will be boys, you know,) listening to the weird far off cries of the sea birds quarrelling on Leigh Sands, and as the night tide ebbed, and gurgled and rippled along the lands of her hollow old clench built bows — the while I smoked the early, forbidden at home, surreptitious pipe of youth, — or cooked the succulent mussel, in a fearfully topheavy cylindrical paraffin stove, which also smoked in an undesired, but by no means surreptitious manner. And then, when the day's work was done, everything made snug for the night, and the huge second-hand tin riding light hung up on the forestay, how trustfully and cheerfully I lay me down to sleep, on my one inch cork mattress, with a rug and an oil-skin coat as a coverlet, and a rolled up spare coat for pillow.

It is not too much to say that this boat made me what I am now, a confirmed, perhaps prejudiced, believer in the small sailing craft, as a school *par excellence* for the production of the genuine salt water cruiser. She was a little too large for the present authorized type of canoe-yawl, which is fondly supposed to be able to win races, be carried about by a couple or three hands with her ballast out as easily as a big portmanteau, be hauled up and down beaches, and over hedges and ditches; in fact, do everything that a boat ought to do, except turn to windward in a *breeze,* a *real* breeze, up or down Sea Reach, or any other reach, and afford a substantial shelter to her owner, dry and snug every night for a month, or three months, if the breeze lasted so long.

No, shipmates! she was a *little* too deep, a *little* too heavy, for she had a hundredweight or so outside and five or six in, and she was a *little* more than a ·5-rater, not much more anyway, but still, outside the charmed circle; and half a dozen good men couldn't have lifted *her* over hedges and into hotel back yards, which was quite as well, for neither she nor her owner ever wanted to do these things. We had no desire to go to places that we couldn't sail into and out of, and we should have looked slightly upon the sailor, who, when the shades of evening fell, and tired and strained to death, with sitting out to windward to keep his craft "on end," besought the aid of the passing stranger to lift his "packet" up into a safe place for the night.

No! the 'Dauntless" wasn't a racer either, but she would get as far to windward in a tide as a "stumpy" barge, and she would sail on her bottom as long as sail could be carried on her without the skipper projecting his lower half dead to windward, and she would let him walk about her tiny waterways to get the anchor, without rolling over and chucking him into the "drink," as the waterman hath it. Yea, moreover, she could be rowed when the breezes came not out of the heavens, — but, alas! she could not be called an authorized CANOE-YAWL.

But, for the work she was expected to do, she was not a bit too large, unless it was when we went up out of the tideway on the Medway, and towing had to be resorted to. At such times, and in such places, she was a bit heavy on the hands of an eighteen year old lad, and I am very decidedly of opinion that this suspicion of unweildyness when up amongst the bushes, kept her and her owner, to waters where there was more room for wind and wave, and thus made a keener salt water man of him, than if the temptations had been all the other way. Nevertheless, it was not seldom that the 'Dauntless' took up her position under the willows below Maidstone, where the attractions of a certain young lady, who now sits opposite me, and who has shared happily the last ten years of my life, added to the other inducements in the shape of good fishing and sketching, minimized my objections to towing and rowing 16 to 18 cwt. of boat, ballast and stores.

All the same; if a man prefers the peaceful up-river work of either Thames or Medway, she is not the type of boat for him. I dare say the sharpie type is quite good enough for this sort of thing, and tents, as well as riverside hostelries, fit in with it. In fact, although my experience of the sharpie is of the smallest, it seems better for this kind of cruising than either the light displacement canoe-yawl of the round bottom sort, or even the Thames gig, if single-handed the owner goes.

For the round bottom canoe-yawl, of 16 or 17ft. overall, with 4ft. 6in. beam, and 4 or 5 cwt. of ballast, is neither one thing nor the other. There is not much room on board of her, and she is not so stiff as the sharpie, nor so fast on the upper waters, whilst below bridge she is not powerful enough, nor roomy enough, nor dry enough, nor comfortable enough for a man to live on board entirely in bad weather, or even moderate weather. It is quite possible she will be as fast, or even faster in fine weather, than the heavier boat of the 'Dauntless' type, but in a breeze when comfort, speed, and power, are things to be sighed for and enjoyed, what chance would she have either of getting where she was bound to, if the wind was ahead, or of accommodating her owner in anything like the same manner as the more powerful and roomy boat?

It is not a question of expense, for one boat can be built very nearly as cheap as the other, if plain fittings keep pace with increase of displacement.

The little 'Wren' (1889), though not a canoe-yawl, (she might easily have been one, for *she* came within the limits of depth, beam, and sail area, and had no outside ballast,) only cost, ready for sea, £38, and her fittings were gorgeousness itself compared with the 'Dauntless.' She had lead ballast something "beyond the dreams of avarice," when I owned that cruiser of blessed memory, beautiful copper riding light, a first-rate spirit stove, galvanized rigging, copper chain plates, &c., &c., and though smaller than need be for single hand work, did give a good deal of dry, roomy cabin space, as well as plenty of room for stores, and sailed remarkably well in a breeze, especially to windward.

But it *is* a question of keeping a man a keen single-hander, such as I presume the canoe-yawl class is intended to foster.

The surest way to "choke off" a promising cruising man of small means, but of large desires, is to put him in possession of a craft that will not keep his "togs" dry in a breeze, and that needs the nautical abilities of a W.B.P. to work her successfully in anything like nasty weather. The average man nowadays has neither the ability, nor the knowledge to successfully utilize a canoe-yawl of the ordinary light round bottom type, nor has he the patience and time to learn to do it. Consequently after a season or two of struggles with refractory tents, dependent on shore assistance, and a series of wettings through, he either gives up canoe-yawling or goes in for real yachts, and becomes lost as a single-hander either way.

To my mind, this is a deplorable thing, believing as I do, that single-handed work is one of the most invigorating exercises, both for mind and body, that a man can go in for, and, provided the craft is suitable, as safe or safer, and healthier than many other pastimes for men, that are nowadays constantly pressing their claims.

When the canoe-yawl class was first introduced I hailed with delight a probable school for good cruisers, that it seemed to me the class would assuredly produce. But it soon became apparent that, when racing was the main object, and that racing carried on mainly up river, or at Hendon, coupled with the limitation of sail area by overall length, cruising capabilities would be crushed out to make room for light displacement and midship sections of small area.

Let me here say that racing qualifications and cruising requisites are incompatible, either in canoe-yawls or small yachts. It will not be necessary to state why this is so, the readers of the *Canoeist* are quite as capable of supplying the answer as I am.

But there must be many men who would become keen and able cruisers, could they find companions and craft to help them. At present I fear that on Thames at least, the canoe-yawl in vogue, and for sale, are not such as are either fit, or safe, for the beginner to venture below bridge in.

On the Humber, and on the Mersey, a suitable type is growing up. Is there any reason why the Thames, a better river in all respects for small cruisers, should be behind hand in this respect? Is it that the racing classes have grown too powerful?

If it is so, and I am inclined to think there is much in the idea, could not a class of *cruising* canoe-yawls, or "canoe-yachts," be fostered, suitable for work in the lower reaches, and the coast as far as Harwich.

In this district, camping on shore is out of the question, as it mostly is on tideways, therefore a boat possessing good accommodation for a single man and his kit is absolutely necessary, and, as the reaches are exposed and open, when wind is against tide, a very nasty short sea is soon raised, a boat of some power and ability is equally imperative. Again, landing is in many cases possible only at wide intervals, and except in the immediate neighbourhood of towns water and other stores are difficult to be obtained, and when got have often to be carried long distances. In short, the sort of canoe-yawl that would be most effective would be one that a man can be *comfortable* in, and that will carry enough water and stores to last a whole week without replenishment.

These requirements can be well got in a boat of not less than 5ft. beam, and from 14 to 16 cwt. displacement, and 16 or 17ft. l.w.l. To obtain sufficient room under deck and hatches, something more than 11 inches of draft must be conceded, if the freeboard is to be moderate *i.e.* not more than 18 or 20 inches.

Therefore in fixing the dimensions of a cruising class, would it not be as well to say that the beam, draft, length, displacement, or ballast and sail area, should not be *less* than certain agreed upon measurements, of course, at the same time fixing limits that may not be exceeded. Should this be done, and perhaps some allowance made to favor clench built craft, as being less expensive, and really better fitted for rough work than carvel or ribbon carvel, (though maybe not quite so fast) a cheap, useful, and sea-worthy class of canoe-yawl might be soon established, a class that could be rowed, sailed, and made little floating homes for week-end cruises or summer holidays.

But, better than a class of boats, a class of *men* would grow up — perhaps an improvement on the somewhat dilletante racing men of to-day who stirs not far from home, and who must have hotel comforts, patent leather shoes, and spotless linen flannels, all very good things in their way, but not easily had in a cruising canoe-yawl.

The man I should like to see filling the class is he who can haul, reef, and steer, who knows by heart the noble river he is privileged to sail on, who can splice, mend his sails, cook his meals, and get his craft in tune like a fiddle, and who, from one week's end to another is content to live a simple healthy life afloat in his canoe-yawl, and lay up health, strength, and cheerfulness, against that enemy, old age, who is surely creeping up under the lee of all of us, and against that time, which will come some day, when to the strongest it shall be said: "And there shall be no more sea."

CHERUB.

1892 had proved a disappointing year for the Scarborough Model Yacht Club in that The Mere was choked with weed, the water was low and there was no wind. Match sailing did not resume after the Spring until October when the water rose above normal, allowing the yachts to be started from the bank rather than requiring their handlers to wade out to float them. The first match was for 20 Tonners for the Commodores prize of an Oil Painting won by T. Franks' MARY. Later in the month, a race was held for "a valuable water colour drawing, kindly presented to the members by Mr Nelson Dawson RBA for which Albert entered JULIA but without success; DOLLIE and CUPID both took part in the final two races of the season but trophies were not to be had.

It is obvious that the development of canoe yawls was a pre-occupation at this time, CHERUB II was being designed and built and Holmes and the other Humber Yawl men had their own ideas which they were actively putting into practice — Holmes in particular designing and building for himself a new craft almost every year during this period. The move to greater displacement and some form of cabin was gaining favour and as is shown by his letter to the editor of THE CANOEIST in February 1893, it was something of which Strange approved:—

DEAR SIR,—It is an adequate, aye, more than adequate payment for labour expended in arguing a somewhat unpopular view of the true functions and equipment of the canoe yawl, or yacht, to find such strong supporters of my opinions as "Tavie" and "Mudlark." When I last had the pleasure of looking round "Sam's" yard at Birkenhead, it was comforting to find that "Cacique" was going in for something weighty *outside,* and to hear of others inclining that way. I believe I am correct when I say that no "sea going" canoe yawl in the Humber Yawl Club, is without the same aid of stiffness, power, and strength.

So it seems that we of the North Countrie, who have perforce to face something like wind and weather, if we wish to get any sailing, are pretty much of a mind on the subject of outside ballast, and moreover we are finding out that we must have some room on board, "to live and move and have our being in."

But don't let us run away with the idea that we are going to do anything against either the full fledged half raters or the sharpie in ordinary racing. If we do, we shall be mistaken. There is not a *cruising* canoe yawl in existence that will finish within 20 minutes on a ten mile course with either a "Wee-Winn," or a "Shadow." Perhaps with the latter, on a five mile dead to windward *sea* course in a breeze necessitating a couple of reefs, the cruiser might have a chance, but not with the thoroughbred "Wee-Winn" and her successors of that ilk. And whether you have your ballast inside or out (even if it is hung on a fin, and four feet below your waterline) the *cruiser* is, from construction, fittings and equipment, hopelessly out of it from a racing point of view, just as hopelessly as the *racing* canoe-yawl, or "half' rater is out of it from a proper cruising point of view. Under existing circumstances brought about by the L. & S.A.

rule, all small racers are a class by themselves and will remain so until they are broken up or sink, they can never be made into cruisers. Consequently the cruisers are also a class by themselves—boats and men.

Whether this state of things is regrettable or not, is not for me to decide, but it points strongly to the fact that cruisers will have to look out for themselves and combine for the purposes of cruising and racing—if they wish it. When it is found out that a considerable number of men wish for something a little more wholesome and roomy than is allowed at present for canoe yawls by what ought to be considered the central authority—probably that central authority will do something for them. If they sit down quietly, and allow the funds which they subscribe to their different clubs for the advancement of cruising, to be devoted solely to the encouragement of uncomfortable racing machines, instead of comfortable cruising machines, they will have themselves to thank.

I still wait for an explanation of the fact, that considering its extreme suitability for cruising, my native river, the Thames, produces a smaller number of cruising enthusiasts, of the very small boat type, than any other larger river. I know both the Humber and the Mersey pretty well and with all due respects to them, they are simply "not in it" with Father Thames as a cruising ground.

But all the same, they, with less advantages, have produced a magnificent crop of boat sailers—the Mersey especially. Although I have always had a strong love for something "with a lid on" I cannot withold my admiration from the open boat men of both rivers, especially the Mersey, and I do not suppose any river in the world can surpass the show that it annually makes (if it can equal it) of men who are past-masters in the art of open boat sailing in open tidal waters—both amateur and professional.

In conclusion, let me quote a supporting authority from the other side of the Atlantic. Towards the end of a most interesting account of a cruise in a small sailing boat, the "Elsa" Mr. II. K. Wicksteed, whose name will be well known to all nautical readers of the *Forest & Stream*, says, "One great drawback experienced was the want of sleeping accommodation aboard. Not that the crew were subjected to any hardship or discomfort, but because of the anxiety which a properly constituted single-hander always suffers when away from his boat. To camp on shore is almost out of the question, so much time being necessary to break camp, and cook. 'Elsa,' or her successor, will be so fitted next summer that the crew can sleep and cook aboard." That is so—and the more a man cruises, the more he will find out the absolute truth of these—to me—truisms.

Besides this extract, there are some very pertinent remarks about rig and size of boat, that fit in with what I have for some time been trying to make clear to the embryo single hander.

But this letter grows long—too long. Let me thank "Mudlark" for his cheering news anent the state of the Thames water. I may, with your permission Sir, also, when time and space serve, try to rake up some of the 'Dauntless's' cruises—would that they were to come over again!

Faithfully yours, "CHERUB."

It is interesting to note from this letter that he still considered himself to be a Thames man and still regarded that water as being superior. In August 1893 it was the Canoe Yawl Rig which exercised his mind and again he addressed the Editor of THE CANOEIST:—

CANOE-YAWL RIG.

THE EDITOR, *The Canoeist.*

SIR,—"Aquatic," opens a very important question, but one also that is not to be positively answered for all conditions.

Having tried the following rigs, viz.: Sprit main with single jib; Lug main with single jib; Battened main lug and mizen; Regular cutter and regular yawl, I have come to the following conclusion:

That for *single handed work* in a ballasted canoe-yawl of good beam and displacement, three sails are best, divided into mizen, main and jib. The main may be either gaff or standing lug, fitted for effectiveness with a boom but for absolute convenience and handiness no boom on the main, but a pair of brails. The sails should be so placed and sized that the boat will work handily under mainsail alone, mainsail and jib, or jib and mizen. It follows that the jib and mizen should be of fair size, say 30 feet mizen and 35 feet jib, if they are to be of any use.

Should the canoe-yawl be manned by a crew of two, the most effective and easily handled rig will be the sloop, gaff mainsail and jib, or lug and jib. The gaff sail is easier set, although there appears to be an advantage so far as speed goes in the high peaked lug. I can see no difference from the point of view of safety, between lug and gaff.

I agree with "Aquatic" that for light displacement canoe-yawls with sails of comparatively small area, the battened main and mizen lugs are the safest, because in this rig there is always a reserve of luffing power when the main sheet is let go. This reserve is very valuable in easily capsized craft, and does not exist in the sloop rig, unless jib sheets only are let go.

But the sloop rig is faster on a suitable hull, as it is well-known that the driving power of the jib is immensely superior to that of the mizen, area for area. In fact it is only its power as a luffer that makes the mizen of any value. For open water work, where there is any chance of a "kick up" happening often, I prefer *unbattened* sails. All fisherman and boatmen swear by the *lifting* power of a working lug, with the tack fast to stem, or on weather bow, and there is little doubt they are right. Such a sail however would be utterly out of place on any sort of canoe-yawl, even for sea work, as it is dangerous and unhandy. But the moral that it points is that for all but smooth water sailing, in light displacement craft, the *lifting* power of a sail, not absolutely flat, is a valuable help, not only for speed, but weatherliness also.

Any arrangement of sail which keeps the weights inboard is a distinct advantage for rough water work, although in canoe-yawls the position of the centre-plate is often a bar to the proper placing of the mast for effective sloop rig, unless much more overhang is given forward than usual, or a bow-sprit is used, as in the Mersey yawls.

Seeing that the formation of the canoe-yawl aft, is such a serious obstacle to the comfortable arrangement of a mizen, often causing more expense and bother over steering gear, mizen bumkins &c., than almost any other part of the ship, and seeing also how very ineffective as a sail the average mizen is, I have often wondered why any double handled yawl bothers with them. But for single handed work I think the arrangement of sails I have before mentioned, jib, mizen and mainsail, is the safest and handiest, although not quite so speedy as either main and mizen, or sloop; and I believe all concessions to comfort, handiness or safety, either in hull or sails, are only made at the expense of speed, pure and simple.

CHERUB,
Humber Yawl Club.

The Model Yachting Season of 1893 opened in Scarborough in February with a muster of thirteen 10 Ton boats coming to the line, some being new boats "of a great length and power" which "on the whole fairly mastered the older and lighter craft, although FLORENCE and JULIA (A. Strange) have seen several seasons racing and are still 'bad to beat'. There is yet a "dark horse" just finished from the Commodore's design, that may prove a troublesome customer, as length and weight have in her been duly taken advantage of, and if she is successful, a great development in these directions may be seen in the Clubs models in the future". JULIA finished second in the match and it is evident that both designing and sailing models remained a considerable interest, even though he had by this time been designing full-scale craft for some six years and was cruising extensively both single-handed and in company.

There can be little doubt that, in common with Dixon Kemp, G.L. Watson and others, he found model design and competition useful as well as enjoyable and that in his usual enthusiastic and capable way, he contributed significantly to the development of an emerging and popular sport. How long this interest lasted, whether or not he was successful in introducing a new class, how he managed to find time for this activity whilst teaching, painting, designing, cruising, writing, lecturing and enjoying family life are questions to which we have no answers but the questions themselves are indicators of the enquiring mind, the full, rich and satisfying life spiced with humour, knowledge and energy which is tangibly obvious to us through the legacy of his paintings, his designs and particularly through those small cruising yawls that are still sailing the creeks, backwaters, estuaries and seas he so loved. To slightly mis-quote Emerson:—"He builded better than he knew; the conscious *wood* to beauty grew."

Appendix 1

The Albert Strange Association

To determine the birth of the Albert Strange Association we have to go back to 1975 when the Honorary Secretary of Scarborough Yacht Club decided to research the early years of the Club with a view to producing a history. In reading the Scarborough newspapers spanning the period 1885 to 1976 one name, that of Albert Strange, stood out prominently in the early years and it soon became obvious that he was a remarkable man in many ways.

In December 1976, an article appeared in YACHTING MONTHLY headed, "Before the Deluge" in which Albert Strange's association with the Humber Yawl Club was mentioned. Scarborough Yacht Club's Secretary was moved to write to the Editor to say that the S.Y.C. was proud to record that Albert Strange was in fact a founder member of the club, and had been chiefly responsible for its formation.

That letter opened the flood gates — a number of readers replied, and in the Spring of 1978 sufficient progress had been made for a weekend meeting to be arranged in Scarborough at which the Albert Strange Association was formed. Unknown to these founder-members there were many enthusiasts in the U.K. and overseas who still cherished and regularly sailed designs from Strange's drawing board. The rest of the story is contained in this book — the production of which was the main aim of the Association — "To trace and preserve the designs and little ships of Albert Strange and to make a permanent record of his life and work" — the completion of which has fulfilled a dream of Herbert Reiach, the founder-editor of YACHTING MONTHLY who was a personal friend of Albert Strange.

The Association now has nearly a hundred members all over the world — not all own Strange designs or paintings of course but each is an enthusiastic admirer of his work. They are still researching and have received invaluable help from Mystic Seaport Museum, Connecticut, which is a member of the Association and holds the W.P. Stephens Collection of Albert Strange plans. The support of readers of like mind would be welcomed — if anyone would like to join them please write to:—

Bill James
Honorary Secretary
Albert Strange Association
Maesycoed
5 Harewood
Molescroft
BEVERLEY HU17 7EF
North Humberside
TEL: (0482) 868147

This is not an owner's Association. Anyone who shares the members' interest in our heritage and feels that it should be preserved can help them in their task. The Honorary Secretary is particularly anxious to hear from anyone who owns or knows of an Albert Strange design or boat which it is thought may not have been traced by the Association.

Appendix 2

A List of Strange Designs (Basic Facts)

This list is based on the researches of the Albert Strange Association. The designs are not all to his original plans, as in Strange's day and even later many boats were built from magazine articles which contained line drawings, and others were slight modifications of these plans, and could be considered the design of the person concerned. Readers will also notice that the entries of UNNAMED designs may have no AS design numbers or dates and in one or two instances the AS design numbers are duplicated. This information is as listed at Mystic Seaport Museum and such later discrepancies *may* reflect Strange's health at that time.

The Association would be pleased to hear from any reader who can add to this list or feels that any of these designs contain inaccuracies or should be attributed to someone else — the Honorary Secretary's address will be found in Appendix 1.

The List is merely a summary of the information in the Association archives. On some designs there is a great deal of information, on others just a sketch, an entry in Lloyd's Register of Yachts, or a passing reference in YACHTING MONTHLY. The members of the Association are constantly receiving new leads which result in the tracing of designs previously unknown. Any reader who would like further details of any particular design is invited to get in touch with the Honorary Secretary who can supply these, if they are available, for a reasonable fee which would be allocated to their funds for further research. It must be emphasised however that Mystic Seaport Museum holds the copyright of all the plans in the W.P. Stephens Collection and is entitled to make a charge to anyone who requires copies of these and/or who intends to build to these designs.

Note
TM = Thames Measurement Tonnage
Displ = Displacement Tonnage
All rigs are Gaff unless otherwise stated and the terms 'canoe', 'transom' and 'counter' refer to the type of stern.

ASA No	Name	Ex	Type	Date of Build	Builder	LOA/LWL/Beam/Draught
001	A'BHERLINN	ex A'BHIRLIN	Yawl	1929	Dickies of Tarbert	30' 6" × 29' 6" × 8' 6" × 5'
002	AFREET		Racing Dayboat Sloop	—		30' × 20' × 6.92' × 4.35'
003	AGUSTINA	LULA	Yawl	1910	A.V. Robertson	25' × 20' × 7.2' × 2.25'
003.1	AILIE		Yawl	1934	J. Skivington, Partick	25' × 22' × 7.7' × 2.5'
	ALCIOPE	see TALLY-HO				
003.2	ALETHEA		Yawl	1923	Abeking & Rasmussen, Lemwerder	25' × 22' × 7.7' × 2.5'
004	ANYNDAH		Cutter now Bermudan	1928	R.T. Searles, Largs Bay	28' × 25' × 8' 6" × 5' 6"
	APRIL	see REDWITCH				
005	ARIEL		Cutter	1925	Anderson, Ridgen, Perkins	25.7' × 22.9' × 8.4' × 3.75'
006	BABY (The)		Cutter	—		28' × 21' × 7.7' × 4.4'
	BANTAM	now ENTERPRISE		—		
	BARBARA	see FANTAN				
007	BARBARA (not CHARM)	see FANTAN				
	BARBARA ANN	see STORNOWAY				
008	BARBARA MARY	JOY II ex CHAA-SZE	Ketch	1927	Hillyards	32.4' × 9.4' × 4.8'
009	BEE (1st)		"A" Class sailing canoe	—		18' × 15.9' × 3.96' × .55'
010	BEE (2nd)		Sloop	—		21' 6" × 20' × 7' 7" × 2' 9"
011	BEE (3rd)		Gaff Sloop	—		19.1' × 17.45' × 6.6' × 3'
	BETTY	see TALLY-HO				
012	BETTY		Yawl	1913	Dickies of Tarbert	31' 6" × 8' 6" × 5' 9"
	BETTY II	see GREY GOOSE				
013	BETTY II		Ketch or Yawl sail-plan	—		63.6' × 50.4' × 13.6' × 8.2'
014	BETTY II		as AS design 139	1914	Stow & Son, Shoreham	63.75' × 50.25' × 13.5' × 8.16'
	BIRDIE	see DORCIS				
015	BLUE JAY		Yawl	1926	W.E. Thomas, Falmouth	38.75' × 30' × 9.58' × 5'
016	BOREAS	IMOGEN	Yawl	1899	Courtney & Birkett	22' × 6.5' × 2.5'
016.1	CANDELA		Berm Yawl	1931	? in Hong Kong	?
017	CATALONE		Ketch	1909	Ray Urstor, Maidenhead	22' LBP × 7' × 4' down
018	CHARM		Yawl alt Bermudan sloop	1921	E.L. Woods, Cantley	33' × 25' × 7' 7" × 5' Enlarged VEN
019	CHARM	BARBARA	Yawl	1927	Richardson, Dublin	30' × 22' × 8.3' × 5'
020	CHARM II		Yawl	1925	E.L. Woods, Cantley	40' × 30' × 9' 2" × 6'
	CHARMIAN	see CHARMINA				
021	CHARMINA	ex CHARMIAN	Yawl alt Bermudan	1923	E.L. Woods, Cantley	28' × 24' × 8' × 4' 3"
022	CHERUB	later SEABIRD	Cutter	1887/8	James Frank	21' × 7' 3"
023	CHERUB II		Yawl then batten-lug	1893	James Frank	20.2' × 17.7' × 5.9' × 1.7'
024	CHERUB III	now REDWING	Yawl	1910/1	Dickies of Tarbert	28' 6" × 23' × 8' 2" × 3' 9"
025	CIRCE		Yawl	1948	Jacht A. Beekman, Holland	32' × 9' × 5'
026	CLOUD		Yawl/ketch	1912	W.E. Thomas, Falmouth	38.75' × 30' × 9.58' × 5'
026.1	CUPID		Model Yacht 10-tons YRA			44" × 6.7" × 9.25"
027	CURLEW	ETHEL	Yawl	1894	R. Kemp, Oulton Broad	18.5' × 6.5' × 2.7'
028	DESIRE		Racing Sloop 6m class	—	—	28.66' × 21.9' × 5.5' × 4.1'
029	DOLLY		Lugsail	—	—	15'
030	DORCIS	BIRDIE	Cutter	1899	J.A. Akcaster, Hornsea	29' 4" × 23' 9" × 7' 5" × 3' 10"
031	DRYAD		Dayboat Sloop	1909	Canadian in Toronto	23' × 17' 6" × 6' 3" × 1' 9"
032	DUNLIN		Sloop	1909	W. Clacherie, Dalbeatie	21' 5" × 19' 6" × 7' × 3' 3"
033	EMERALD		Yawl	1938	Wms & Parkinson, Deganwy	28' 6" × 23' × 8' 2" × 4' 6"
034	ENTERPRISE	BANTAM	Cutter	1928/9	Chute & Bixby, N.Y.	28' × 25' × 8' 6" × 5' 6"
	ESCAPE	see TALLY-HO				
	ETHEL	see CURLEW				
035	FAN TAN	BARBARA	Sloop (Fishing/shooting)	1920	Sam Bond, Birkenhead	26.1' × 23' × 8.5' × 2.6'

	Sail Area	Original owner	Owner 1990	AS Design No	Mystic Ref.	Comments
oe, TM 7	500	W. Macintyre, Glasgow	Steve Thomas, ASA member	—	—	Believed based on SHEILA II
l 2.45, counter	440	—	—	—	1.718	Comp 12 YM Vol 12 1912
oe C.B.	553	M.C. Mattinson, B. Aires	—	102/1909	1.754	CATALONE/ZIF possibly sisters
TM 5	400	Duncan Ferguson	—	—	—	Sister to MINGULAY Jt des McLean Gibson
TM 5	400	1927 Richard B. Brown	—	—	—	Possibly inspiration for Clyde CC 1 Des
som, displ 8	519	Norman Ford, Adelaide	Harry Cook, Vale Park, S.A.	To 137	1.677	Sister to PHANTOM
som, TM 5	480	W.A. Lister, London	Jim Maynard	To 112	1.730	Based on CHERUB III
	430	—	—	—	—	Nursery Class — YM June 1917
				—	—	
				—	—	
				—	—	
vel	558	Arthur Hobson	Tony/Pat Webb, ASA membs	—	—	Attrb Hillyard who built JOY I
oe, displ 745 lbs	150	—	—	—	1.702	2nd Prize YM Comp. No 9 1909
som, displ 2.67	327	Des. for D.W.H. MacPherson	—	142/1914	1.684	1917 amend shows daggerboard
ast keel	250	Intended for himself	—	142/1914	—	Sent to HB 1917 — see YM by HB
				—	—	(See 010 also)
oe	—	Sam Strang	Phil Risby	—	—	J.A. McCallum claims design
nter TM 38		Charles Hellyer	—	139/1913	1.688	See also Myst 1.717 = BETTY II
nter	1864	for Chas Hellyer	—	138/1913	1.717	Sail plan only & YM 1915
oe, displ 10	836	T.N. Dinwiddy, Dartmouth	James Griffin, Mission	125/1912	1.711	Built to design of CLOUD
. Canoe TM 3	250	—	Peter Collett	—	—	Not IMOGEN ex IMOGEN II
noe stern	—	—		—	—	Escaped in war from Singapore to Padang
. Canoe TM 4	300	C.T. Ricardo, Bembridge	—	—	—	Believed 1.754. Destroyed 1966
nter, TM 6		N.R. Suffling	Richard Child, ASA member	—	—	See YM Oct 1923. Needs rebuild
noe TM 6		Arthur Richardson	Harry Murphy, ASA member	—	—	Loosely based on SHEILA II
nter, TM 10	—	Sufflings & partners	Watson and Cohen	—	—	Enlarged VENTURE
noe, TM 6	430	Arthur Filby, Lymington	Richard Rouse, ASA member	—	—	Based on CHERUB III?
nsom, 2 centreboards		Albert Strange	—	—	—	Last heard owned D.A. Gordon
. Canoe, O/B rudder, dis 22cwt	249	Albert Strange	—	—	1.729	"My most beloved boat" — AS
noe, displ 4.6	480	Albert Strange	Jeremy Burnett, ASA member / Lying Maryland	112/1910	1.730	Draught now 5' 2"
noe	—	—		—	—	For sale via "Wooden Boats"
noe, displ 10	846	A.W. Gush & G.D. Stanford	—	125/1912	1.711	Orig des for YM Competition 1908
nsom, keel				—	—	1st Prize Des Comp June 1891
. Canoe, displ 3	250	R.H. Calvert, London	—	4/1894	—	Built to WREN Design
nter		—	—	?/1908	1.743	YM Competition 1909
.		Albert Strange?	—	—	—	No proof AS Design. See YM 1915
nter, displ 4½	621	S.G. Radcliffe, HYC	—	—	—	HYC Yearbook 1900
. TM 3	397	T.S.H. Guest, Toronto	—	101/1909	1.732	2 sail plans in Mystic
. TM 4	298	W.H. Armistead	—	87/1908	1.691	Solway Class q.v.
6	650	Mr & Mrs (Catherine) Cooke	Joe Pennington, ASA member	—	—	Based on CHERUB III
pl 8	732	Lewis S. Chanler, N.Y.	Stan/Leonard Sinowitz ASA member	To 137	1.677	Based on PHANTOM
				—	—	
				—	—	
nsom C.B.	450	C.A. Robinson	—	129/1912	1.683	Last heard Holyhead 1969

ASA No	Name	Ex	Type	Date of Build	Builder	LOA/LWL/Beam/Draught
036	FAY Class		Dinghy to BRA 12' Class rules	—		12'
037	FEI-LIM		Cutter alt Bermudan	1936	Hop Kee, Hong Kong	30' × 25' × 8.5' × 5'
038	FIREFLY		Yawl	1922	J.W. Brooke, Lowestoft	34' 6" × 24' × 8' × 4'
039	FLAPPER		Racing Sloop	—		24.2' × 17' × 5.6' × 3.2'
040	FLORENCE		Sloop	1920	R. Pandurang, Bombay	19'(?) × 6.5'
041	GALATEA		Gaff now Bermudan cutter	1929	Anderson, Rigden, Perkins	25' 9" × 8' × 4'
042	GANNET	PSYCHE ex MAYBIRD	Yawl	1912	W. Roberts & Son, Chester	27' 6" × 8' 2" × 2' 11"
043	GEISHA			—		
044	GRAYLING		Yawl	—		
045	GRETTA		Yawl, canoe stern	1912	M. Mahoney, Kingston	25.9' LBP × 23' × 8.2' × 3.8'
046	GREY GOOSE	ISABEL ex BETTY II	Schooner formerly ketch	1914	Stow & Son, Shoreham	63.75' × 50.4' × 13.5' × 8.16'
047	HAWK		Dinghy			12'
048	HAWKMOTH		Yawl	1908	Dickies of Tarbert	31.75' × 22.33' × 7.6' × 5'
	HERVOR II	see THERESA II				
049	ILONA		Sloop alt from yawl	1928	G.W. Lavis, Exmouth	21' 5" × 19' × 7' 6" × 3'
050	IMOGEN	IMOGEN II	Yawl	1911	Lukes, Hamble	25.9' × 22.5' × 7.9' × 4'
	IMOGEN	see BOREAS				
051	INNISFALLEN		Cutter	1910	Dickies of Tarbert	41' 9" × 32' × 10' 4" × 6' 5"
	ISABEL	see GREY GOOSE				
052	JILT		Cutter	—		30' × 26' × 8.41' × 4.75'
053	JOVANNA		Yawl	1913	M.M. Gallimara, Leghorn	31' 7" × 24' × 8' 6" × 4' 11"
	JOY II	see BARBARA MARY				
	KOTIK	see PINCHER				
054	LEONA	BLUE JAY ex LEONA	Yawl	1906	Bundock, Leigh-on-Sea	24.6' × 7.1' × 2'/5.5'
055	LOFOTEN FISHERIES		Cutter	—		31' 6" × 9' 10" × 3' 2"
	LULA	see AGUSTINA				
056	MARY		Sloop	1912	W. Roberts, Chester	23' × 17.5' × 6.3' × 3.1'
057	MAY		Ketch	1912	Robertson, Sandbank	
	MAYBIRD	see GANNET				
058	MEG		Sloop, cutter in 1914	1909	A.V. Robertson, W'bridge	21.7' × 19' × 7.2' × 3.75'
059	MERVYNA		Bermudan Yawl	1934	A.M. Dickie, Bangor	40' × 32' × 10.7' × 5'
060	MINGULAY	MORAG	Yawl	1934	J. Skivington, Partick	25' × 22' × 7.7' × 2.5'
060.1	MINNA		Yawl	1934	J. Skivington, Partick	25' × 22' × 7.7' × 2.5'
061	MIST		Yawl	1907	P. McKeown, Belfast	26.5' × 20' × 7.1' × 4'
062	MONA		Gunter sloop	1897	G. Webster, Lincoln	22.8' × 17.7' × 6.7' × 1.63'
063	MONA (not 062)		Lugger	1893	A. Burgoine, K. on Thames	17' 3"
	MORAG	see MINGULAY				
064	MOTH II		Yawl	1912	Luke & Co, Hamble	28.5' × 21' × 7.6' × 4.1'
064.1	MULDONICH		Yawl	1930	J. MacDonald, Oban	30' × 22' × 6.6' × 4.5'
065	MYTH		Cruiser/racer sloop	—	—	33' 9" × 23' × 7' 11" × 3' 6"
066	NIRVANA OF ARKLOW	NIRVANA	Yawl	1925	John Tyrell, Arklow	35.75' × 27' × 8.66' × 5'
	NORMA	see SHULAH				
067	NORMA	not SHULAH	Yawl	—	—	20' 6"
068	NORSEMAN		Ketch	1912	Sam Lee, Hong Kong	22' 5"LWL × 8' × 4' 6"
069	NURSEMAID The		Sloop	—	—	28' × 21' × 7.5' × 4.2'
070	OTTER		Yawl	1899	A. Make, Longueil, P.Q.	24.9' × 22.5' × 7.8' × 2.2' (5.2' down)
071	PHANTOM		Cutter	1920	White Bros Ltd, Southampton	28' × 25' × 8' 6" × 5' 6"
073	PINCHER	KOTIK	Cutter	1902	W. Jones, Milford Haven	23.8' × 21.6' × 7.4' × 3.4'
	PSYCHE	see GANNET				
	PUFFIN II	see WOOZLE				

	Sail Area	Original owner	Owner 1990	AS Design No	Mystic Ref.	Comments
nsom				97	1.697	Priced at £18-10s-10p
nsom?		Mr Nesbitt	Ann Stinson, Maryland	—	—	
unter TM 7	490	Robert Lamb	Jim A. Clay, ASA member	119/1911	1.744	Design 119, modified Harrison Butler?
unter, displ 27 cwt	265	—	—	?/1912	1.747	YM Comp No 15 1912/3
ons	250	John Munster, Bombay	—	—	—	No details available
nsom, TM 6		Alfred Morgan Hughes	Rich'd/Jane Blomfield ASA membs	To 112	1.730	Built to ARIEL's plans
3. Canoe O/B rudder TM 6½	425	Lieut Norman Jones RNVR	—	122/1911	1.735	Believed burnt at Bridlington
				—	1.749	No details available
				—	—	2nd prize HYC Comp 1905
1 6	531	S.T. Robinson, Dublin	—	—	—	Wrecked Mersey mid-1950s
	1864	C. Hellyer JP, Brixham	—	—	—	Dinghy for HAWKMOTH?
noe TM 6	535	Walter Ibbetson Beaumont	—	85/1908	1.680	
				—	1.679	Believed in Mallorca
3. transom TM 4	315	C.F. Ombler?	Ian Whitaker, ASA member	142/1914	1.684	AS wanted to build her but never did
ansom TM 6	400	—	—	116/1910	1.687	See YM Oct 1930
				—	—	Not IMOGEN ex IMOGEN II
unter TM 15	1122	Beauclerk-Upington, C. Town	—	95/1909	1.678	Sank off Duiker Pt 1941
ansom	530	Des. for G.A.E. Clarke	—	150/1917	1.681	AS Des not proven-cf YM Dec/18
noe TM 7	545	H. Dubs, Rome	—	117/1910	1.722	Same lines as SHEILA II
				—	—	
3. Canoe TM 4	298	W.F. Wilson, London	Jamie Clay, ASA member	—	—	Very similar OTTER
uble-ender, Norwegian type	553	Des. for S.A. Fangen	—	110/1909	1.377	Alt draught 4'
				—	—	
3. TM 3	285	E.A. Eborall, Liverpool	—	—	—	
ton		Frank Gilliland (RCC)	—	—	1.706	Some confusion at present
ansom TM 4	297	Dr H.P. Helsham, Beccles	—	97?	1.700?	Last heard — G. Loveless 1968
noe TM 18	746	Mrs Edith Coote, Barmouth	Terry Adams	Not AS	—	Designed by Dickie with AS inf
3. TM 5	400	J. McC. Thomson, Paisley	Anthony Holdich, ASA member	—	—	Joint des. with McLean Gibson
3. TM 5	400	D.Q. Archer Bates, Stirling	Searching	—	—	Sister to MINGULAY Jt des McLean Gibson
noe, displ 3.3	654	Bryan R. Waite	Searching	78/1906	1.712	Larger version of SHEILA ?
3. Counter TM 3		G. Webster	Jasper Bagshaw	—	—	AS met Webster on L'coln canal, cf HYC
3.		A. Burgoine	—	—	—	Lloyds 1895/9 — des by Burgoine
noe TM 5	410	H.H. May	—	126/1912	1.721	See YM Vol 35
1 5	416	W.K. Chalmers, Glasgow	—	—	—	Des by G.L. Watson based VENTURE/YM 1931
spl 4.2	700+	—	—	76/1906	1.676	For Trent/Ouse/Humber
noe TM 9	748	A.W. Mooney	Peter Clay ASA member	144/1914	1.724	See YM 1934
3. Canoe O/B rudder	258	Des. for George Holmes	—	118/1911	1.750	
		—	—			Few details available
1 5	505			?/1917	—	"Nursery Class" YM June 1917
3. Canoe 10.5 cwt iron keel		R.J. Durley, HYC & RStLYC	—	40/1898	1.748	Last heard Montreal 1921
ansom, TM 8	619	John S. Trench	—	137/1913	1.677	See YM/Vol 17 p297 August 1914
3. TM 5		W. Jones		—	—	Few details
				—	—	
				—	—	

APPENDIX 2 — A List of Strange Designs (Basic Facts) cont.

ASA No	Name	Ex	Type	Date of Build	Builder	LOA/LWL/Beam/Draught
074	QUEEN BEE		Gaff yawl	1912	? in Hong Kong	22.7'LWL × 8' × 5.1'
075	QUEST II		Ketch	1906/7	Dickies of Tarbert	44' × 36' × 11.5' × 7.3'
076	QUEST II (Dinghy)		Dinghy	—	—	11' × 4' 2"
077	RED DAWN II		Sloop later Ketch 1953	1923	Geo Sinden, Fishbourne	27.5' × 19.2' × 6.35' × 3.8'
	REDWING	see CHERUB III				
078	REDWITCH	APRIL	Yawl later alt Bm Yawl	1914	W.E. Thomas, Falmouth	36' 3" × 30' 6" × 9' × 5' 9"
079	REVERIE		Bermudan sloop	1924	R.B. Brown, Auckland	29' 6" × 7' 11" × 4' 6"
080	SEA BREEZE		Yawl	1904	Robert Caine, P. St. Mary	25' × 19' 6" × 6' 9" × 3' 5"
081	SEA HARMONY		Yawl	1937	E.L. Woods, Horning	33' × 25' × 7' 6" × 5' 3"
	SEABIRD	see CHERUB				
	SEABIRD II	see GANNET				
082	SEAL		Yawl	—	—	30' 9" × 8' × 4' 1"
083	SHEELAH II		Yawl	—	—	30' 9" × 8' × 4.1'
084	SHEENAN		Yawl	—	—	40' × 32' × 10.7' × 5'
085	SHEILA		Yawl	1904/5	Robert Caine, Pt St Mary	25' × 19' 6" × 6' 9" × 3' 5"
086	SHEILA II		Yawl	1911	Dickies of Tarbert	31' 7" × 24' × 8' 6" × 4' 11"
087	SHULAH	ex NORMA	Yawl	1914	Sam Bond, Birkenhead	25' 5" × 20' × 7' 2" × 3' 4"
088	SHULAH II		Yawl	1934	A.M. Dickie, Bangor	40' × 32' × 10.7' × 5'
089	SOLWAY ONE DESIGN		C.B. Sloop	—	—	21' 6" × 19' 6" × 6' 9" × 2' 3"
090	SPINDRIFT		Gaff Cutter	1913	Woolacott, Dartmouth	28' 5" × 26' 5" × 9' 6" × 6'
091	STORMFINCH		Bermudan yawl now cutter	1902	Ashent Kilner	28' × 24' × 7.5' × 4.75'
092	STORNOWAY	BAR ANN ex VAERINGER	Cutter	1926	Dauntless Shipyard, Conn	33' × 11'
093	TALLY-HO (now ESCAPE)	ALCIOPE ex BETTY	Cutter	1910	Stow & Son, Shoreham	47' 5" × 44' 1" × 12' 8" × 7'
094	TARA		Cutter	?	?	31.7' × 29' × 10' × 5'
095	TAVIE II		Yawl	1896	Sam Bond, Birkenhead	22' 2" × 18' × 6' 4" × 1' 10"
096	TERN	sister to REDWITCH	Yawl then sloop	1914	W.E. Thomas, Falmouth	36' 3" × 30' 5" × 9' × 5' 9"
097	TERN III		Cutter	1914	Whitstable Shipping Co	53' × 44' × 12.4' × 7.5'
098	THERESA	MALIA	Yawl	1907	A. Taylor, Sandown	20' × 6' × 2.8'
099	THERESA II	HERVOR II ex THERESA	Yawl	1914	Bundock Bros, Leigh/Sea	25' 6" × 20' 5" × 7' 6" × 3' 7"
100	THORN		Yawl	—		25' × 20' 5" × 7' 3" × 3' 6"
101	THRASHER		Lug	—	—	23'
102	TOPSY		Dayboat sloop	—	—	17' × 16.4' × 6' × 2.5'
103	TUI		Sloop	—	—	30' × 24' × 8.58' × 4.92'
104	UNNAMED 101		Sloop	—	—	29' × 23' 4" × 7' 4" × 3' 6"
106	UNNAMED 102		Yawl	—	—	35' × 28' × 9' × 5.6'
107	UNNAMED 103		Cutter	—	—	47/48'
108	UNNAMED 104		Sloop	—	—	20' 6"
109	UNNAMED 105		Humber Yawl	—	—	12.6' × 4.8'
110	UNNAMED 106		Lug rigged yawl	—	—	14'
111	UNNAMED 107		C.B. open single lugsail	—	—	17' 6" × 6' × 1' 8"
112	UNNAMED 108		Yawl	—	—	28' 6" × 23' × 7' 1" × 4' 7"
113	UNNAMED 109		Yawl	—	—	21' 7" × 19' 5" × 7' 1" × 2' 1"
114	UNNAMED 110		Ketch	—	—	36' 7" × 30' × 10' 2" × 5'
115	UNNAMED 111		Racing sloop	—	—	26' × 17' 6" × 6' 5" × 2' 10"
116	UNNAMED 112		Racing sloop	—	—	26' 2" × 6' × 4' 7" down
117	UNNAMED 113		Racing sloop	—	—	26'
118	UNNAMED 114		Cutter	—	—	30' × 8.5' × 4.9'
119	UNNAMED 115		Gaff sloop	—	—	20' 9" × 6' 11" × 3' 3"
120	UNNAMED 116		Yawl	—	—	51' 6" × 40' × 13' 5" × 7' 3"
121	UNNAMED 117		Sloop	—	Edward E. Cox	18' × 5' × 3' 7" down

	Sail Area	Original owner	Owner 1990	AS Design No	Mystic Ref.	Comments
noe TM 21	1000+	C.W. Adderton	—	—	—	Owned by John Illingworth 1927
s. transom centre-board	—	C.W. Adderton if built	—	—	Yes	No Mystic no, but plans there
unter TM 4	336	Gordon Sinden, I.O.W.	Chris Staples, Hants	—	—	1990 based Hamble Nr Bursledon
				—	—	
noe TM 10	713	—	—	133/1913	1.755	Last heard London 1952, Sister to TERN?
5	450	Dr Chesson	John Davis, ASA member	—	—	See "Little Ships" by R. Carter
noe TM 4	330	W. Booth?	—	70/1904	1.752	Sister to SHEILA
unter TM 6	546	N.A. Suffling	Betsy/Dan de Leiris ASA	—	—	Based on VENTURE/CHARM 017
				—	—	
noe TM 9.9	740	—	—	—	—	2nd in YM Comp. No 3 March 07
		—	—	98/1908	1.703	Sketched for L. Vilmour, Morlaix
noe TM 18	745	—	—	—	—	Believed sister SHULAH II
noe, displ 3.6	330	Robert Groves	Mike and Jane Burn	70/1904	1.752	Well documented
noe, displ 7.7	545	Robert Groves	Mike Bourice, Auckland	117/1910	1.722	Needs restoration after damage
noe TM 4	365	G. Norman Jones	—	110/1910	1.750	Lost in gale 1941 Menai Sts
noe TM 18	745	R.D. Briercliffe	—	Not AS	—	Designed by Dickie with AS influence
nker transom displ 2	298	see DUNLIN	—	87/1908	1.691	DUNLIN only boat built to des
ansom TM 9	570	—	—	—	—	Beken has colour photo, cf Lloyds 1954
noe TM 5		—		—	—	Doubtful AS cf Lloyds 1938/1952
noe O/B rudder			Dana Hayden	114/1910	1.709	Al Peterson circumnavigated
ansom TM 20	1686	Charles Hellyer	Dave and Joy Olson	96/1909	1.695	Salv in Raratonga, now at Brookings, O'gan
noe O/B rudder, Norweg'n type	593	Des. for Claud Worth	—	114/1910	1.709	STORNOWAY was to same design?
3. canoe O/B rudder	260	John D. Hayward	—	—	—	Last heard Rosyth 1921
1 10	811	Herbert R. Cooper	—	133/1913	1.755	Lost 1928 at Poole Harbour Bar
unter TM 28	1400	Claud Worth	Wrecked Antigua 1960	—	—	Joint design with Claud Worth
3. now keel TM 3			Anthony Richards, ASA	—	—	No proof AS but influenced
noe TM 4	409	C. Walton	Bill McKenna, ASA member	139/1913	1.685	Original plans = THERESA II SA 363.5
noe displ 3.6	450	No proof ever built	—	—	1.751	2nd in Comp. HYC Yearbook 1909
B. transom		F. Webster?	—	123/1911	1.686	No evidence built
nker straight stem, transom	250	Albert Strange?	—	—	1.704	2nd in HYC Comp 1908 (redrawn 1912)
noe TM 7	614	Des. for W. Hopkins	—	145/1915	1.726	No evidence built
	490	—	—	39/1898	1.727	
spl 10.5	700	—	—	?/1909	—	
ansom		Des. for Chas Hellyer	—	96/1909	1.695	Also in Mystic as 1.746
ansom		Des. for Dr Helshaw	—	97/1909	1.740	Also in Mystic as 1.700/1.710?
B. canoe, clinker		Des. for Dr W.H. Macpherson	—	100/1909	1.694	Also in Mystic as 1.725
noe		Des. for Dr W.H. Macpherson	—	104/1909	1.699	No trace built
ansom	175	—	—	115/1910	1.753	
anoe displ 6	450	—	—	118/1910	1.739	Also in Mystic as 1.750 = NORMA
B. transom		Des. for Dr. W.H. Macpherson	—	146/1915	1.698	See also Des. 87, 142 and 146 (HYC)
anoe displ 11	665	Des. for G.H. Cooke	—	147/1915	1.737	Cf YM 1916
	345	—	—	148/1916	1.713	
B.		—	—	149/1916	1.690	See also 1.696 1.713 and ASA 117
		—	—	149/1916	1.696	See also ASA 116
ransom		Des. for Capt G.A.E. Clarke	—	150/1917	1.681	See also JILT
ransom	305	—	—	150/1916	1.693	Based on Dickie design 1894-AS
M 28		—	—	151/1917	1.736	Mystic has amnd to 56' as ketch
anoe O.B. rudder displ 846 lbs		Des. for Edward E. Cox	see comments	154/1917	1.742	Is this boat with Dave Morgan?

ASA No	Name	Ex	Type	Date of Build	Builder	LOA/LWL/Beam/Draught
122	UNNAMED 118		—	—	—	98′ × 60′ × 18′ × 10′
123	UNNAMED 119		Sloop/yawl sketch			34.6′ × 24′ × 8′ × 4.25′
124	UNNAMED 120					45′ LWL × 13.7′
125	UNNAMED 121		Racing sloop?	—	—	17′
126	UNNAMED 122		Yawl	—	—	32′ 7″ × 24′ × 8′ × 4′ 9″
127	UNNAMED 123		Sailing dinghy, single lugsail	—	—	9′ 3″ × 4′ 2″
128	UNNAMED 124		Yawl			53′
129	UNNAMED 125		French Nat, 6½ metre			6.5m × 5.5m × 1.8m
130	UNNAMED 126		Motor dinghy	—	Stow and Son, Shoreham	14′
130.1	UNNAMED 127		Motor launch	—	—	17.2′ × 16.2′ × 5.4′ × 2.0′
130.2	UNNAMED 128		Sailing dinghy	—	—	16′ × 5.7′
130.3	UNNAMED 129	2 separate designs	Yawl	—	—	18′ 7″ × 16′ also 20′ 11″ × 18′
	VAERINGER	see STORNOWAY				
131	VENTURE		Yawl alt Bermudan	1920	A. Wooden, Oulton Broad	29′ 4″ × 22′ × 6′ 9″ × 4′ 4″
132	VIKING		Lug Yawl	1886	J.A. Akester, Hornsea	18′ × 17.6′ × 5′ × 2.5′
133	WAWA		Humber Yawl	1895	James Frank, Scarboro'	19′ 3″ × 5′ 9″ × 1′ 7″
134	WE TWO		Yawl	1912	Sam Lee, Hong Kong	28′ 5″ × 22′ 2″ × 7′ 6″ × 4′ 7″
135	WEC CLASS ONE DESIGN		C.B. Dinghy	—	—	14′
136	WENDA		Yawl	—	—	24′ 9″ × 19′ 3″ × 6′ 5″ × 2′ 3″
137	WHITE CLOUD		Cutter	1931	Chute & Bixby, N.Y.	30′
138	WOOZLE	PUFFIN II	Motor Boat, yawl	1910	G.E. Ramsey, Shipley	44′ 6″ × 39′ 6″ × 9′ 1″ × 3′ 5″
139	WREN		Yawl	—	—	15′ 6″ × 15′ × 5′ 6″ × 2′ 6″ (plate down)
140	ZIF		Cutter	1911	A.V. Robertson, W'bridge	22′ × 20′ × 7′ × 4.2′

	Sail Area	Original owner	Owner 1990	AS Design No	Mystic Ref	Comments
nter displ 78				None	1.734	Mystic plans in AS hand, hull only
nter TM 7	567	Des. for an E.C. Yachtsman	—	119/1911	1.744	
34.4				—	1.741	Unsigned hull design only
nter 'dish' shaped				None	1.707	
oe TM 6	550	Des. for G. Thomp Scactro?	—	?/1910	1.720	Similar to Hawkmoth — AS
nsom, dagger board	44	Des. for G.H. Cooke	—	?/1916	1.738	
				?/1917	1.689B	
pl 1259 kilos				—	1.708	
		Charles Hellyer		—	1.723	No date traced
aight lead keel 2438 lbs	210	Des for Dr W.H. MacPherson	—	75/1904	—	
		Des for Dr W.H. MacPherson	—	140/1913	—	
canoe	213	—	—	4/1891	1,733	See also CURLEW ex ETHEL
nter displ 4.3	410	H.J. Suffling	Ian Taggart, ASA member	?/1917	1.728	AS last design — finished ANO — Suffling?
canoe OB rudder TM 1.5	160	—	—	—	—	Now attrib. John Hamilton Jnr
canoe O/B rudder TM 2	220	Henry Hayes	—	—	—	See AS's "Parody of Hiawatha"
6	535	V. Goulbourne	—	—	—	Last heard Hong Kong 1921
nsom, vertical stem	—	Des. for Dr. W.H. Macpherson	—	128/1912	1.692	West of England Conference
canoe displ 30 cwt	295	Des. for J. Bennett ARIBA	—	45/1899	—	cf "The Sailing Boat" by Folkard
nsom stern, O/B rudder			J. Brigardi, M. Brasset, NY	—	—	Similar to ENTERPRISE — awaiting details
oe TM 13	340	G.C. Waud	—	108/1910	1.719	Last heard 1955 at Scarborough
nsom displ 11 cwt 5 qtr	116	—	—	—	—	See THE FIELD Dec 1889
canoe TM 4	360	F.S. Antliff, HYC	Peter Stone, Kent	102?	1.754?	These design Nos not proved

APPENDIX 3

A list of Paintings and Sketches

As with the LIST OF STRANGE DESIGNS in Appendix 2 this list has been compiled by the ALBERT STRANGE ASSOCIATION and does not pretend to be complete. There must be many more of Strange's paintings throughout the world and the Association would welcome the help of readers in tracing them. Please get in touch with the Honorary Secretary if you can make the list more complete.

Title	Description	Owned by	Date	Size	Type	Notes
1) Fishing Boats beating to windward		Humber Yawl Club	1895	19½″ × 13″	WC	Signed
2) Castle Rock from South Sands		Scarborough Council		13½″ × 20½″	WC	In Mayoress' Parlour, Scarborough LO96
3) Middlesborough Docks		Scarborough Art Gallery		9″ × 13″	WC	Grey grisaille/White 81/44
4) Berwick-on-Tweed		Scarborough Art Gallery	1888	19″ × 28″	WC	Ref 134
5) View from Across Fields		Scarborough Art Gallery		6″ × 9½″	WC	Signed: Simple treatment of simple subject, 30 min demonstration sketch, 81/24
6) Landscape	Study of tone values	Scarborough Art Gallery		6″ × 9½″	WC	Signed: Simple painting, 30m demonstration sketch, 81/25
7) Filey Bay		Scarborough Art Gallery		8″ × 13″	WC	Monochrome 81/45
8) St Vulfrain, Abbeville seen from Rue Voltaire		Scarborough Art Gallery	1880/1	20″ × 30″	WC	82/4
9) Sea Fog lifting Loch Keills		Scarborough Art Gallery		7½″ × 12″	WC	83/86
10) Dick and Dorothy Scarborough Harbour		Scarborough Art Gallery		9″ × 13½″	WC	82/5
11) St Valery		Scarborough Art Gallery		8″ × 10½″	WC	82/6
12) Warkworth Castle Northumberland		Scarborough Art Gallery		9¾″ × 6¼″	WC	82/7
13) Moorland Scene		Scarborough Art Gallery			WC	Unframed
14) Harbour Scene		Scarborough Art Gallery			WC	Unframed
15) Coast Scene		Scarborough Art Gallery	1910	8″ × 10½″	WC	83/87
16) Sea Shore and Clouds		J.W. Cadbury III USA		7¾″ × 10¼″	WC	Signed

Title	Description	Owned by	Date	Size	Type	Notes
17) Isle of Man		J.W. Cadbury III USA		10½″ × 8″	WC	Signed
18) Loch Ranza		,,		9⅞″ × 6½″	WC	Signed
19) Landscape		,,		9¾″ × 7″	WC	Unsigned Att AS
20) "Deserted"	No 957					R. Academy Exhibit 1882
21) "End of the Voyage"	No 907					R. Academy Exhibit 1883
22) "Midsummer Eve"	No 1051					R. Academy Exhibit 1883
23) "Moonrise and Sea Mist St Valery"	No 1161					R. Academy Exhibit 1886 (See also 84)
24) "A Quiet Haven — Mist Clearing Off"	No 1182					Royal Academy Exhibit 1887
25) "The Still Pool above Weir" No 750	Overbeck Scarborough	Family in Devon	1888	30″ × 20″	Oil	Royal Academy Exhibit 1888
26) "Boats Ashore — Winter"	No 383		1889			Royal Academy Exhibit 1889
27) "Kelso"	No 1280		1890			Royal Academy Exhibit 1890
28) "The Whispering Reeds"	No 1328	8 Granville Sq. Scarborough	1891			Royal Academy Exhibit 1891
29) "A Fisherman's Haven"	No 1328		1897			Royal Academy Exhibit 1897
30)	River Derwent from Train					Referred to by Horace Alexander USA
31) "The Scarborough Fishing Fleet"		Bootham School Donated by daughter of Frederick Gillman		14″ × 9½″	WC	Signed in full
32)	Shore Scene(a)	Dr Gwendoline Knight	1905	6½″ × 9½″		Signed
33)	Shore Scene(b)	,,	1905	6½″ × 9½″		Signed
34)	Unknown Scene	,,	1905	8″ × 10″		Wedding present to Frank Knight Bootham School Staff
35) "Bridlington Lugger" Leaving Bridlington		?		24″ × vert		
36) Evening, Crinan Sands		Private Collection			WC	Signed in full
37) Coastal scene		,,			WC	Signed in full
38) View of Scarborough Harbour		Scarborough Y.C.		18″ × 13″	Oil	
39 Scarborough South Bay looking north towards Castle Hill		Atholl J. Wallis Scarborough		13½″ × 9½″	WC	Signed
40) Scarborough South Bay looking south towards White Nab		,,		13½″ × 9½″	WC	Signed
41) Beached Fishing Boats outside Scarborough Harbour		,,		13½″ × 9½″	WC	Signed
42) River Scene (Norfolk?)		,,		9½″ × 6″	WC	Signed
43) River Scene (Norfolk?)		,,		9½″ × 6″	WC	Signed

Title	Description	Owned by	Date	Size	Type	Notes
44) Blakeney Church, Norfolk		Atholl J. Wallis Scarborough		9½″ × 11½″	WC	Signed
45) Scottish Seascape		,,		9½″ × 6″	WC	Signed
46) Scottish Seascape		,,		11½ × 7½″	WC	Signed
47) Scottish Scene		,,		14½ × 9½″	WC	Signed
48) Scottish Mountain Scene		,,		11½″ × 7½″	WC	Signed
49) Loch Ranza (?)	Landscape	Martin Strange	1870	20¼″ × 13¼″	WC	Signed Large version of 18?
50) Shore Scene		,,		13¼″ × 9¼″	WC	Signed Original framing?
51) Landscape		,,		9½″ × 6″	WC	Signed
52) The Inner Harbour Scarborough		,,	1900	14¼″ × 9¼″	WC	Signed
53) Doctor, Doctor		,,		4¾″ × 7¾″	WC	Initialled AS Monochrome vertical
54) Tal-y-bont	Landscape	,,		6½″ × 4½″	WC	Painting removed from sketchbook on grey paper
55)	Cliff Scene (a)	,,		6½″ × 4½″	WC	Sketchbook painting on grey paper
56)	Cliff Scene (b)	,,		6½″ × 4½″	WC	,,
57) "Entrance to Loch Carron"		G.W. Johnson York	1904	14″ × 7″	WC	Signed in full
58) Menai Straits (?)		Chris Rowntree		11½″ × 7¾″	WC	Signed — monochrome
59) Landscape of lake foreshore (Lake and Trees)		,,		14½″ × 9½″	WC	Signed — monochrome
60) "Ferry House and Pier, Loch Fyne"		Bill James	1912	12″ × 8″	WC	Signed
61) "Across Kilbrennan Sound"		,,	1914	12″ × 8″	WC	Signed
62) "Talybont"		,,		7″ × 5″	WC	Sketchbook painting
63)		Kathryn Fozard			WC	
64)		,,			WC	
65)		,,			WC	
66) British Fishing Boats leaving Ardglass		Eileen Hart (Step-niece of AS)			WC	On John Sell Cotman paper
67) Holy Island, Northumberland		,,			WC	On John Sell Cotman paper
68) A Steamer in the Thames Estuary		,,	1881		WC	Signed AS Mono wash with white, David Cox paper

The above 3 watercolours (66, 67, 68) are small.

Title	Description	Owned by	Date	Size	Type	Notes
69) The Fringe of the Moon,	Norwood Lodge, No 810		1879/80		WC	£8.8s
70) Study of Boats No 367			1886/87		WC	£5.5s

Title	Description	Owned by	Date	Size	Type	Notes
71) The Sands, Mont St Michel, Normandy			1887/88		WC	£10.10s

The above 3 (69, 70, 71) were exhibited at the R. Society of British Artists in the years shown.

Exhibited at the Walker Art Gallery, Liverpool

Title	Description	Owned by	Date	Size	Type	Notes
72) At Rest			1878		WC	8 gns
73) Becalmed			1879		WC	3 gns
74) In Holland			1880		Oil	5 gns
75) Whitby Old Town			1880		Oil	42 gns
76) A Rockbound Coast			1880		Oil	10 gns
77) In Quiet Haven			1880		Oil	10 gns
78) On the French Coast			1881			7 gns
79) On the Ferry			1881			15 gns
80) Summer Twilight			1882			12 gns
81) The End of the Year			1882			25 gns
82) The Return of the Boats	Fécamp, Normandy		1882			6 gns
83) A Summer Morning — Whitby			1885			12 gns
84) Moonrise and Sea Mist, St Valery			1886			21 gns

Title	Description	Owned by	Date	Size	Type	Notes
85) Fishing Boats		M.J. Day, London		14″ × 10″	WC	Unsigned
86) Huzzah Rocks, Eyemouth		,,		14″ × 10″	WC	Signed
87) Scottish Seascape		,,		13″ × 9″	WC	Signed
88) Loch Craignish		T.A.W. Holdich, Cherry Burton		12″ × 8″	WC	Signed
89) Country scene at Ayton		Geoff Hill, Scarborough		12″ × 8″	WC	Signed
90) Seascape (E. Coast?)		,, ,,		12″ × 8″	WC	Signed
91) Herring fleet at Scarborough		,, ,,		3″ × 10½″	WC	Signed in red
92) Scarborough Harbour from seaward		John Howarth		14″ × 6½″	WC	Signed in full
93) Staithes		Wenda Steer, New Zealand			WC	
94) Cranborne House		Unknown	1883	22″ × 15″	WC	Signed in full

Book Illustrations

J.S. Fletcher's "Picturesque History of Yorkshire" includes:—

Middlesbrough by Night
The Docks, Middlesbrough
The Tees below Middlesbrough
Redcar Sands
Old Saltburn
Redcliff from Huntcliff
Staithes
Runswick Bay
Sandsend
Whitby Sands looking West
Whitby Harbour, Moonrise
The Scour, Whitby
Robin Hood's Bay
Robin Hood's Town
The Peak
Beast Cliff
Cloughton Wyke
Scarborough from the Sea — Evening
The North Bay, Scarborough
The Herring Fleet, Scarborough
Castle Hill and Harbour, Scarborough
Filey Bay
Filey Brigg
The Harbour, Bridlington Quay
Bridlington Sands and Flamborough Head
Withernsea
On the Holderness Coast

HUMBER YAWL CLUB YEARBOOKS:—

1892 Pen Sketches — CHERUB's Cruise 1891
1893 Pen Sketches — Easter Cruise Notes
1894 Dutch Estuary Scene   WC
        Daisy on the Zuiderzee 1893   WC
1895 CHERUB — A Weighty Problem WC
        A Passing Squall — Grimsby   WC
1896 Fishing Boats off a Harbour   WC
        "Luff Boy!" CHERUB in a heavy squall of Walberswick
1897 In Blakeney Harbour   WC
1898 Humber Yawl — untitled   Oil
1900 Northeast Coast — pen sketches
1905 Scottish Cruise — pen sketches

HYC YEARBOOK Covers

1897 1899 1900 1901 1902 1903 1904 1905 1906 1907
1908 1909 1910 1911

YACHTING MONTHLY CRUISE Accounts

'A Winter's Tale' (1882)

Outside the Somme
Abbeville
St Valery-sur-Somme
Bay of the Somme at St Valery — Low Water
A sail bag under her bilge
She rode pretty well
We lay alongside the barge
Our last sail in QUEST

'A Single-handed Cruise in the North Sea' (1895)

Bound for London
Rocked in the cradle of the deep
Off Grimsby
Athwart hawse of a barque
We overtook and passed a cutter yacht
Ferriby Sluice
Doctor! Doctor!
Althorpe
Below Lincoln
What the Hades are you doin' off here?
Going over Blakeney Bar
A mournful little procession
Old Walberswick Pier
CHERUB II H.Y.C.

'My Last Cruise in CHERUB II' (1896)

Entrance to Wootton Creek
A Relic of the Past
The Looe Overfalls
Running Up-Channel
A Solitary Barge
On the Gridiron, Folkestone
Bawleys at work on the Blyth Sands — Dawn
Queenborough Swale
Smelt Fishers at work
Barges leaving the Medway — evening
Bawleys boiling Shrimps
Chatham Reach
Cement Works on the Medway
Rochester Bridge

'A Cruise on the Elbe and Baltic' (1897)

On the Alster
On the Upper Elbe, near Lauenburg
Nightfall on the Lower Elbe
Lauenburg
Sunset on the Upper Elbe
On the Elbe, above Fliegenburg
Lauenburg
Fliegenburg
A Pleasure Party
On the Kaiser Wilhelm Canal
In Kiel Bay
On the Baltic Shore
Kappeln, Schleswig Fiord
Here lie many brave Germans and Danes
Sonderborg
Running into Augustenborg Fiord
Farmhouse at Nybbol Nor
Wischaven

'A Sketching Cruise on the Irish Coast' (1906)

Rogerstown Bar and Lambay Island
In Ardglass Harbour
Dundrum from the North Spit
Dundrum Lough at Low Water
Sand Boats at Dundrum
Dundrum from the Hill
Wrecks at Strangford Lough
Ashore on the North Rock
A Little Fishing Boat: Ballywalter
Ailsa Craig over the Fog

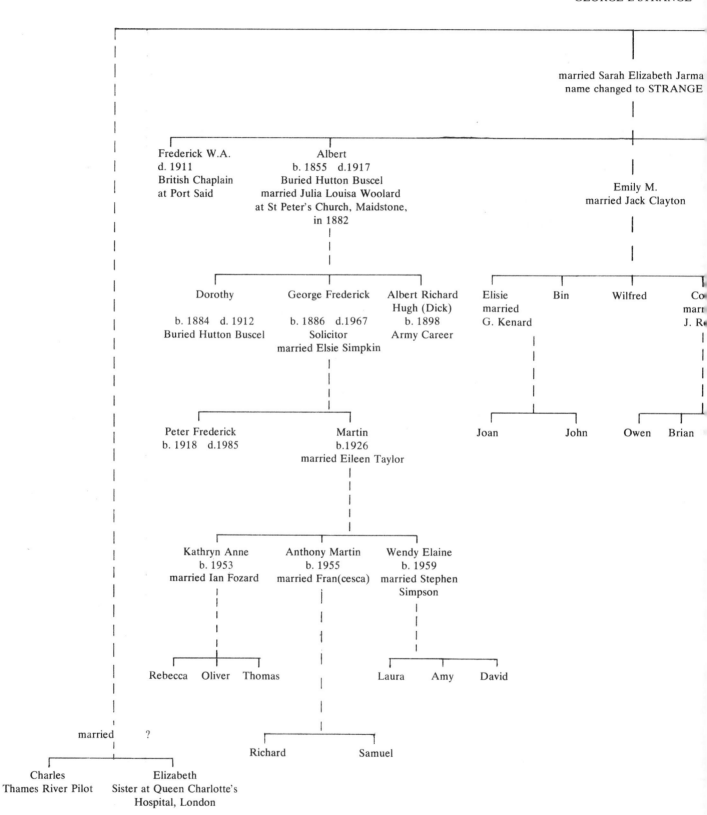

married Sarah Elizabeth Jarma
name changed to STRANGE

Frederick W.A.
d. 1911
British Chaplain
at Port Said

Albert
b. 1855 d.1917
Buried Hutton Buscel
married Julia Louisa Woolard
at St Peter's Church, Maidstone,
in 1882

Emily M.
married Jack Clayton

Dorothy
b. 1884 d. 1912
Buried Hutton Buscel

George Frederick
b. 1886 d.1967
Solicitor
married Elsie Simpkin

Albert Richard
Hugh (Dick)
b. 1898
Army Career

Elisie
married
G. Kenard

Bin

Wilfred

Co
marr
J. R

Peter Frederick
b. 1918 d.1985

Martin
b.1926
married Eileen Taylor

Joan

John

Owen

Brian

Kathryn Anne
b. 1953
married Ian Fozard

Anthony Martin
b. 1955
married Fran(cesca)

Wendy Elaine
b. 1959
married Stephen
Simpson

Rebecca   Oliver   Thomas

Laura   Amy   David

married   ?

Richard   Samuel

Charles
Thames River Pilot

Elizabeth
Sister at Queen Charlotte's
Hospital, London

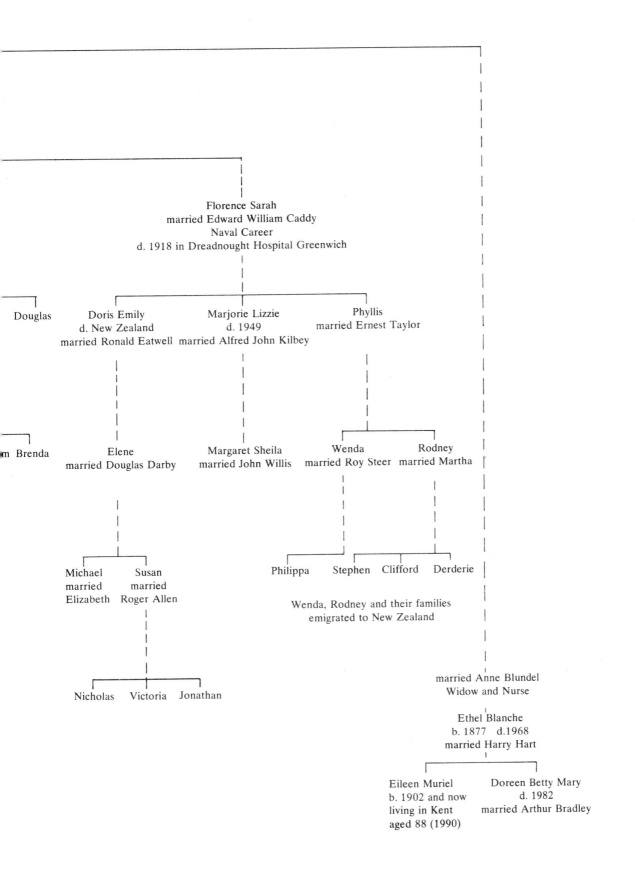

Douglas

Florence Sarah
married Edward William Caddy
Naval Career
d. 1918 in Dreadnought Hospital Greenwich

Doris Emily
d. New Zealand
married Ronald Eatwell

Marjorie Lizzie
d. 1949
married Alfred John Kilbey

Phyllis
married Ernest Taylor

m Brenda

Elene
married Douglas Darby

Margaret Sheila
married John Willis

Wenda
married Roy Steer

Rodney
married Martha

Michael
married
Elizabeth

Susan
married
Roger Allen

Philippa   Stephen   Clifford   Derderie

Wenda, Rodney and their families
emigrated to New Zealand

Nicholas   Victoria   Jonathan

married Anne Blundel
Widow and Nurse

Ethel Blanche
b. 1877   d.1968
married Harry Hart

Eileen Muriel
b. 1902 and now
living in Kent
aged 88 (1990)

Doreen Betty Mary
d. 1982
married Arthur Bradley

APPENDIX 5

Bibliography and further reading

Albert Strange Association. Yearbooks 1978-1989. Published by the Hon Sec
Atkin, William. Of Yachts and Men 1949 & 1985 (No 114)
Beken of Cowes have in their library a number of excellent photos of AS Designs
Blomfield, Richard. 'A Designer of Influence' — Yachting Monthly October 1983
Carter, Ronald. Little Ships. Pub. in Auckland, New Zealand
Chatterton, E. Keble. Fore & Aft Craft. Seeley, Service & Co Ltd., London 1922
             Through Brittany in CHARMINA. Rich & Cowan, London 1933
             To the Mediterranean in CHARMINA. Rich and Cowan 1934
             CHARMINA on the Riviera. Hurst & Blackett, London 1937
             Yachtsman Pilot. 1937
Classic Boat May/June 1988 (George Holmes' ETHEL) (+ all issues Jan/87 onwards
       Waterside House, Ponsharden, Falmouth TR10 8BE)
Cooke, Francis B. The Corinthian Yachtsman's Handbook 1913 (CHERUB III)
          Cruising Hints 4th Ed 1928, 5th Ed 1935 (CHERUB III)
          The Single-handed Yachtsman 1946 (VENTURE)
Die Yacht published in Germany
Field, the (on WREN). 21st Dec 1889 pub London by Horace Cox
Fletcher, J.S. A Picturesque History of Yorkshire Vol 6 1889-1901, Caxton Pub
Folkard, H.C. The Sailing Boat, 5th Edition 1901, Edward Stanford, Ldn.
       (OTTER/WENDA)
Forest & Stream. Forest & Stream Publishing Co, New York. (Still researching)
Fox, Uffa. Sailing, Seamanship & Yacht Construction. P. Davies 1934 (on G. Holmes' EEL)
          Thoughts on Yachts and Yachting. P. Davies 1938, (on SHEILA II)
Graves, Algenon, FSA. Dictionary of Artists exhibited in London Exhibitions 1760+
Griffiths, Maurice. 'The Father of the Yawl' — Yachting Monthly 516 Vol 86 Apr 49
            Little Ships and Shoal Waters. Conway Mar. Press London 1988
            Sixty Years a Yacht Designer. Conway Mar. Press 1988
Harrison Butler, T. Cruising Yachts — Design & Performance. Adlard Coles 1958
Hayter, Adrian, SHEILA in the Wind. Hodder and Stoughton, London 1959 (SHEILA II)
              The Second Step. Hodder & Stoughton, London 1962 — Autobiography
Hemming, Charles. British Painters of the Coast and Sea. Victor Gollancz 1988
Hughes, John Scott. Eternal Wave. Temple Press Ldn 1951. (BLUE JAY sister to CLOUD)
Humber Yawl Club. Yearbooks 1892-1918
James, Bill. Scarborough S.C. Scarborough Y.C. A History. Pub privately
Kemp, Dixon. Yacht Architecture. The Field, Horace Cox c. 1891 (on WREN)
          Manual of Yacht & Boat Sailing. 7th Ed 1891. (Several canoe designs)
Kirkpatrick, J.B. Little Ship Wanderings 1933 (ARIEL)
Leather, John. Sail and Oar. Conway Maritime Press, London 1982
Mallalieu, H.L. The Dictionary of British Watercolour Artists up to 1920
Model Yachtsman & Canoeist. Vols 1-7 1884-1894. Pub by Thomas Brassom, Hull
Mystic Seaport Museum. Connecticut (W.P. Stephens' Collection of Ship's Plans)

Petersen, Marjorie. STORNOWAY East and West. Publisher Van Nostrand & Co 1966
    Trade Winds and Monsoons Published by Van Nostrand, N.Y. 1966
The Royal Society of British Artists 1824-1893 & New English Art Club 1888-1917
    Published by Antique Collectors Club
Rudder. Pub in New York. (Researching-believed at one time edited by W.P. Stephens)
Small Boat Journal, 2100 Powers Ferry Road, Atlanta, Georgia 30339
Smyth, H. Warington. Mast and Sail in Europe and Asia. 1st Ed 1906, 2nd Ed 1929
Stephens, W.P. Traditions & Memories of American Yachting. Int Marine Pub. U.S.A.
        (CHERUB II, EEL, VITAL SPARK,, VIKING, SNICKERSEE, CHERUB
        III, NORMA, SHEILA II)
        50th Anniversary Edition. Pub by Wooden Boat 1989
Taylor, Roger C. Good Boats 1977 (EEL, SHEILA II, CHERUB II, NORMA, SEAL,
        CHERUB III)
Watts, A.V., The Humber. Lockington Publishing Co Ltd., 1980
Wood, Herbert. Spare Time Sailing (PSYCHE)
Wooden Boat No 47/1982 John Gardner 'Whose Right?'
        No 64/1985 'Albert Strange and the Canoe Yawl SHEILA'
        No 80/1988, Mike O'Brien — Shoal Draft Yawls. Designs by AS & Bolger
        'Thirty Wooden Boats' — a Catalogue of Building Plans incl WENDA 1988
Worth, Claud. Yacht Cruising (on TERN III and No 114) 4th Ed J.D. Potter Ldn 1934
        Yacht Digest, Casa Editrice Scode, CSO Monteforte N36, 20122 Milan, Italy
        Yachting published in America
Yachting Monthly. London, Vol 1 May 1906 to Vol 25 October 1918 and later
        Nov 1924 — Refs to CHARM & HAWKMOTH in adverts
Yachting World Feb 1933. Advert for RED DAWN II
        Feb 1982 (SHEILA)
Yachtsman, The. Vol 2 1892 (on Des No 4 & AS's lecture on Single Handed Cruising)

INDEX

	Page
Adam, John, Gourock	2
Adderton, C.W.,	80, 100, 101, 105
AFREET	81
Albert Model Yacht Club, Hull	169, 172
Albert Strange Association	180, 190
Alden, John G. (American) designer of LA GOLETA	34
Aldous & Son, Brightlingsea	2
Allen, J., Poole	2
Appleyard, Fred	25
ARIEL	84
AUSTRALIA (Sydney Cutter)	9, 76
AYAH	4
Baden-Powell, Warington	5, 6, 8, 26
Bathe, Sir Henry de	5
Bawley ELIZA	92
Bawley at Queenborough	93
Bayly, H.E., Exmouth	3
Beardsley	156
Beaumont, W.I.	21
BEE	35, 80, 139, 140, 141
Beechy, Capt Richard	144
Bentall, E.H., Sailing yacht designer	75
Berwick on Tweed	147 (PLATE), 154
BETTY later TALLY HO	34, 80
BETTY II	135, 136, 137, 138
Binks, Thomas, Hull	146
Birchbark, Canadian Indian	4
BIRDIE	49
Blake, H.P., Southampton	2
Blakeney Bar, Going over (painting)	45
BLUE JAY	80
Boating Monthly later Yachting Monthly	77
Bond, Sam, Rock Ferry	2, 8, 176
Bonington, Richard Parkes	146
Booth, W.	78
Bootham School, York	21
Bristow, H.H.	96, 101
British Canoe Association	18
Brooks, Thomas, Hull	146
Bruce Prize Designing Competition	170
Burgoine, C. and A., Kingston on Thames	8
Burnham Yacht Building Co., Burnham-on Crouch	8
Butler, T. Harrison	10, 25, 81, 98, 101, 103, 104
Caine, W.S. a Member of Parliament	16
Caine, Robert, Port St Mary	78
Canoe stern — alleged first use by Strange 1891	9
Canoe sterns — Strange and others' views on	96 et seq.
CANOEING by Dr John Hayward	6
Canoeist, The	176, 177

Carter, H.B., Whitby	146
CASSY	27
CATRIONA (Sanderson)	9, 72, 73
Chambers, George, Whitby,	144, 146
CHARM I	81
CHARM II	81
CHARMINA (Keble Chatterton)	1
Chatterton, E. Keble	1
CHERUB I	17, 18, 27, 28, 163, 169
CHERUB II	18, 19, 20, 28, 29, 85, 176
CHERUB II's Cruises 1894/1896	30, 39, 41, 42, 43, 44
CHERUB III	21, 35, 64, 65, 66, 82, 83, 84, 160 (PLATE)
Cherub's Cruise 1891	28
Clark, J. Pain, London	3, 76
Claymore Challenge Cup (RCC)	80
Clayton, C.P., Southampton	2
Clayton, Harold, Penarth	2, 32, 34
CLOUD	80, 121, 122, 123
Clyde 17-19s	101
Cockburnspath School of Painting	146
Cole, Robert, Scarborough	156, 163, 169
Cole, Miss of Scarborough	156
Collister (QUEST's hand)	105, 114
Corinthian yachtsman	77
Cox, David, Norwich	146
Crane, Walter	156
Cranfield and Carter, Burnham on Crouch	82
Cruising in the Wash, Notes on — by Strange	31
CUPID (Model Yacht)	170, 171 (PLATE), 172, 176
DAISY	27, 28
DAISY in full Flight — painting	28, 29
DAISY, Dutch cruise with Geo Holmes	28
DAISY on the Zuiderzee 1893 — painting	153 (PLATE), 154
Dandy Rig (Dundee = French for a Ketch)	4
DAUNTLESS	14, 15, 71, 96, 174, 177
Dawson, Nelson, RBA	176
Design No 146/1915	35
DESIRE (6 metre Int Rating Class)	32, 81
Dickie's of Tarbert	21, 24, 80, 81, 82, 84, 105
Die Yacht	78
Dinwiddy, Norman	80
Doblemen on the Medway	94
DOLLIE (Model Yacht)	176
Doyle, J.E., Kingstown	2
DRYAD	61, 62, 63, 81
Dufferin, Marquis of	4
Dutch estuary scene	151 (PLATE), 154
East Coast Challenge Shield	170
EEL (Geo Holmes')	18, 19, 24, 26, 31, 31, 75
EGERIA	2, 14
ETHEL	See WREN/ETHEL

Falmouth quay punts   98
Fastnet Cup 1927   34
Fay, J. and G., Southampton   10
Field, The   162
FIREFLY   81, 161 (PLATE)
Fishing boats beating to windward   147 (PLATE), 152
FLAPPER   81
Fletcher, J.S. Picturesque History of Yorkshire   152, 156
FOAM II   3
Folkard's 'The Sailing Boat'   21, 31
Forbes, Stanhope   146
Forest and Stream   8, 18, 177
Forrestt & Co., Limehouse and Wivenhoe   2
Frank, James, Scarborough   17, 28, 30
Frank, T.   176
Froude — wave line theory   84
FULMAR   32, 101, 102, 103

Gibson, G. McLean   32
Gilliland, Frank   102, 103
GLORY   4
GODIVA   28
Grassam, Thomas, Hull   162
Gravesend   13
GRAYLING   32
Grimshaw, Atkinson   146, 156
Groves, Robert E.   32, 78, 82
GULL   32
Gush, Lt A.W., RN   80

Hamilton Jnr., J.   32
Hardy Corinthians   6
Harris, E.P. and P.T., Rowhedge   2
Harvey, John, Naval Architect   75
HAWKMOTH   21, 32, 55, 56, 57
Hayter, Adrian   83
Hayward, Dr John (His book 'Canoeing')   6, 7, 19
HEATHEN CHINEE   28
Hemy, Charles Napier   146
Herring Fleet, The, Scarborough   149 (PLATE), 152
Hilditch, J., Carrickfergus   2
Holmes, George F.   8, 10, 17, 19, 24, 25, 26, 27, 28,
                                                      29, 30, 31, 32, 35, 36, 71, 156,
                                                      162, 172, 176

Hope, Linton, Greenhithe   2, 8
Hornsea Mere   32
Howard, John T., Maldon   2
Hughes, Henry   30
Humber Canoe Yawl 1895   47
Humber Sailing Club   32
Humber Yawl Club   4, 17, 18, 19, 21, 24, 25, 26, 27,
                                                      28, 29, 31, 32, 35, 71, 74, 78, 81,
                                                      82, 96, 154, 162

Humber Yawl Club Yearbook covers   156, 158 (PLATE),
                                                      159 (PLATE)

Hunt's Yachting Magazine	77
Hutton Buscel churchyard, Strange's grave	25
Huzzah Rocks	152
IMOGEN later BOREAS	76
Indians of N.E. America	4
Ingleby, J.F., RYYC	32
INNISFALLEN	58, 59, 60, 81
Inskip, J. Henry	25, 150
Jackett, T., Falmouth	2
Jarman, Sarah Elizabeth (mother of Albert Strange)	13
Johnson, Charles V	10
JOLIE BRISE	34
JOVANNA	84
JULIA (Model Yacht)	170, 176, 178
JULLANAR	9, 75, 76
KATE (W.E. Middleton's)	4, 166
Kayak, Eskimo	5
Kemp, Dixon	9, 10, 71, 102, 162, 178
Kingston Model Yacht Club, Hull	169
Knight, Laura, Staithes	146
KOTIK (later PINCHER)	32
L'Strange, George (father of Albert Strange)	13
LA GOLETA	34
LADY HERMIONE (Marquis of Dufferin's)	4
LADY MARTIN	18, 87
Lake and Trees	152 (PLATE), 154
Laws, G. Umfreville, London	2, 8
Leicester College of Arts and Crafts	16
Leslie, Robert — Marine Artist	3
Liverpool College of Art	16, 148
Lloyd's Register of Yachts	181
Lloyd's Register of American Yachts	8
Loch Fyne cutter	101
Long, Ardagh E., Jarrow-on-Tyne	170
LORA	76
Luff Boy — painting	29, 30 (PLATE), 154, 157 (PLATE)
MacGregor, John	4, 5, 6, 26, 39, 166
MacKenzie, Landseer, Bournemouth	3, 28
Mackey, Charles, Staithes	146
Manual of Yacht and Boat Sailing (Dixon Kemp)	10, 71
MARIE	108
Marine Painting in Britain	144
Marlborough, E. & Co	162
MARY (Model Yacht)	176
Mason, Frank H.	25, 144, 150, 156
Mast and Sail (Warington Smyth)	102
MAY	98, 99, 103 (Robertson's)
Mayall, Frederick, Staithes	146

McAlister, R., Dumbarton   2
McMullen's boats   39
McWhirter, Erith   6
Mead, Harley, East Cowes and Falmouth   2
Middleton, Lieut.   162, 166 et seq.
Middleton, W.E.   4
Mills, A.   26
MISCHIEF (Model Yacht)   163 et seq.
MIST   78, 79, 113
Model yachts — Letters in The Model Yachtsman   163 et seq.
Model Yachtsman and Canoeist, The   14, 162, 163, 168, 169, 170,
                                                       172
MONA   30, 81
Motor Boat and Yachting   77
Motor Launch 75/1904   50
Mule   98
Munro, H.   26
Murdoch, W., Campbeltown   22
Musslewhite, Tom, Poole   2
Mylne, Alfred   102
Mystic Seaport Museum, Connecticut   24, 25, 70, 180, 181

Nautilus type canoe   26
Newlyn School of Painting   146
NIRVANA OF ARKLOW   161 (PLATE)
North Sea Coast, Notes on the — by Strange   31
Norwegian lifeboats and pilot boats   102
NURSEMAID   81
Nystrom and parabolic curves   101

Oliver, Ernest Hicks, Editor Lloyd's Register   24
OPOSSUM   28
OTTER   48, 71, 72, 74, 75, 76, 77, 78
Oxford University Sailing Club   7
Oxford canoe-yawls   8, 27

Parabolic curves   101, 102
Passing Squall, A., Grimsby   154, 155 (PLATE)
Payne, Alfred, Southampton   2, 3, 10
Payne, Arthur E., Southampton   2, 3, 10, 77
Pears, Charles   25, 39, 150
Penzance lugger   102
Peter Boat   14, 96
PHANTOM   124, 125, 126
Place, Francis, Scarborough   144
Plymouth hookers   98
Pocock, Nicholas   144
Pryor, Naval architect   75
PSYCHE   115, 116

Quakers, Society of Friends   16
QUEST   16, 105, 107, 108, 109, 110,
                                                       112, 113, 114
QUEST II   80, 100, 105, 114

Redmore, Henry, Hull	146
REDWING ex CHERUB III	84
Reiach, Herbert	10, 36, 102, 180
ROB ROY (canoe and the later yawl)	4, 5, 6, 26, 74, 166
ROB ROY Canoe, A Thousand Miles in the	5
ROB ROY, The Cruise alone in the	5
Robertson, Alex	103
Rodmell, Harry Hudson	156
Roller reefing	82
Rowntree, Joshua, M.P.	163
Royal Academy, The	16, 148
Royal Canoe Club	5, 6, 26
Royal Cruising Club	80
Royal Society of British Artists	148
Royal Yorkshire Y.C.	10, 17, 32, 78, 96
Rudder, The	77, 78
Sailing Dinghy (No 140/1913)	127, 128
Sailmaker, Isaac, London	144
Sanderson, Louis N.	9, 72, 73, 96
Scarborough Art Gallery	152
Scarborough Fishing Fleet	150 (PLATE), 152
Scarborough Gazette, The	163
Scarborough Harbour, Scottish Fishing Boats	145 (PLATE), 152
Scarborough Model Yacht Club	163, 168, 169, 172, 176
Scarborough Sailing Club later S. Yacht Club	18, 19, 24, 25, 27, 32, 180
Scarborough School of Art	16, 17, 148, 148 (PLATE), 150
Scott, Samuel	144
SEA BELLE	14
SEA HARMONY	81
SEAL	51, 52, 53, 54
Searl, boatbuilders, Lambeth	5
Settle, William, Hull	146
Seven ton Auxiliary Sloop (1911)	117, 118, 119
Sewell, H., Promotor Scarborough Model Yacht Club	163
SHEELAH II	32
SHEILA	21, 32, 72, 74, 78, 82, 160 (PLATE)
SHEILA II	67, 68, 69, 82, 83, 84
Sheila in the Wind by Adrian Hayter	83
Sibbick, Charles, Cowes	2
SINAH	104
Single hander cruiser design 1891	97
Single-handed Cruise in the North Sea	31
To Single-handers, Notes by Strange	31
Slade School of Art	16, 148
Smith, Harry, Oxford and Burnham-on-Crouch	2
Smith, Theo and Harry	7, 8, 10, 27
Smyth, Warington	102
SKICKERSNEE	74, 75
SNIPPET	24
Society of Marine Artists	150
Solent fishing cutters	3
Speed, Henry and Lancelot Fiennes	6

St Valery	145 (PLATE), 148
Staithes School of Painting	146
Stalbridge, Lord	34
Stanford, G.D.	80
Steer, Philip Wilson	146
Stephens, William P.	8, 9, 18, 22, 24, 25, 30, 70, 74, 75, 96, 180, 181
Stewart, Walter	6, 8
Stone, Douglas, Erith	2
Stow and Son, Shoreham	2
Strange, birth, boyhood and family	13 et seq
Strange as 'boy on racing yachts on Thames 1860s	14
Strange — studying and painting in France 1870s	16
Strange — marriage to Julia Louisa Woolard 1882	16
Strange — headmaster of Scarborough School of Art	16
Strange — birth of Dorothy and George Frederick	17
Strange's Design No 4/1891	29
Strange — birth of Albert Richard Hugh 1898	19
Strange — heart weakness limiting his sailing 1910	21
Strange — death of Dorothy 1912	21
Strange — visit to England of W.P. Stephens 1913	22
Strange — shelling of his house by Germany Navy 1915	24
Strange — retirement from Scarborough School of Art	24
Strange — death on July 11th 1917	24, 25
Strange — his library given to Scarborough S. Club	25
Strange — his planimeter & wooden dividers to THB	25
Strange — his design plans at Mystic Museum	25
Suffling, H.J. and N.R.	81
Summers and Payne Ltd., Southampton	4
TALLY HO (ex BETTY)	34
TAVIE II	30
TEAL (Arthur Payne's)	4
TERN	132, 133, 134
TERN III	
22, 23, 81	
THERESA II	129, 130, 131
THETA	102
Thomas, W.E. of Falmouth	80
THORN	32, 33, 34
TOPSY	32, 34, 80, 120
Tredwen, E.B.	6, 8
TRENT (Geo Holmes')	32
TROTTER	32
TUI	84
Turk, Kingston on Thames	8
Turner, J.M.W.	144, 146
Velde, Wilhem Van de	144
VENTURE	1, 80, 81, 142, 143
VIPER	74
VITAL SPARK	7, 74
Walker Gallery, Liverpool	148

Ward, John, Hull   146
WATER RAT (Fiennes Speed brothers)   6
Watson, G.L.   162, 170, 178
Watson, Harry   25, 150
WAWA   30
Weatherill family, Whitby   146
Whistler, James McNeil (American)   146
Wicksteed, K.   177
WIDGEON   4
Winter's Tale, A (1st of AS's cruise accounts) 16
Woolard, Julia Louisa (wife of Albert Strange) 16
Worth, Dr Claud   22, 81, 100
WREN/ETHEL   10, 29, 96, 174
WREN (not ETHEL)   71
Wyllie, William Lionel   146

Yacht Architecture (Dixon Kemp)   10
Yacht Cruising by Dr Claud Worth   81, 100
Yachting   77
Yachting and Boating Monthly   18, 37
Yachting Monthly   10, 18, 24, 31, 36, 37, 77, 78, 80,
                                                81, 85, 96, 102, 154, 180
Yachting World   77, 78
Yachtsman, The   9, 10, 72, 77, 78, 172
YANKEE   87

ZINITA   34
Zulu types   104